IMAGES
of America

BROCKS GAP

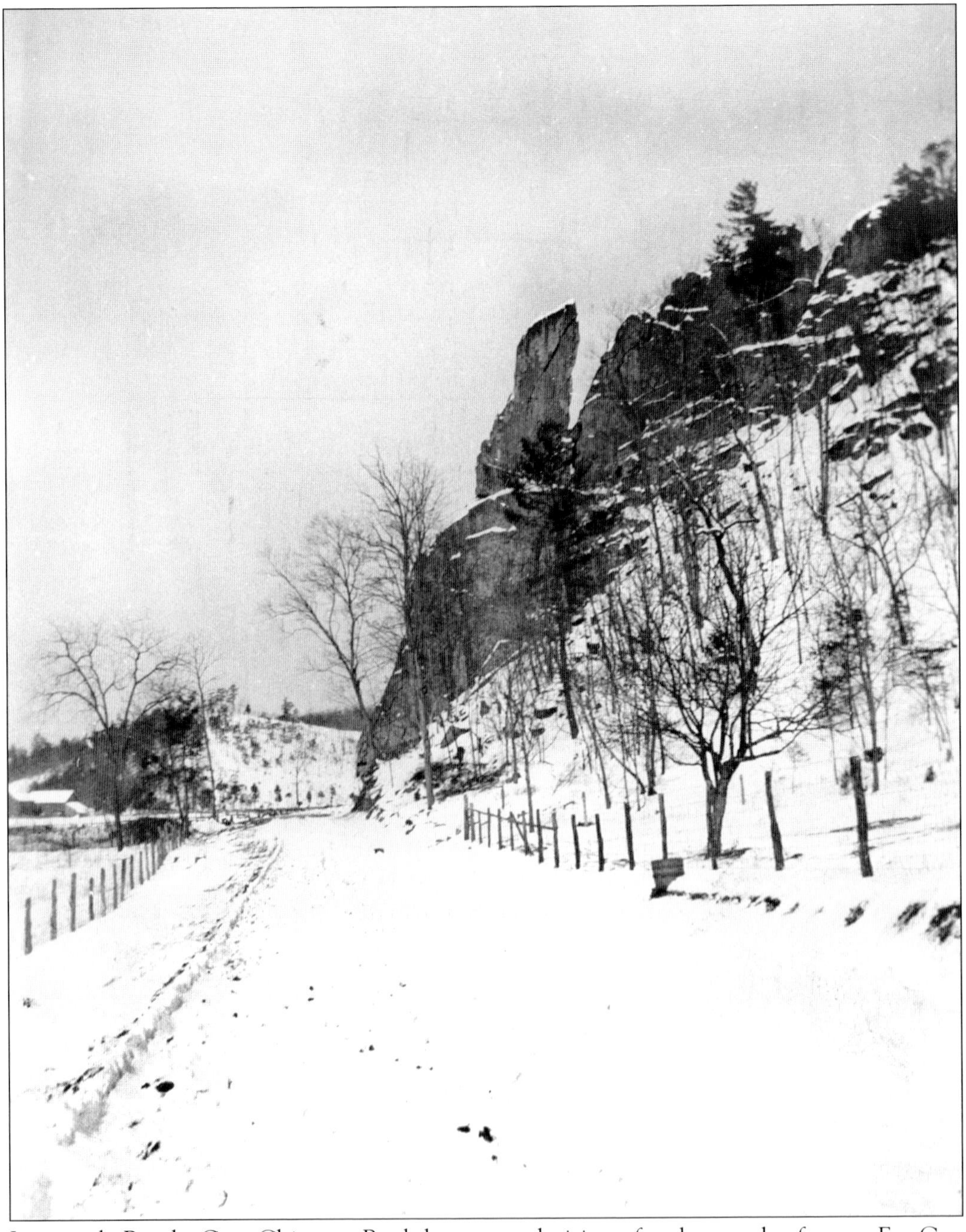

Just inside Brocks Gap, Chimney Rock has greeted visitors for thousands of years. For Gap residents, it is a visible symbol that they have come home. The mountains and generations of family relationships have given Gap residents such a feeling of safety and belonging that when they leave the Gap, they say they are going "out" or "out the way." In this snowscape, horse droppings and the lack of telephone poles date the photograph to 1900 or before. (Helen Fulk collection.)

IMAGES
of America

BROCKS GAP

Lena Albrite Turner
Pat Turner Ritchie

ARCADIA
PUBLISHING

ISBN 978-0-7385-4166-2

Published by Arcadia Publishing
Charleston, South Carolina

Printed in the United States of America

Library of Congress Catalog Card Number: 2005927801

For all general information contact Arcadia Publishing at:
Telephone 843-853-2070
Fax 843-853-0044
E-mail sales@arcadiapublishing.com
For customer service and orders:
Toll-Free 1-888-313-2665

Visit us on the Internet at www.arcadiapublishing.com

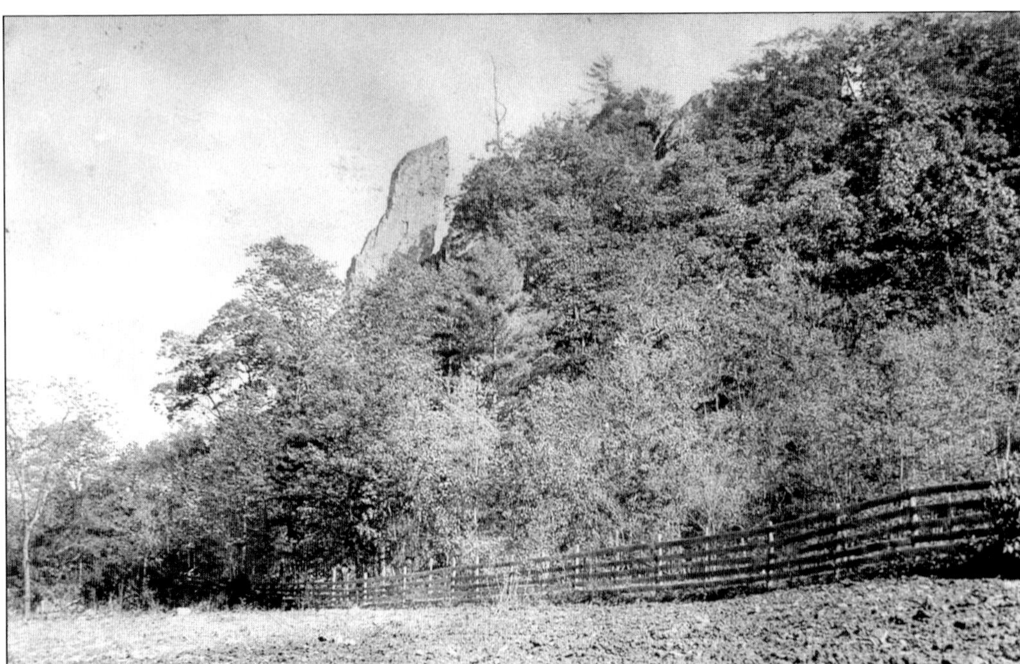

Chimney Rock was included in an 800-acre survey conducted for Benjamin Borden in 1734. This was one of the first surveys made of Brocks Gap land and was described as "near the Gapp where the river runs between the mountains . . . Chimney Rock." Before the 1920s, the road passed next to Chimney Rock. The five-board fence along the road dates this Chimney Rock photograph to the 1920s.

Contents

ACKNOWLEDGMENTS

We have spent pleasant times with friends and neighbors looking through old picture boxes and reminiscing about people and events long ago. When we started our photograph collection 40 years ago, we did not foresee how many photos we would accumulate or how fuzzy our memories would become, and we did not record enough information. If we have left out a donor's name from this list, it was unintentional. The following people deserve special recognition for this project: Ruth Ritchie Baker, Marvin Bare, Kammie Bare, Sharon Smith Bollman, Thelma Ritchie Bowers, Joyce Wilkins Branner, Susan Brown, Billy Chapman, Dan Chitwood, Mrs. Branson Conley, Velma Turner Cooper, Lillian Runion Crider, Luther Crider, Jennie Cullers, Diane May Custer, Millard D. "Pete" and Naomi Fulk Custer, Carol DeHart, Ava Reedy Dove, Lonzo Dove, Luke Dove, Velma Crider Dove, Lona Dove, Laura Custer Early, Geraldine Deavers Eaton, Jean Yankey Estep, Donna Kline Estep, Rev. R. Dean Fawley, Janice Shoemaker Fulk, Carl Fulk, Dr. Floyd L. Fulk, Earl and Vada Custer Fulk, Georgia Custer Fulk, Helen Fulk, Nova Roadcap Fulk, Vita Souder Fulk, and Pauline Carr Fulk. Thanks also go to Lennis Moyers Garber, Bennie Getz, K. B. Getz, Vivian Hiser Knepper, Carl G. Hoover, Nancy May Hoover, Paul C. "Jack" Kiser, Virginia Ann Fawley Hulvey, Anna Lee Wittig Lantz, J. Day Lantz, Barbara Loomis, Mabel Albrite Mathias, Goldie Turner May, J. Ellwood May, Rhoda Fulk Turner May, Matthew E. "Bud" Miller, Shirley G. Cullers Miller, Trovillo S. "Bill" Miller, Vivian Turner Miller, Helen Whetzel Moyer, Lois May Rhodes, Nellie Siever Ritchie, Ruth Ritchie, Roy Ritchie, Gloria Turner Ritchie, Viola Ritchie Sager, Peggy Ann Shifflett, David L. Smith, Floyd A. Smith, Wilma Stultz Smith, Warren J. Souder, Virginia Fitzwater Souder, Eugene Souder, Magdaline Heatwole Stewart, Leota Moyers Stultz, Vonnie Swindle, Carol Hepner Turner, Debbie Estep Turner, Garner Turner, Garnett R. Turner, Granvil J. Turner, Lula Fulk Turner, L. Webster Turner, Mary Fulk Turner, Ruth A. Turner, Reuel Tusing, Miller Whetzel, Goldie Ketterman Whetzel, Jesse Wittig, Emma Whetzel Wittig, Mary Ann Yarsinske, Lewis H. Yankey, Irene Smith Yankey, and Violet Cullers Yankey.

Two others need special recognition for this project: Ronald W. Turner, who taught Lena how to use the darkroom and scan photos, and Dale MacAllister, who gave us articles on Brocks Gap from old newspaper microfilm.

INTRODUCTION

The photographs in *Brocks Gap* cover the 1860s through the 1950s. However, the story of Brocks Gap begins much earlier.

Brocks Gap, a gap in the Little North Mountain range through which the North Fork of the Shenandoah River flows, consists of 200 square miles in northwestern Rockingham County, Virginia. Primarily German pioneers settled it as early as the 1740s. These first settlers claimed good land along the river and stream bottoms, and their descendants are still there. Most of the families have lived in Brocks Gap for 200 to 250 years and, because of the cultural and physical isolation of the area, most of the families are interrelated. Some people still spoke German until the 1950s. In fact, there are a few adults today who were taught German ("Pennsylvania Dutch") by their parents.

Although tucked into the mountains, Brocks Gap has had important visitors. George Washington spent the night in 1784 on his return trip from checking his western properties. Rev. Francis Asbury, a founder of the Methodist Church in the United States, and Rev. Christian Newcomer, a founder of the United Brethren Church, traveled through and visited with Gap families. Jed Hotchkiss, famous mapmaker of the Confederate army, marveled at the abundant water supply in Brocks Gap and at the settlers who were retaining their German speech and ways.

The numerous streams, rivers, and mountains in the Gap isolated the settlers in many ways. Before paved roads and bridges were built in the 1920s, it was necessary to ford streams many times in order to travel to Broadway, the nearest small town with train service. "I'll be there if the creek don't [*sic*] rise," was a common expression for a common problem. Communities in Brocks Gap were 5 to 35 miles away from Broadway. One resident, born in 1903, related that he was 12 years old before he made the 20-mile trip from his Criders home in Brocks Gap to Broadway.

"Modernization" was late in coming to the Gap. Electricity was not available until the late 1930s. Indoor plumbing in homes was not common until the 1960s and 1970s. Two-room schoolhouses were open until 1958 in Criders and 1961 in Fulks Run. Before satellite service, televisions could receive only one channel.

Brocks Gap is composed of distinct communities. To give an idea of the size of the present-day unincorporated communities, each "town limit" sign is on two sides of the same post at the current post offices of Fulks Run, Bergton, and Criders. Each of these post offices has distinct sub-communities. For instance, Fulks Run covers the former areas of Tunis, Genoa, Hoover, and Palos (names of former post offices). Bergton, originally named Dovesville for an early family, consists of the sub-communities of Crab Run, Bennetts Run, and Overly Hollow. Most, if not all, of Criders used to be known as "Germany" in county records.

Until recent years, families from one community seldom moved to a different community or married outside of that community. Since most families have lived in the Gap for many generations, it is common to know personally five, six, and even seven generations of one's own family and of the neighbor's family. Traditions and community memories have been passed on for generations.

Brocks Gap residents were self-sufficient, doing their own doctoring, baby delivering, and entertaining. There was a strong sense of community and safety because of the mountains. Even today, when we talk about going to Broadway or the county seat in Harrisonburg, we say we are going "out" or "out the way." Everyone in the Gap knew everyone else, and everyone knew everyone else's business.

"Help for help back" was the theme as neighbors helped each other with harvests, corn shucking, apple butter boiling, and threshing. The highlight of the year for many Brocks Gap families was the annual hog-butchering day. Before the automobile age, hogs provided most of a family's meat supply; in 1870, a Fulks Run farmer wrote of butchering 20 hogs. Each family in a community owned some, but not all, of the implements necessary to butcher and, by working together, all benefited. To prepare for the big day, they would borrow the rest of the tools, such as scalding troughs, from the neighbors. On butchering day, neighbors would come to assist. Some people were especially skilled at a particular job, such as stuffing the sausage casings or cutting up the meat, and would perform that job at several households.

Peer pressure was not a term early Brocks Gap residents would have used, but they were familiar with the theory, as they encouraged one another to adhere to community standards of behavior. Before the 1920s, the "encouragement" sometimes took the form of tarring and feathering. In some church denominations in Brocks Gap, it was customary for the leaders of the church to visit every member before Communion Sunday to question them not only about their faith but about their relationship with other church members as well. If a member was found to be having a dispute with another member, they were counseled until the issue was resolved.

Even though he did not grow up in Brocks Gap, songwriter Dan Chitwood captured the values of the area in his song "Taking the Cure." He wrote, "Having faith and a family is the measure of worth." Family relationships have been important to Gap families with extended families providing support for each other. By sharing these photographs of our Brocks Gap families at work and play, we invite you to "tuck yourself in those mountains so safe and secure" and become one of the family, at least for today.

One

Brocks Gap Culture

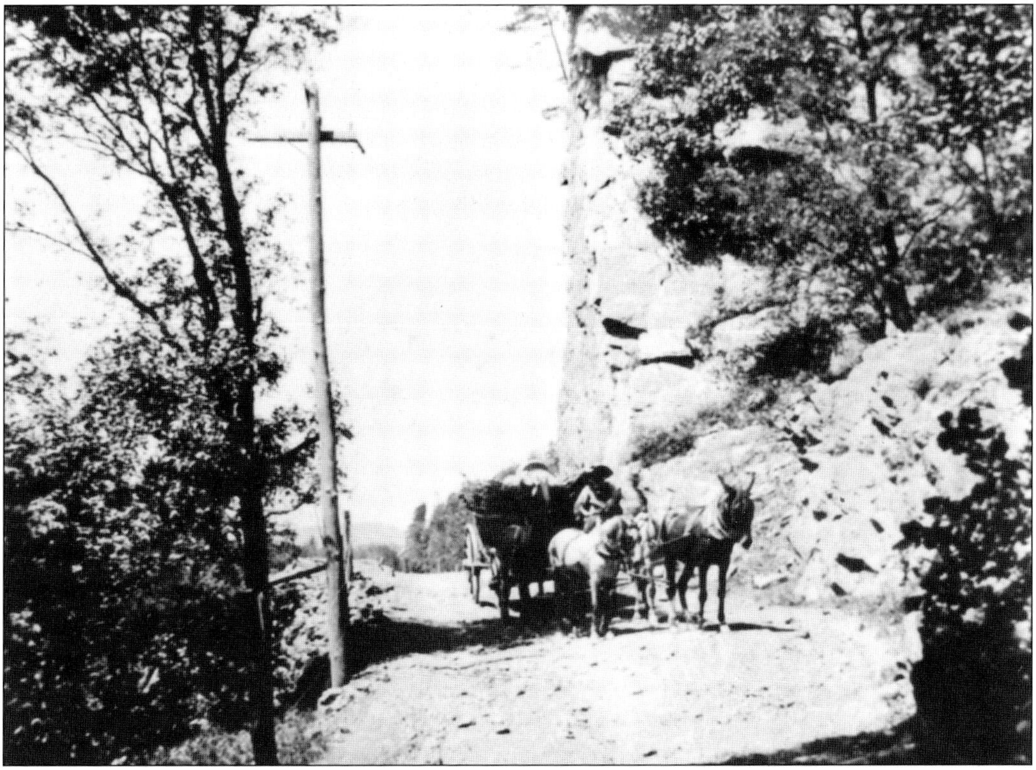

Forests provided housing, firewood, and cash for Brocks Gap residents. The 1880s were boom times for the lumber industry in the Gap. An 1885 article in the *Spirit of the Valley* said that "to see the loads of lumber, ties, hoop poles, and wagon spokes going from the Gap, a person would think the whole outside world depended upon the Gap for these articles." (Private collection.)

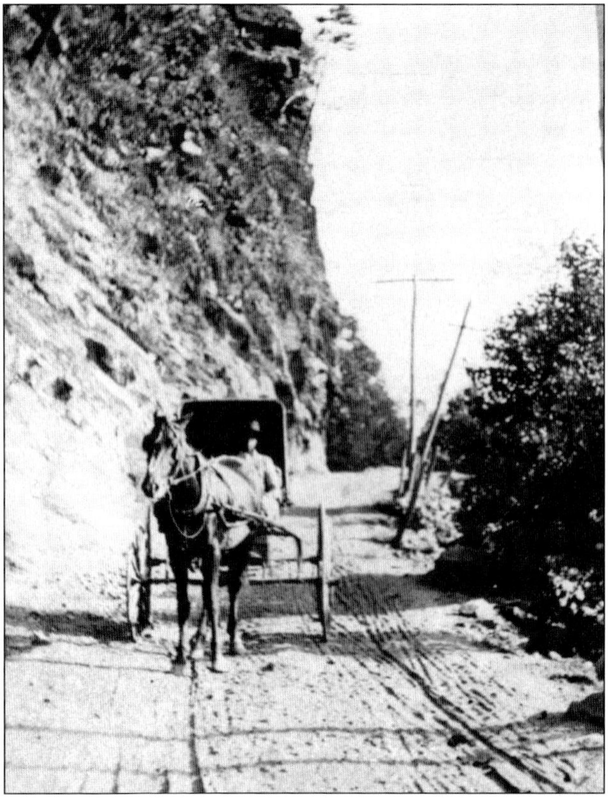

In earliest records, Brocks Gap was called "The Gap of the North Mountain upon Shannandore." By 1753, it had taken on the name of the Brock family who owned 400 acres inside the Gap. Roads followed streams and were often muddy and impassible, but the road is in fair enough shape for this horse and buggy at the Gap rocks. (Leafy Runion Miller collection.)

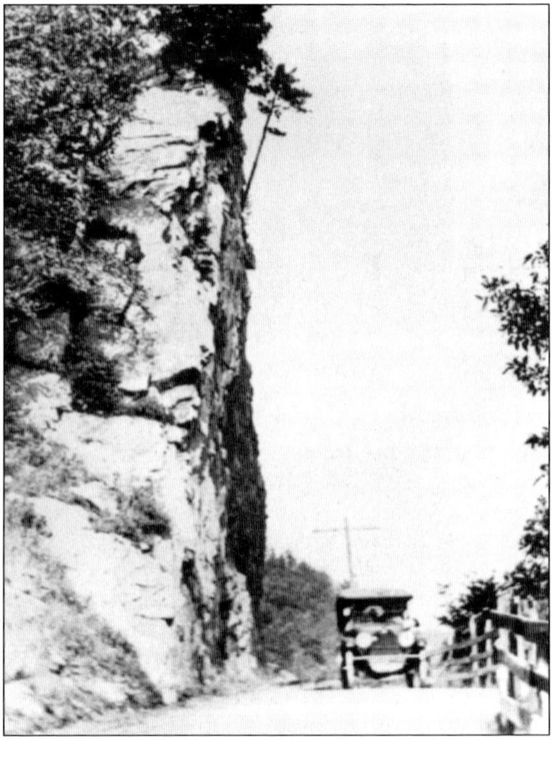

In the same view as above, this Model T drives on a paved road around the Gap rocks. Notice the wider road and board fence. When the road was improved during the 1920s, bridges were built on the main road, eliminating the need to ford the rivers. Now going "out the way" (out of the Gap) did not depend on the river level. (R. Dean Fawley collection.)

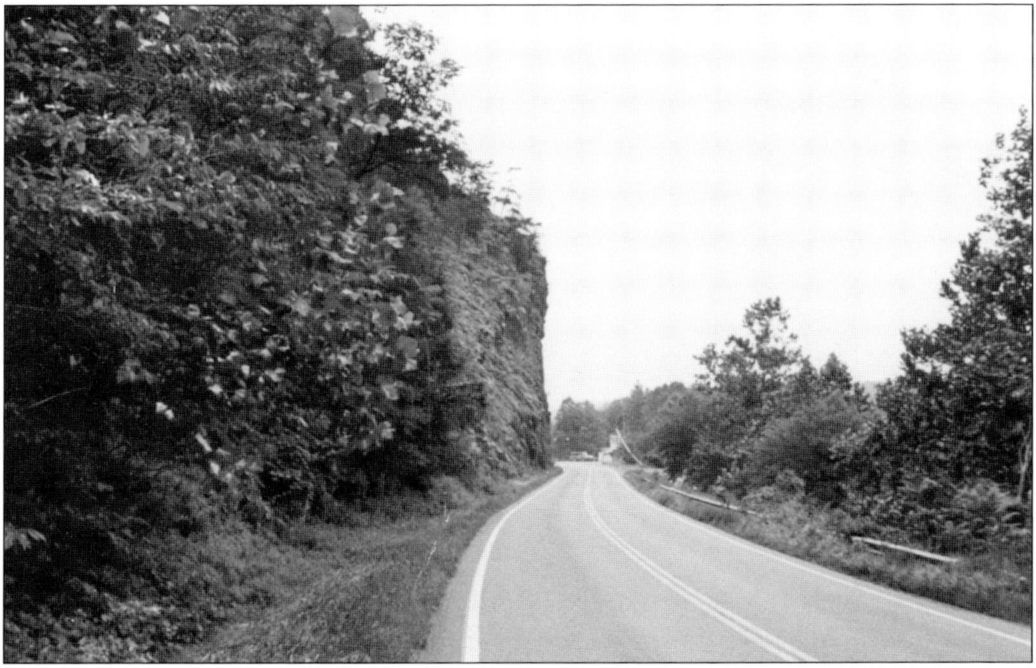

By 1989, falling rocks at the Gap entrance and increased traffic necessitated widening the road at Brocks Gap. Much of the rock wall was blasted away in 1989 and used to widen the road. The rocks that were blasted were used as fill for the road and to level a nearby field. (Ronald W. Turner, photographer.)

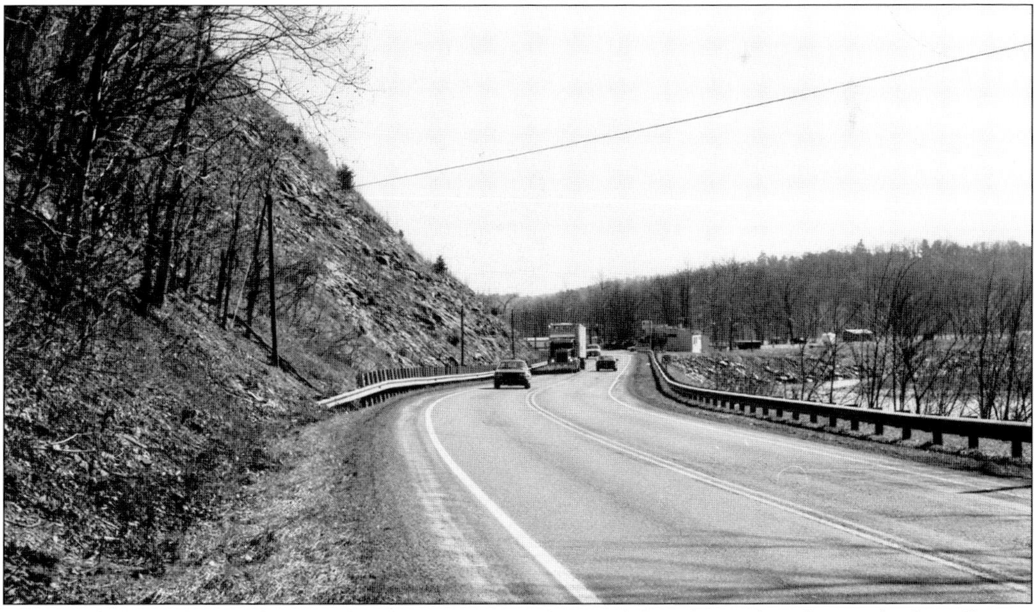

The road through Brocks Gap has been a main thoroughfare from the Shenandoah Valley to western Virginia from Native American times to the present. Highway 259 is heavily traveled today by tractor-trailers. The good road system has made it possible for Brocks Gap residents to commute daily to jobs in Broadway, Harrisonburg, and beyond. This 2001 photograph shows the road as it is today in Brocks Gap. (Pat T. Ritchie, photographer.)

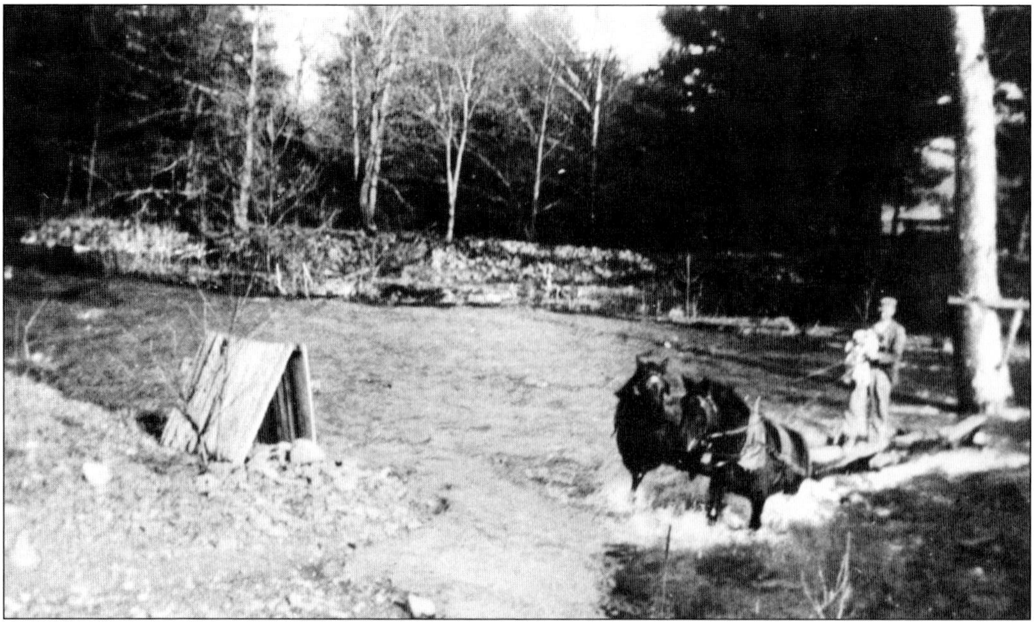

The Shenandoah River and its tributaries were a big attraction for settlers, but the streams also isolated Brocks Gap families. Before bridges were built in the 1920s, travelers had to ford streams. The expression, "I'll be there if the creek don't [*sic*] rise," was not a joke. Above, Casper L. Moyers fords the German River near Criders holding a bag of buckwheat freshly ground at Carl O. Whetzel's mill. (Leota Moyers Stultz collection.)

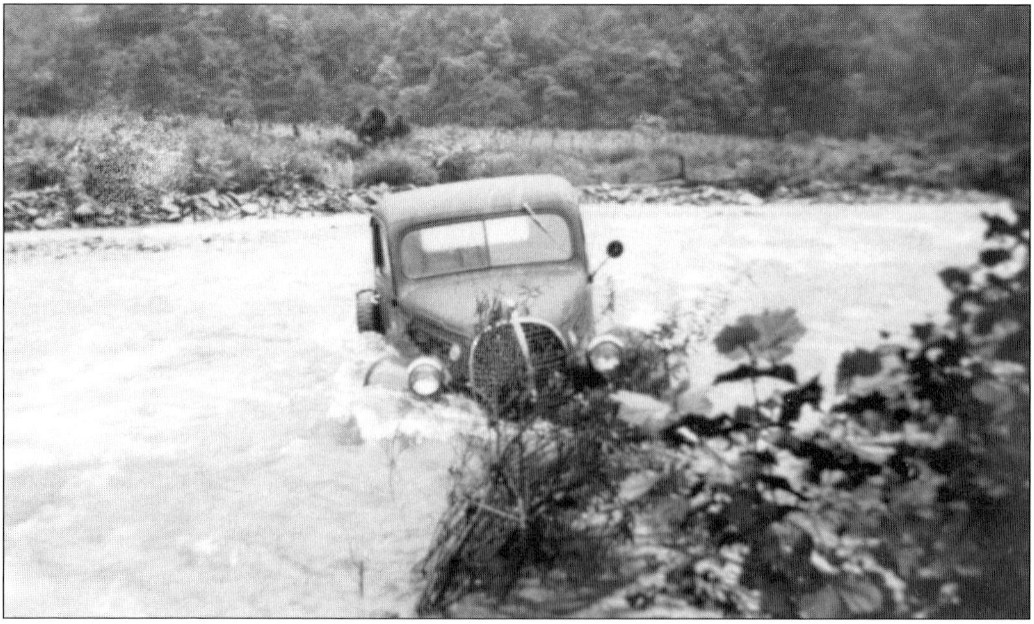

The creek did rise (this time it was the German River), and this driver from Criders did not make his destination. Fortunately, most public roads in the Gap had single-lane iron bridges across fords by the 1930s. When multi-ton feed trucks began delivering feed to poultry houses in the 1970s, they had to ford the German River instead of traveling on the iron bridges that could not support the weight. (Thelma Ritchie Bowers collection.)

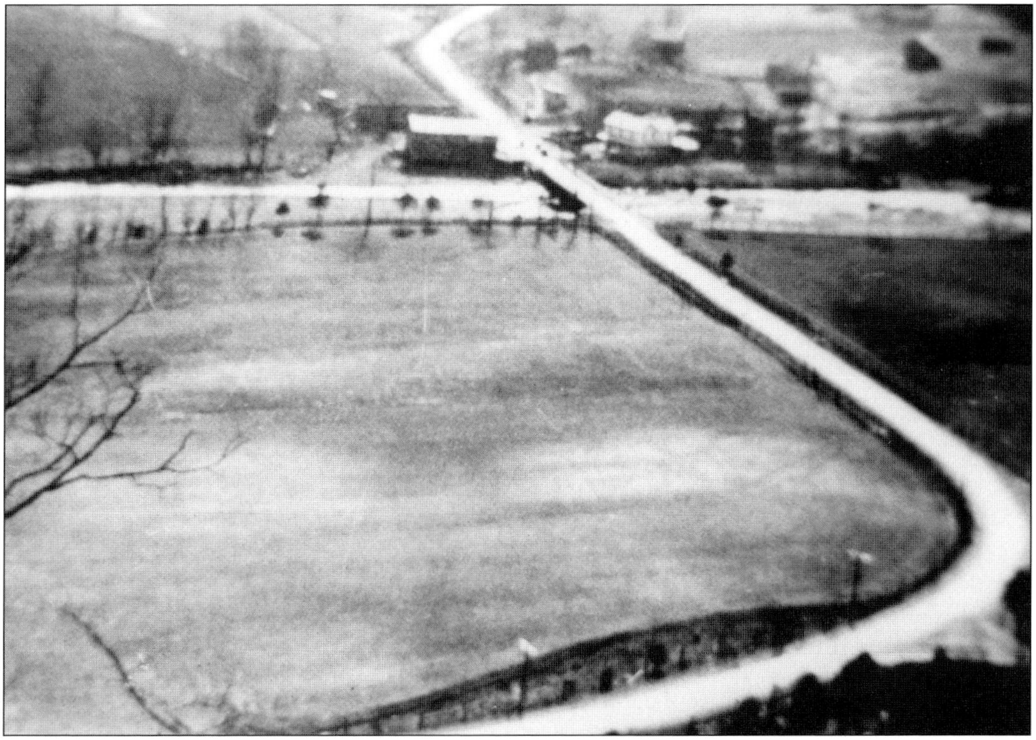

Runions Creek is at flood stage in this view of Highway 259, probably taken from Chimney Rock, when the road passed next to the rock formation in the early 1920s. The white house pictured above is still standing. (Matthew E. "Bud" Miller collection.)

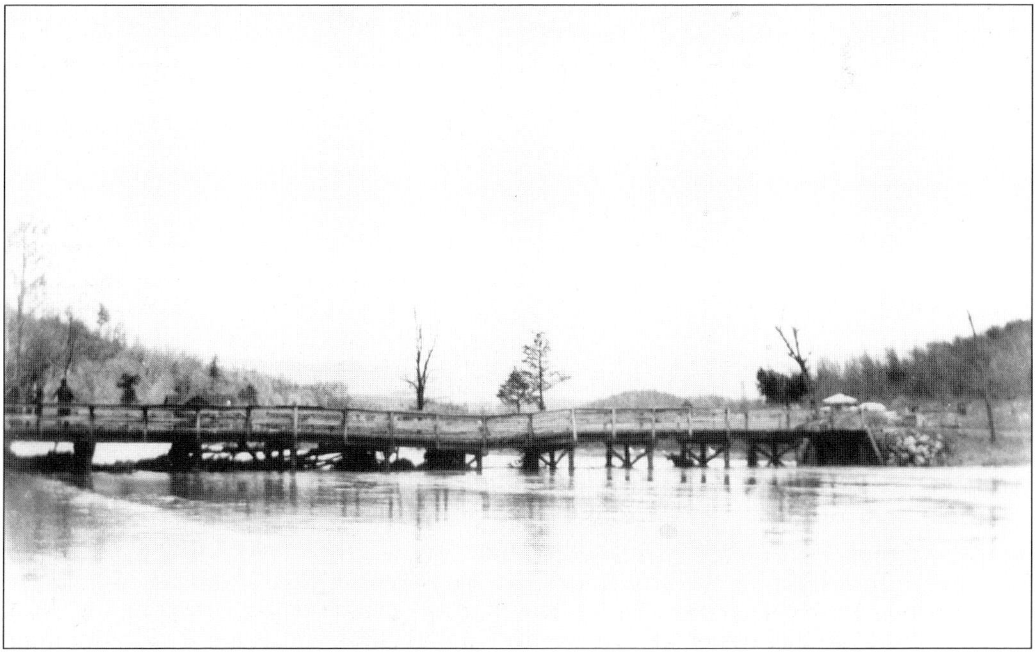

The wooden bridge over Runions Creek had a "dip" in the middle caused by high water. This view looks upstream during a flood, probably in the 1920s. (Matthew E. "Bud" Miller collection.)

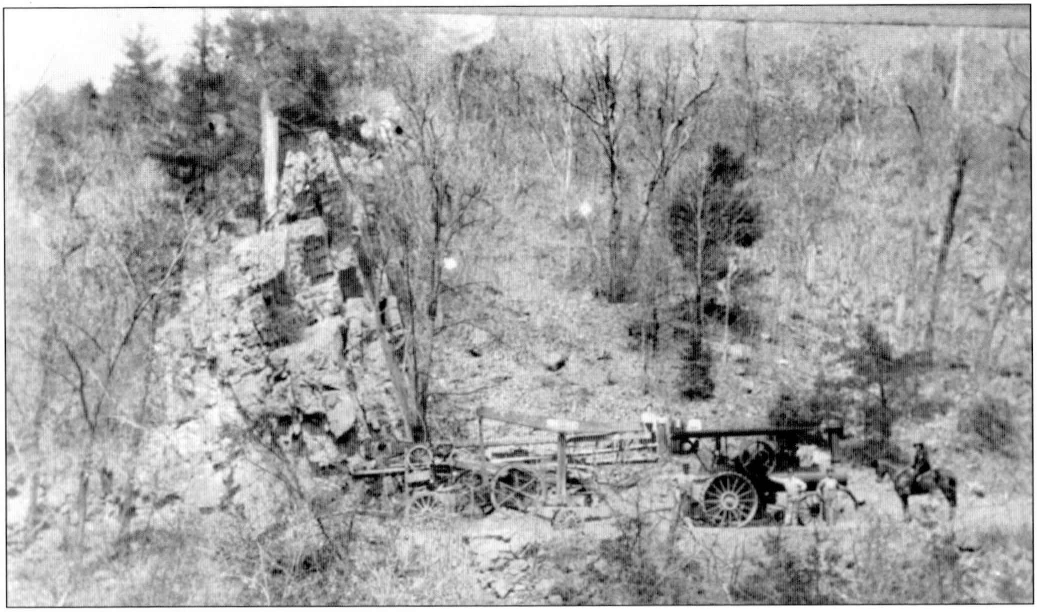

In the early days, going out of Brocks Gap required fording the North Fork three times. In 1848, Elder John Kline proposed cutting down the Gap rocks, making a road on the cut, and erecting a bridge across one of the fords. During his lifetime, part of the plan was enacted. In 1880, a new road and bridge, paid for by private subscriptions, eliminated the other two fords at the Gap. (Paul "Jack" Kiser collection.)

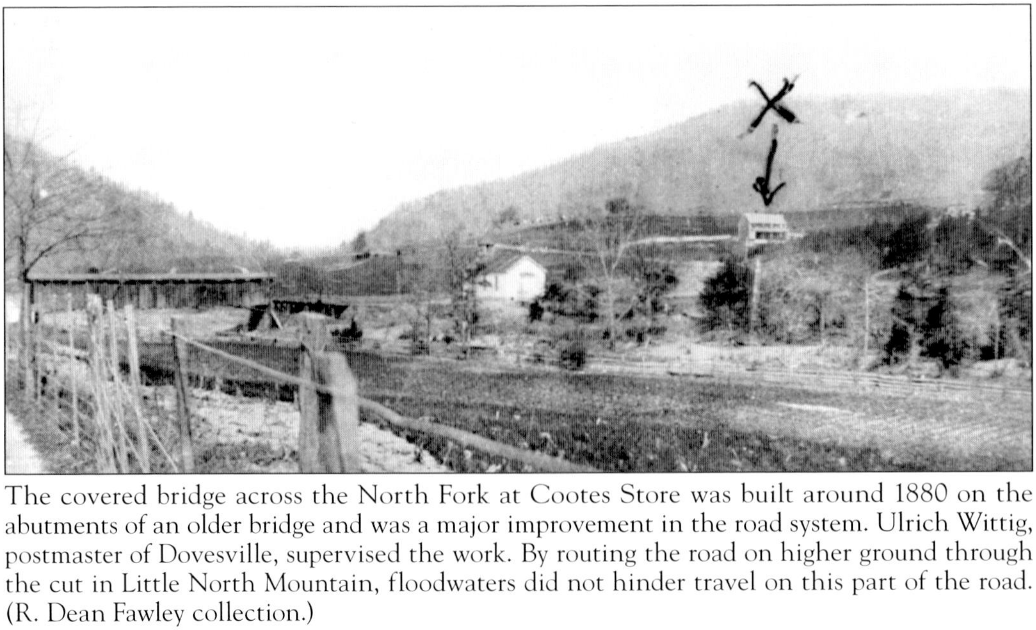

The covered bridge across the North Fork at Cootes Store was built around 1880 on the abutments of an older bridge and was a major improvement in the road system. Ulrich Wittig, postmaster of Dovesville, supervised the work. By routing the road on higher ground through the cut in Little North Mountain, floodwaters did not hinder travel on this part of the road. (R. Dean Fawley collection.)

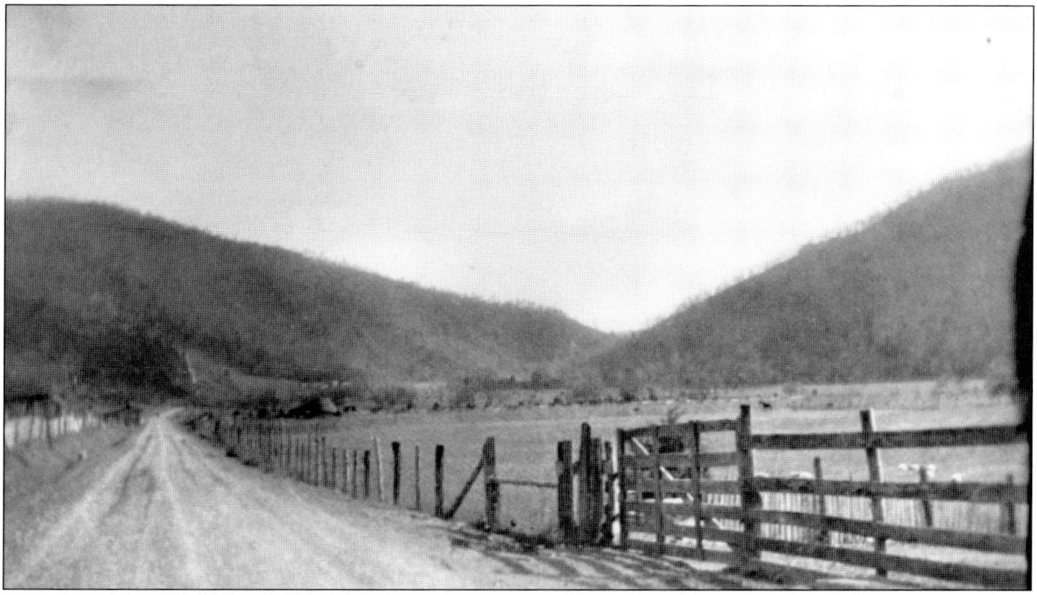

This is Brocks Gap Road, now Highway 259, when it was a dirt road. The lack of telephone poles dates the photograph to before 1908. Chimney Rock is visible at the end of the road, and the building in the distance is probably the tollgate. (Magdaline Heatwole Stewart collection.)

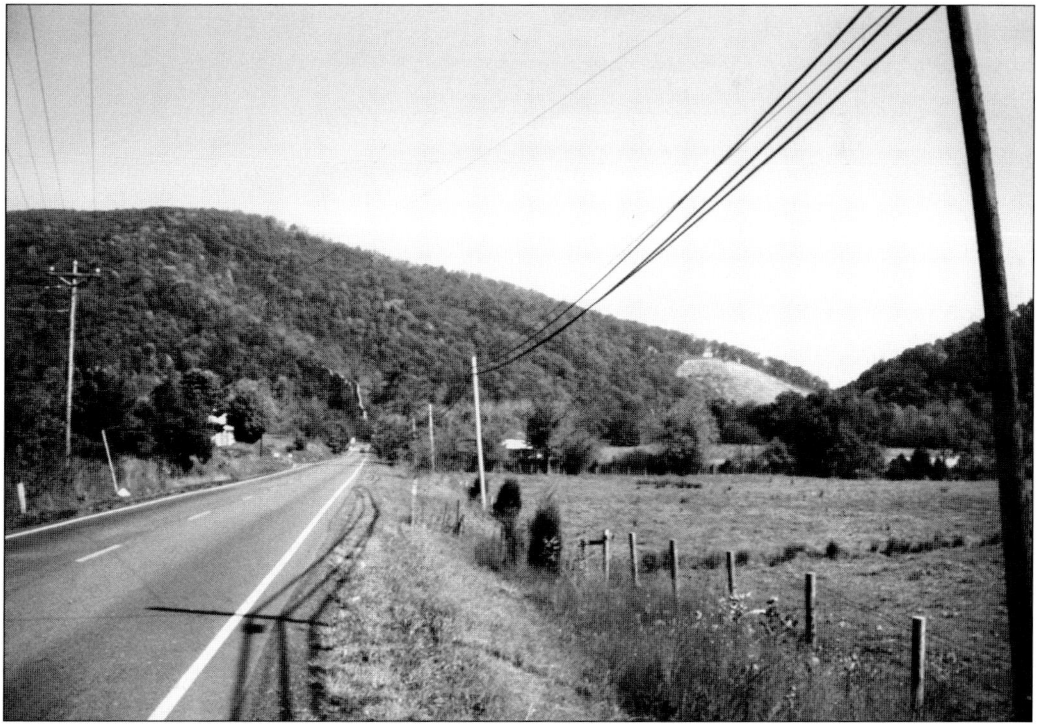

This is Brocks Gap Road in 1995. Chimney Rock is visible at the end of the road. The rocks at Brocks Gap were blasted away to widen the road in 1988 and 1989. (Pat Turner Ritchie, photographer.)

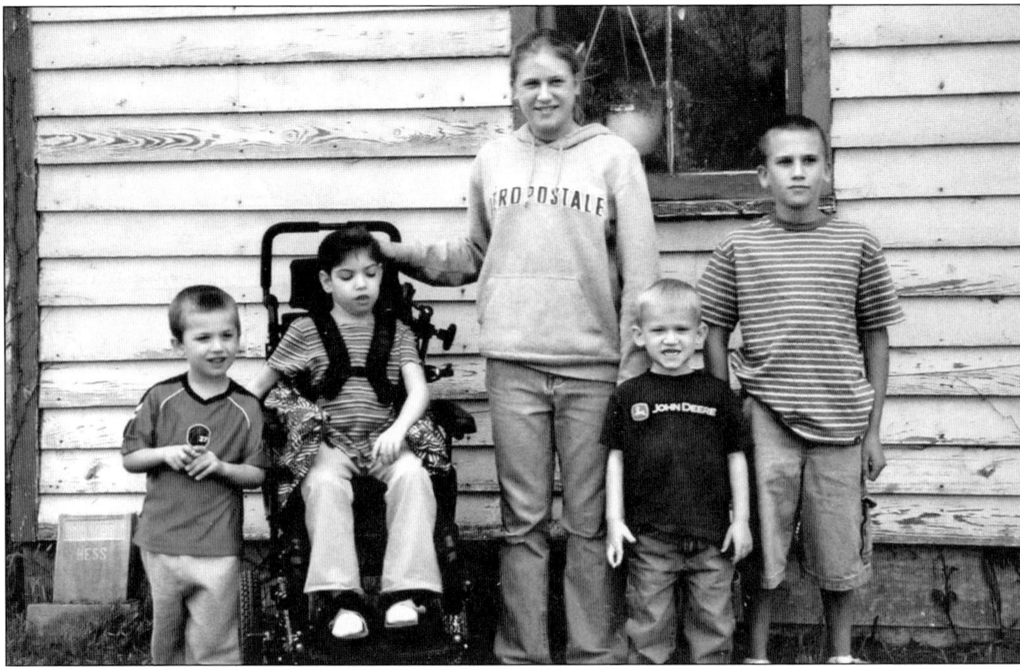

The first settlers came to Brocks Gap in the 1730s. A German settlement formed when the Cains, Shoemakers, and others arrived by 1742. In 1745, the Custer and Humble families moved from Pennsylvania. Logan, Haley, Morgan, Brad, and Daniel Custer (pictured above from left to right) are the 11th generation of the Custer/Humble family in Brocks Gap. The Custer farm with its family graveyard remained in the family from 1765 until 1976. (Diane Custer, photographer.)

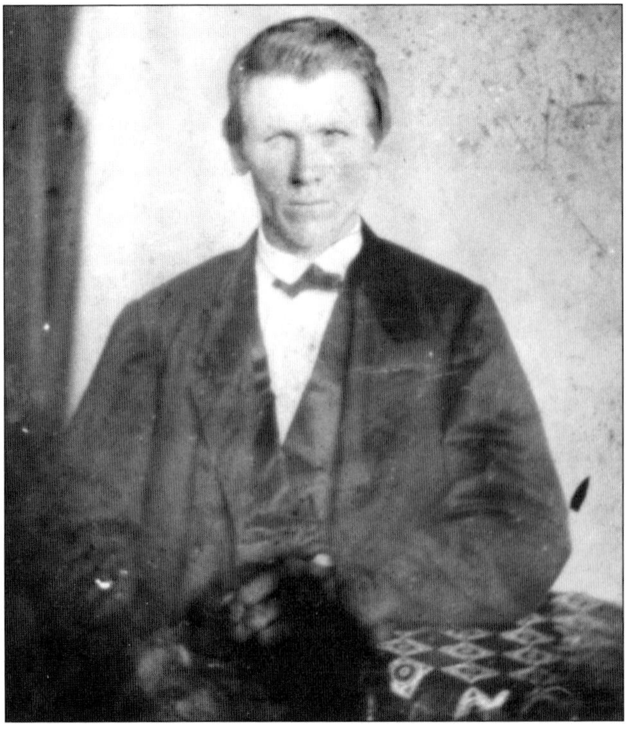

German-speaking settlers continued to arrive in Brocks Gap. Around 1800, the Fawley, Smith, Ritchie, Souder, Wean, Lantz, and Sonifrank families and others moved from Loudoun County's German settlement. The last family to come directly from Germany was Ulrich Wittig's family in 1837. His three oldest children, including Henry Wittig Sr., shown here, were born in Germany. A large landowner, Ulrich was the first postmaster at Dovesville and owned a store and mill. (Jesse Wittig collection.)

German or "Pennsylvania Dutch" was spoken for generations, particularly in the Criders and Bergton areas, known as Germany in county records. In fact, some adults living today were taught Pennsylvania Dutch by their parents. Jacob Crider's family spoke "Dutch." The following members of the Crider family are pictured here from left to right: (seated) Jacob and Franklin; (standing) Martha Wittig Crider, Minnie, Mary, Lula (smallest girl), and David R. Crider. (Mabel A. Mathias collection.)

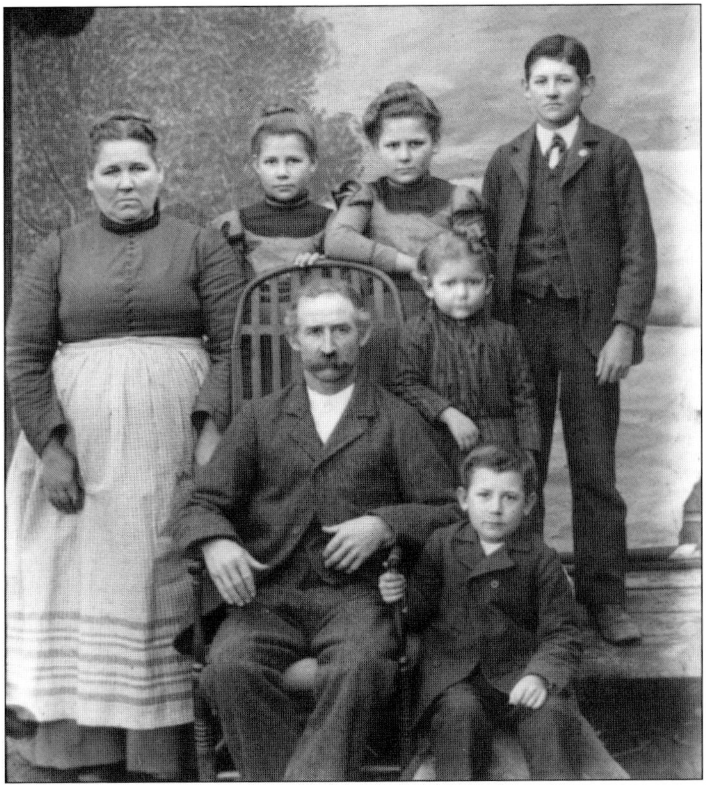

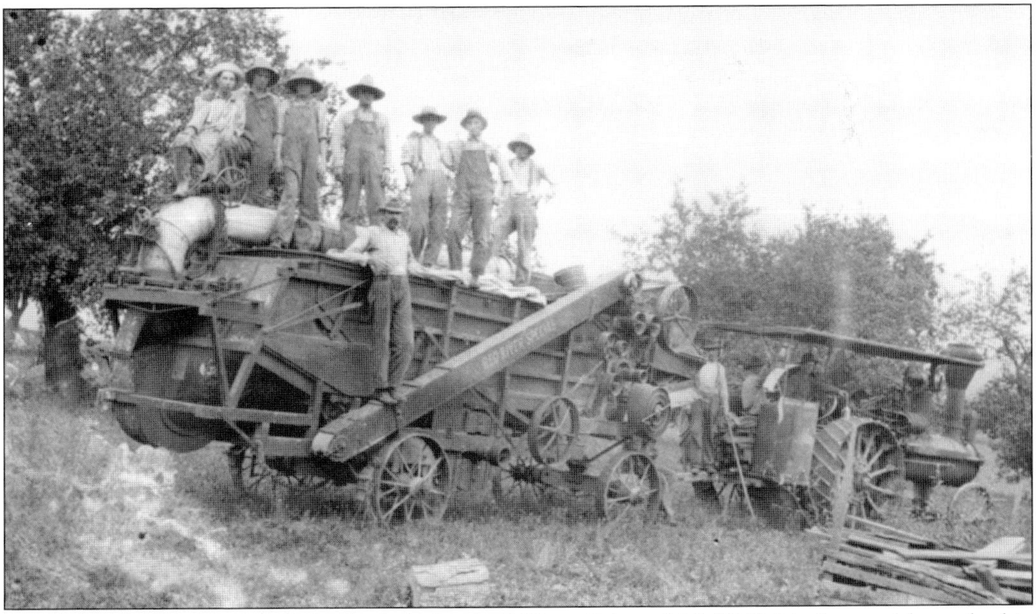

Rural families practiced "help for help back." When Edward N. "Ed" Lindamood brought his steam engine and threshing machine from North Mountain, neighbors would go from farm to farm to help thresh wheat. Ten to twelve men fed the machine, ricked the straw, and hauled the wheat to the wheat bin. While men threshed, several women prepared the meal, because feeding the workers was customary. (Vivian Hiser Knepper collection.)

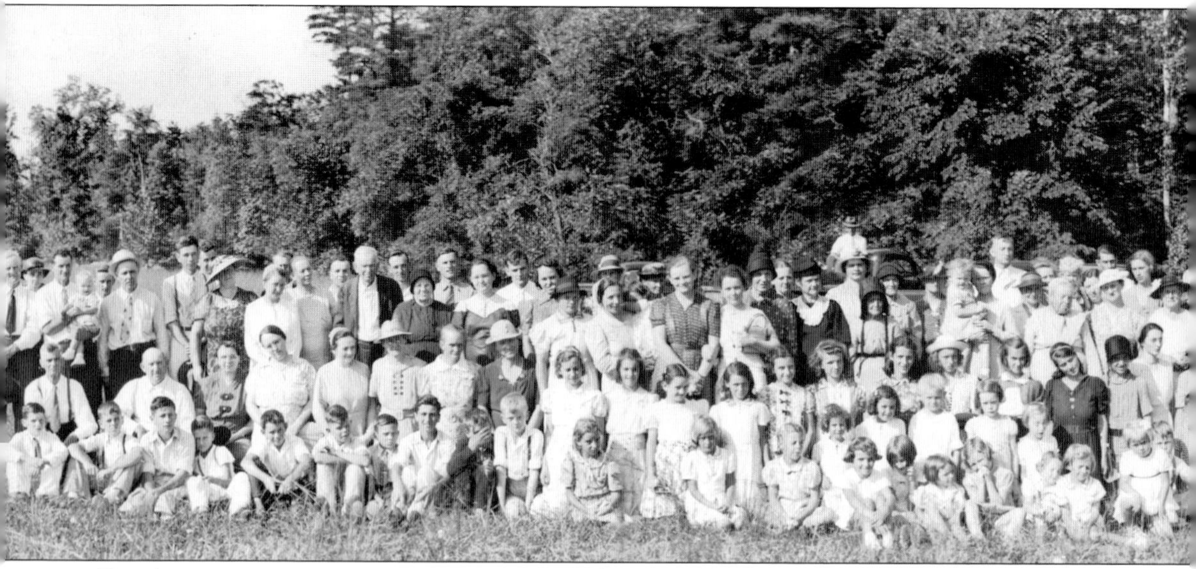

Family connections are very important to Brocks Gap folks. Family historian Goldie Turner May wrote that when meeting a stranger, her father would interrogate them at length to see if some relationship could be established. Sixty years later, she found herself asking, "as [her] father before [her], over and over of people, 'Who are your parents and grandparents?' or 'Who did you marry and where do your people live?'" Goldie May also wrote that she learned the names of all her

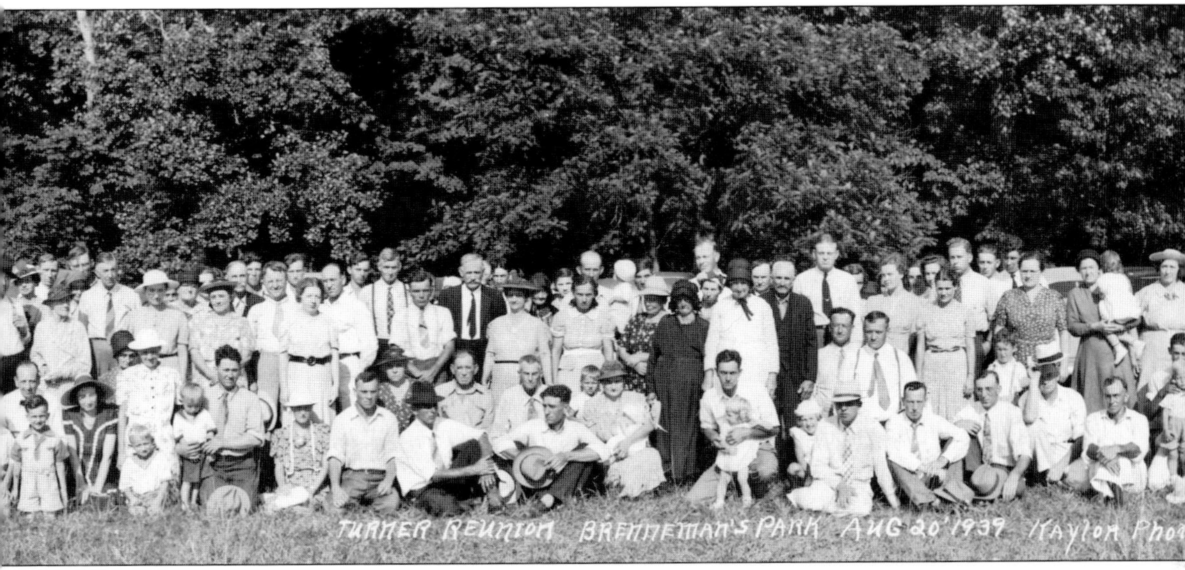

uncles, aunts, and their spouses, as well as the names of her 97 first cousins. Her brother C. C. Turner organized the Turner reunion, pictured here, at Brenneman's Park in 1939. Descendants of all the Turners of Brocks Gap were welcome, even though some of the attendees were fourth or fifth cousins. (Ruth A. Turner collection.)

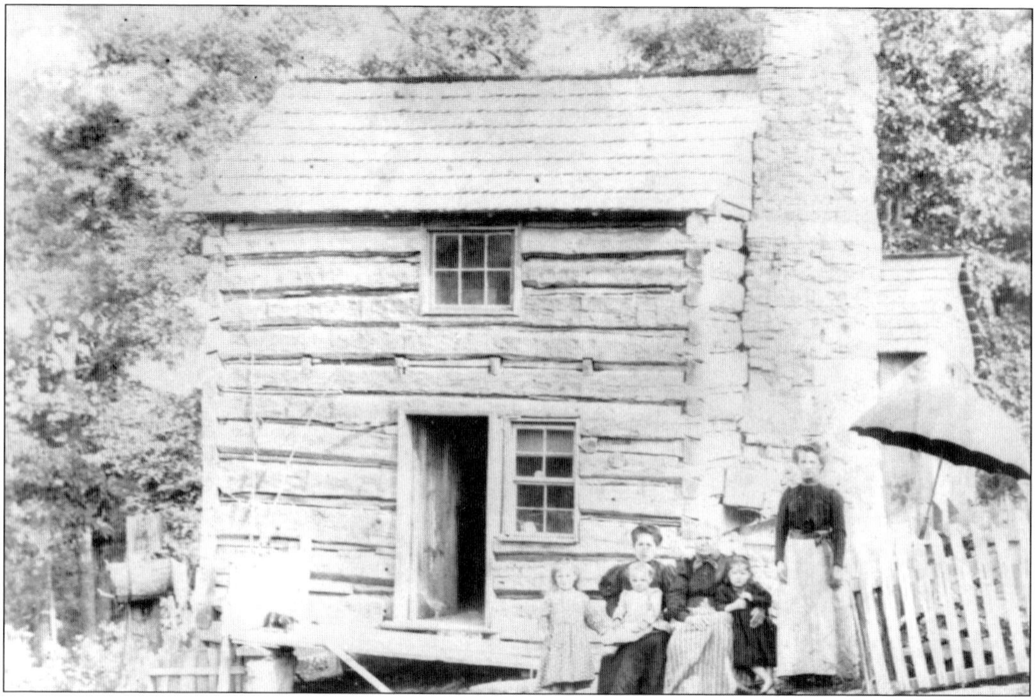

Emanuel "Man" Smith's home on Bennetts Run near Bergton is an example of a mountain farm around 1900. The two-story home is made of squared logs and has a wooden shingle roof and stone fireplace. A picket fence separates the family's yard from the farm. Pictured from left to right are Bertha V. Crider, Sarah "Lizzie" Dove Crider holding Herbert Crider, Clara Dove Ritchie, Bessie L. Crider, and Dorcas Mook. (Shirley Cullers Miller collection.)

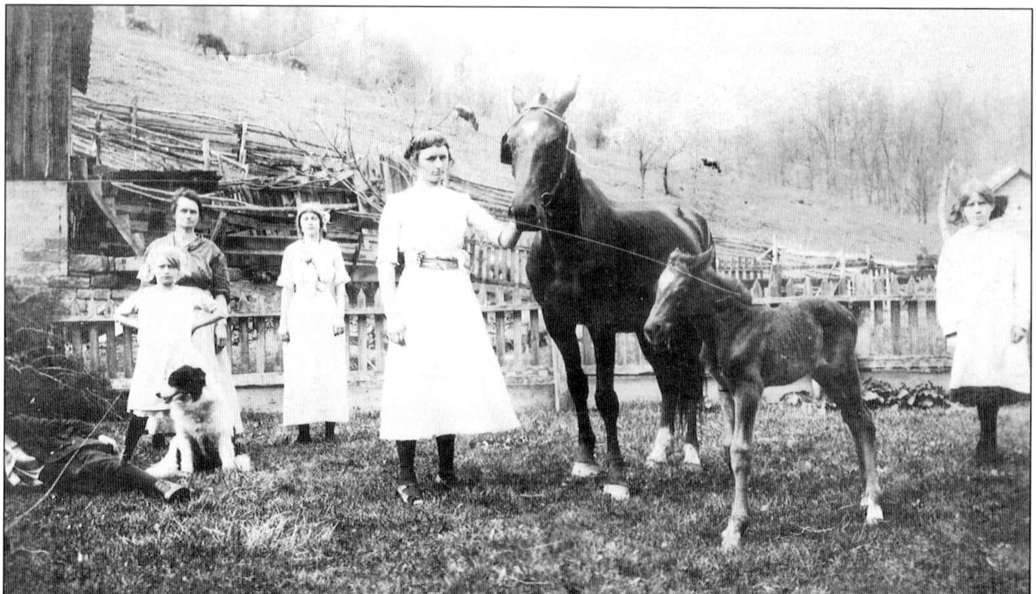

This is another farm scene familiar to anyone who grew up on the Shenandoah Mountain. Cattle grazing on a steep hillside, picket fences, buildings with stone foundations, and neat yards were typical of mountain farms even in the 1930s and 1940s. (David L. Smith collection.)

Two

EVERYDAY LIFE

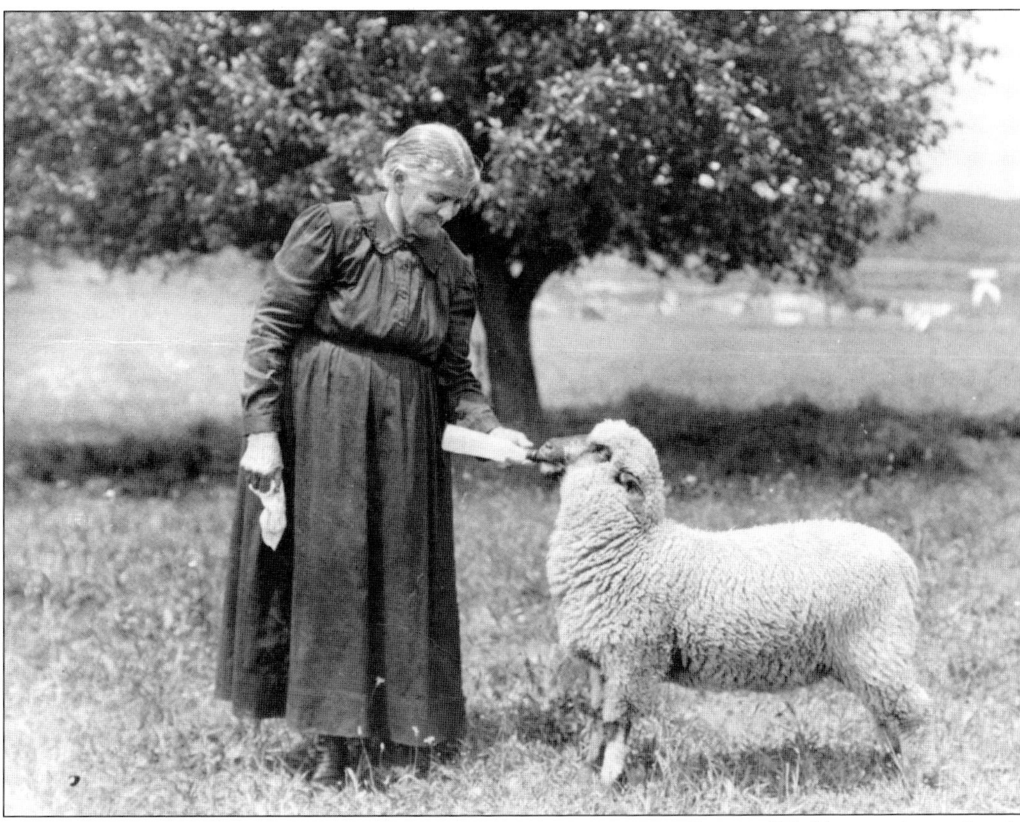

Long after the lamb had grown up, Mary Virginia "Jennie" Basore Albrite still fed her pet from a bottle. The Albrites lived in the Riverside Church area where Jennie and her husband, J. Mosee Albrite, reared their 12 children and took care of elderly relatives. (Lena Albrite Turner collection.)

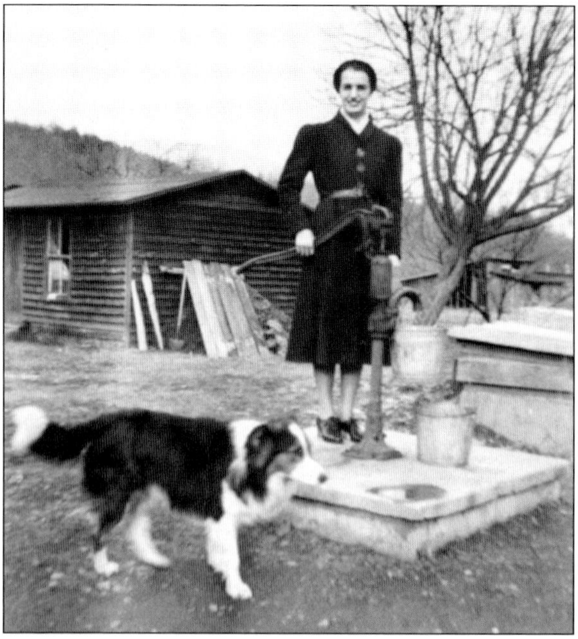

A hand pump was a great invention and eliminated numerous daily trips to the spring. This hand pump was in use at Frank and Ida Nesselrodt Ritchie's home in Criders. Even though she is dressed for church, pumping water was a necessity for Frank's daughter Thelma Ritchie Bowers. (Thelma Ritchie Bowers collection.)

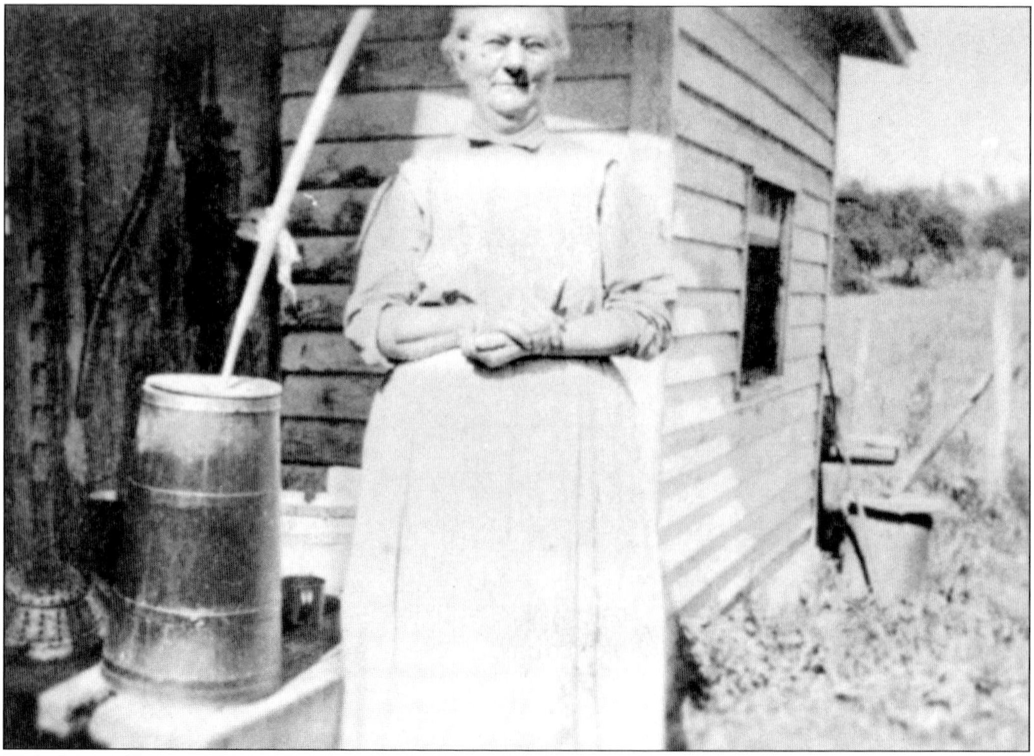

Isabella "Bell" Hess (1857–1931) was the sixth generation to live on the Custer homestead on Dry River. Her porch was part of her dairy operation where she used the up and down butter churn and cottage cheese colander. The hand pump and tin cup are visible in the shadows behind the churn. Bell was first married to Erasmus Jacob Mathias and later to Robert Calvin Miller. (Matthew E. "Bud" Miller collection.)

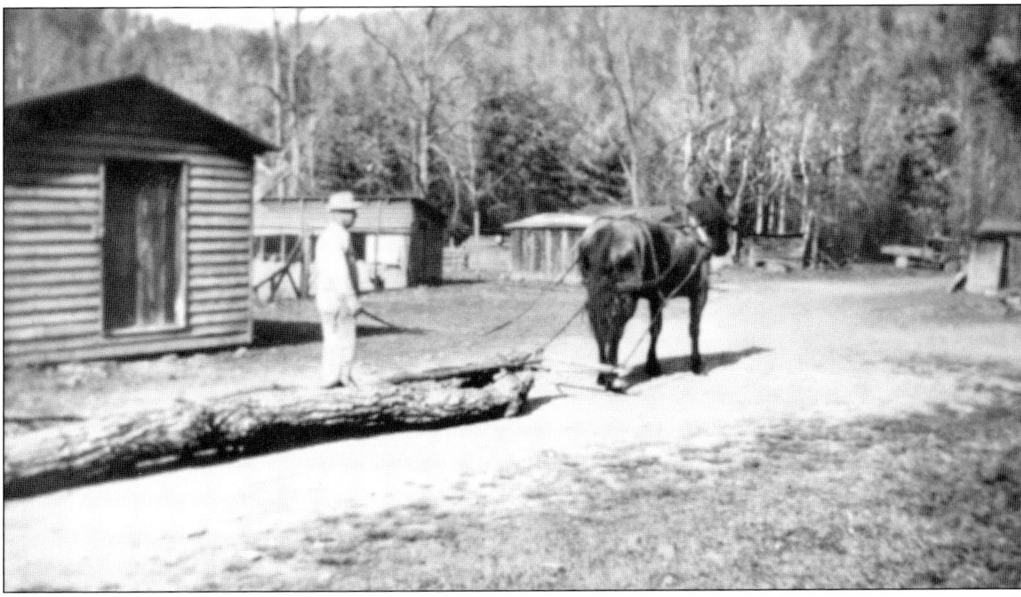

Wood was necessary for heating and cooking, and men worked throughout the year to supply enough wood for the family's stoves. Earl Ritchie uses his horse to bring in a log from the woods. His father's 1922 Ford Model T truck is in the distance. Originally, there was no truck cab, and Frank had to sit on the gas tank; Harvey Dove built the cab for Frank. (Thelma Bowers collection.)

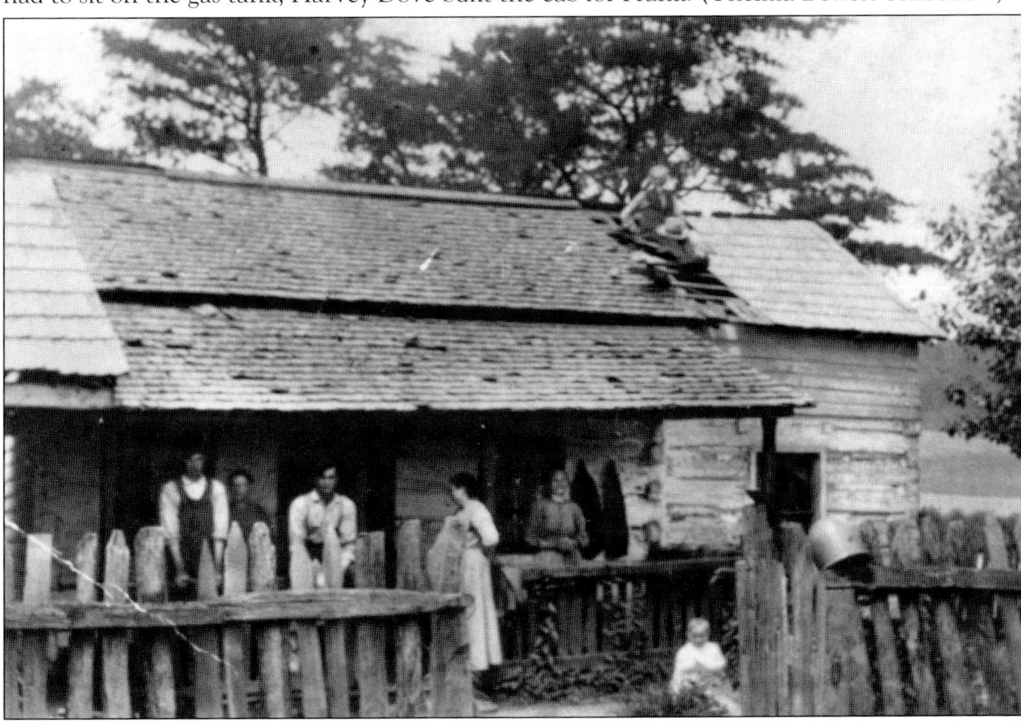

Regardless of the type of home, repairs are sometimes required. Even though he was about 76 years old, Confederate veteran Isaac Turner (1835–1913) is on the roof replacing shingles in this 1911 photograph. Isaac's grandson Ralph C. Fulk is the baby pictured. The log home was near the Genoa school. (Rhoda Fulk Turner May collection.)

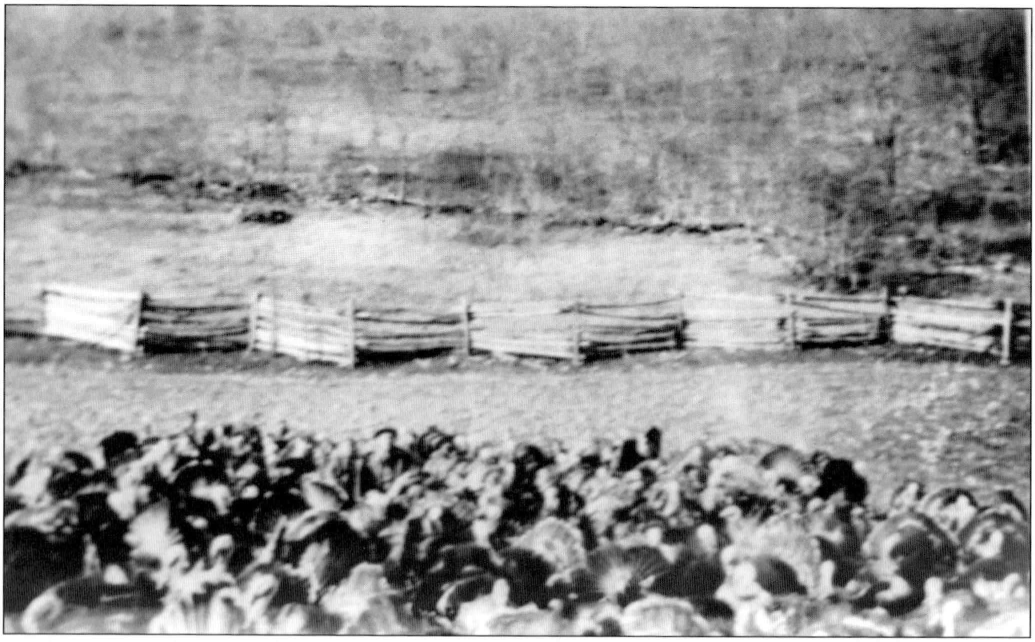

Poultry provided cash to farmers. In the second decade of the 20th century, Elder Daniel Turner raised about 50 turkeys to sell, with turkey hens setting on eggs in individual coops in a field. To feed the poults (turkeys), Dan cut up cooked chicken eggs, shells and all. When they could eat oats, bugs, and grass, they were turned onto the range. This view of turkeys on the range is in Criders. (Luther Crider collection.)

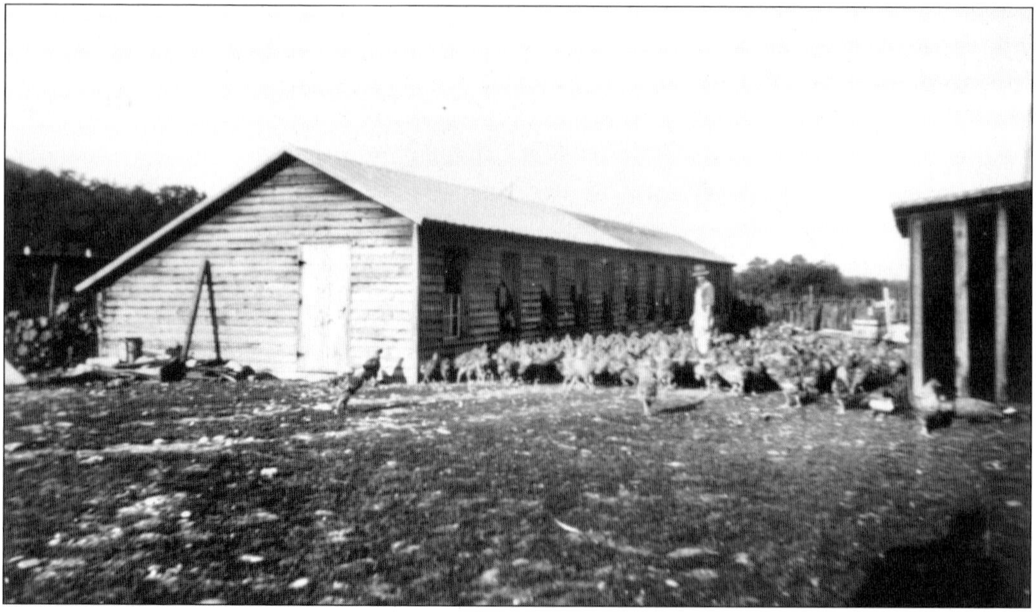

Frank Ritchie of Criders raised chickens in five houses like this one. At first, water was carried by hand and stored in wooden barrels outside each house. Later trenches were hand-dug for water pipes to the houses. When this photograph was taken, chickens were allowed to range near the chicken houses. In later years, Frank's grandchildren raised chickens here to earn money for their school expenses. (Thelma Ritchie Bowers collection.)

Poultry was a source of protein and a cash crop. Guy C. Stultz of Criders is inside a poultry pen with a mother duck and family about 1920. Country stores bought eggs from local people. In 1880, a large goose egg was worth a penny. The "Personals" column of the *Daily News-Record* also reveals that "borrowing" chickens from the neighbors' chicken houses late at night was not uncommon. (Leota Moyers Stultz collection.)

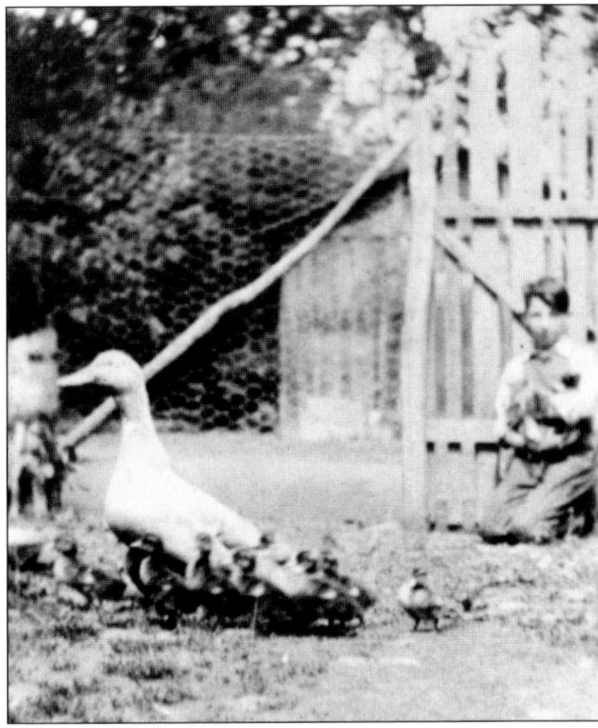

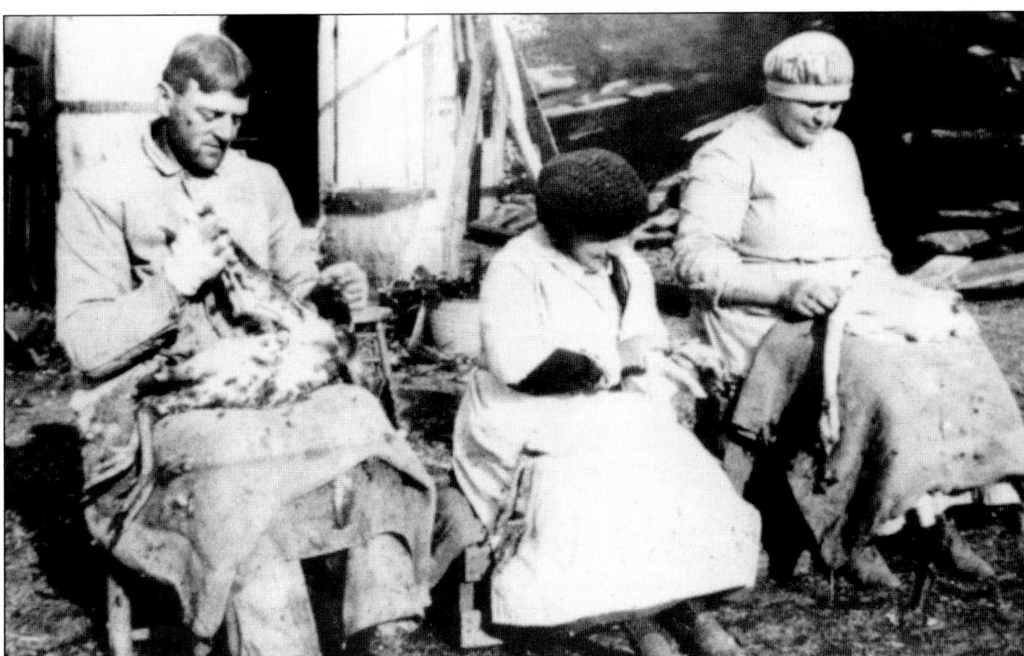

Abram G. Fulk, his wife, Lura Neff Fulk, and Bertha "Byrd" Fawley pluck turkeys, perhaps to sell. In the fall, families who raised extra turkeys would butcher them, pluck the feathers, take out the entrails, and hang them in a cool spot overnight. The next day, the turkeys would be packed in wooden barrels and taken to Broadway by wagon for train shipment to a large city. (Mary Fulk Turner collection.)

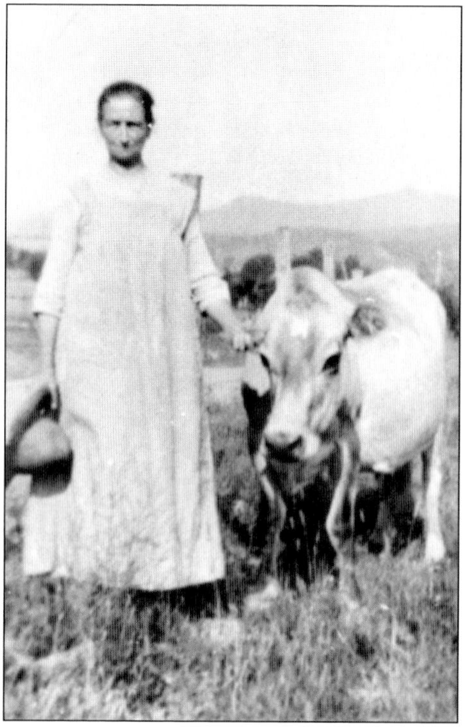

Milking and making butter and cheese was a time-consuming chore as Sophia Custer Fawley Turner could testify. Butter was traded at local stores for other goods. At Michael Baker's store near Fulks Run in the early 1800s, 23 different people sold butter to the store, from 2 to 33 pounds at a time. An 1823 store journal entry says that they sold the butter in Richmond. (R. Dean Fawley collection.).

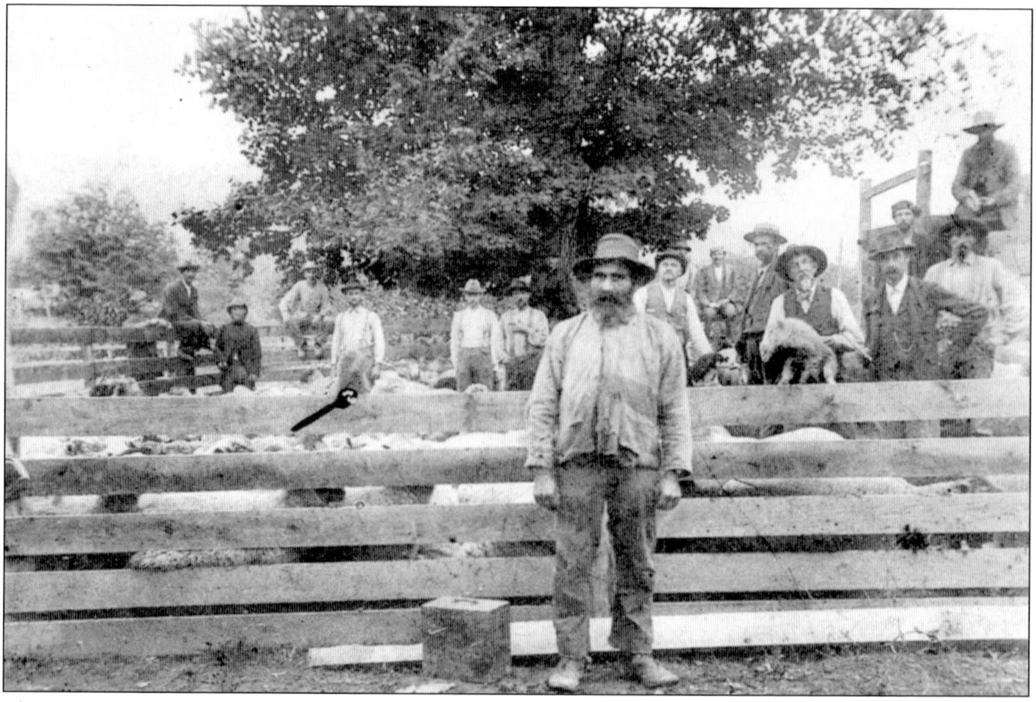

Sheep were raised for wool and food. Surplus wool could be exchanged at the local store. From 1804 until 1823, Michael Baker's store sold three sets of wool cards (necessary to prepare wool for spinning), bought lambs' wool from three individuals, and sold lambs' wool to eleven other customers. These men have probably gathered to buy and sell sheep before 1890. (Carl Fulk collection.)

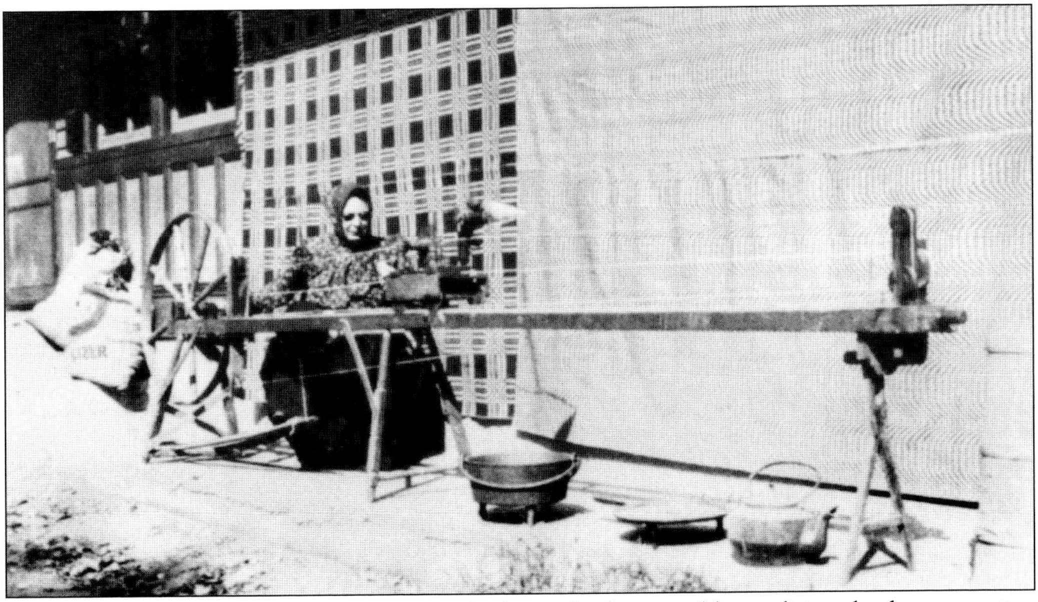

In this 1920s photo, Virginia "Dare" Turner Stultz paid tribute to older traditions by demonstrating the cottage spinning wheel and displaying hand-woven coverlets and other antiques. Some women were especially talented and sold their work. In 1804, Caty Fulk sold eight yards of cotton she had woven to Michael Baker's store, while others sold knitted caps and made clothing to order. (Leota Moyers Stultz collection.)

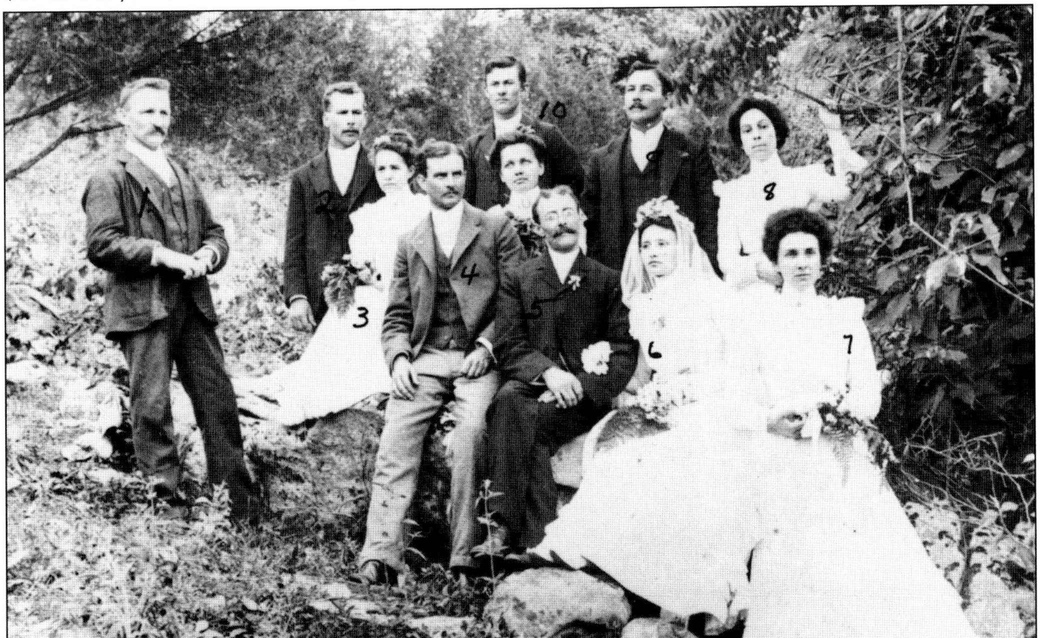

Rev. J. H. Lutz, minister at Phanuel's Lutheran Church in Bergton from 1894 to 1904, supported holding the first Christmas tree service in 1896, which needed congregational approval. In 1898, the church furnished a buggy and harness for his use and paid for feed for Maud, the pastor's horse. Members of the wedding party are unknown except (1) Reverend Lutz, (2) James Webster Dove, and (9) Lee May. (Goldie Turner May collection.)

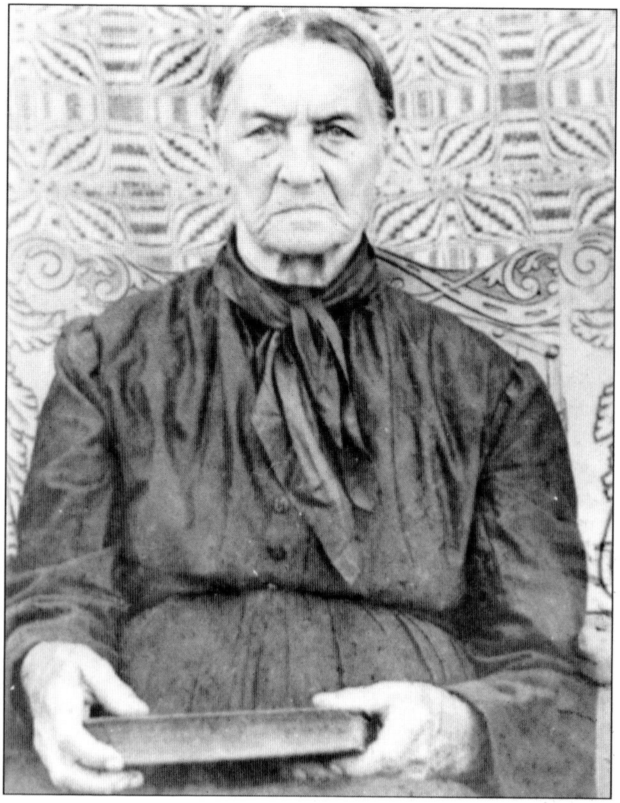

Local midwives delivered babies in Brocks Gap until the 1940s. County birth certificates from 1912 to 1917 showed that 52 Brocks Gap women delivered babies. Katherine "Kate" Fulk Dove traveled by buckboard from Fort Seybert, West Virginia, to Criders to deliver nine babies during this period. In 1919, when she was delivering a baby in the E. A. Caplinger family, she contracted pneumonia and died soon after. (Vonnie Swindle collection.)

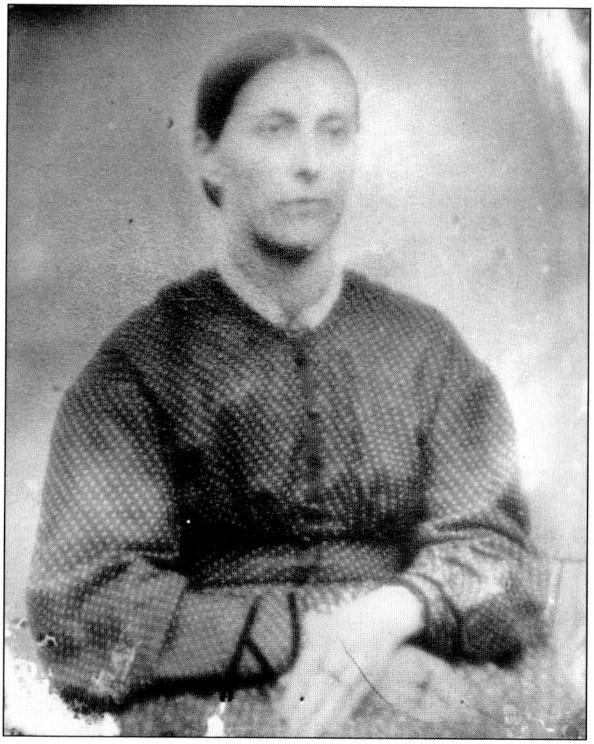

Life before modern medicine was hazardous to children. In 1900, there were 152 mothers in Bergton and Criders. At this time, nearly half of them had lost at least one child. Pictured at right, Rachel Blizzard Wittig, wife of George Wittig Sr., had lost six of her seven children; two other mothers had lost five children each; and two others had lost four children each. (Matthew E. "Bud" Miller collection.)

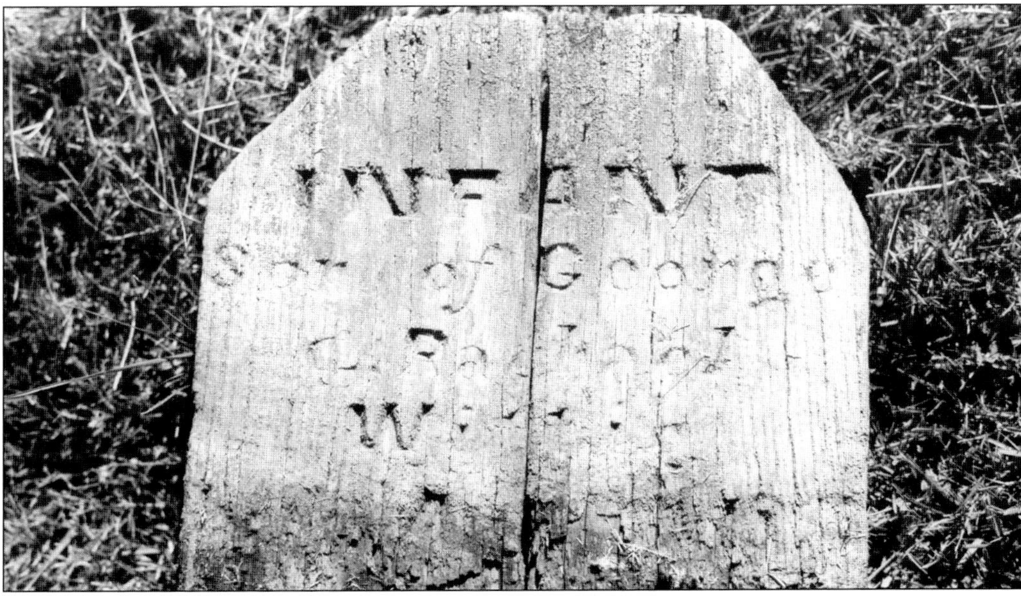

Several families bought tomb boards for their loved ones instead of tombstones in the 1870s. Samuel B. Jordan of Forestville made a set of tomb boards for the Souder family in 1878 for $3, plus 50¢ for delivery to Dovesville. This tomb board for an infant son of George and Rachel B. Wittig at Martin Luther Lutheran Church was replaced with a concrete marker around 2001. (Pat Turner Ritchie, photographer.)

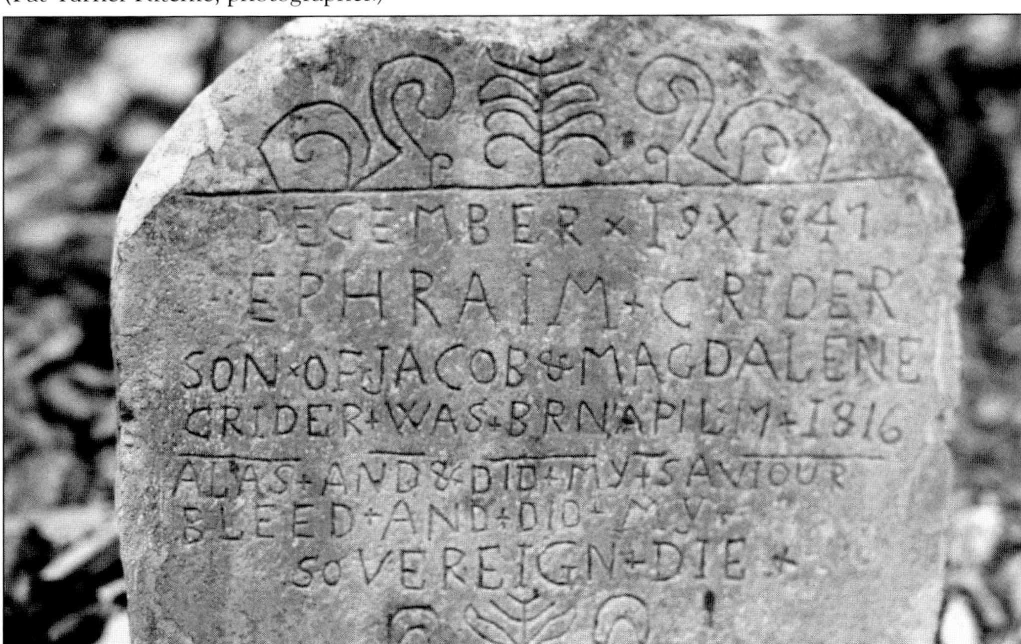

Before 1900, burials usually took place in a family plot, often on hills overlooking the homeplace. At Fulks Run, most early graves were marked with uncarved field rocks. However, Bergton and Crider families frequently marked their family graves with hand-carved and decorated stones. Ephraim Crider's stone in Criders has his dates (1816–1847), names of his parents (Jacob and Magdalene Crider), artwork, and religious statements. (Garnett R. Turner, photographer.)

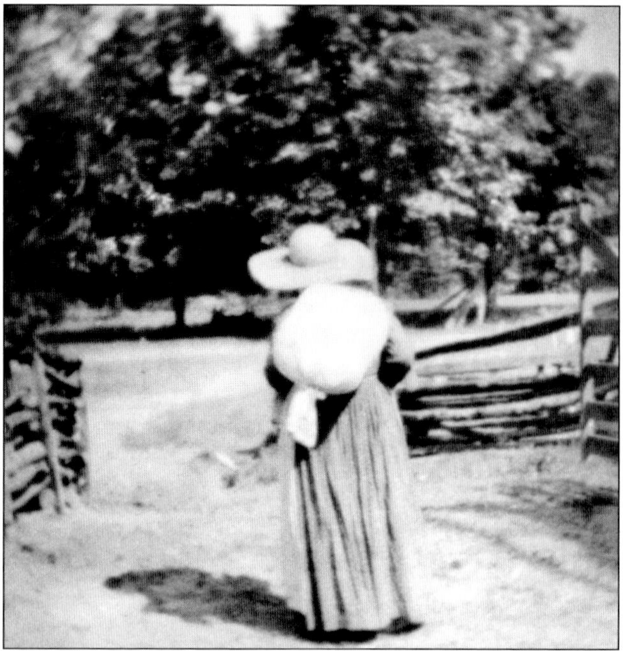

Born about 1832 in Dry River, Susie Bible would spend a few weeks with a family, then pack her belongings in a bundle and walk to the next kind family's home. One time, A. G. Ritchie heard sounds from the Bible cemetery on his farm and found Susie crying at the graves of her loved ones. She died in the Harrisonburg poor house on August 31, 1912. (Madeline Heatwole Stewart collection.)

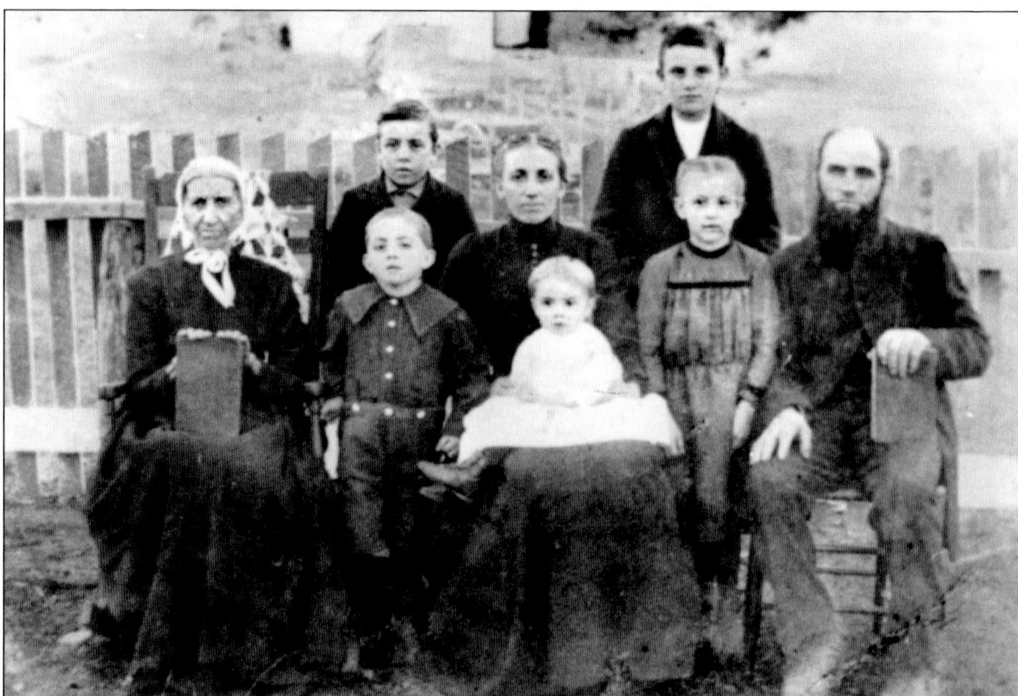

Orphan George H. Fulk lived with Jacob Fawley's family. Worried that he was going to the poor house, George sought reassurance from Jacob, who pointed to the full grain house and told him that as long as there was wheat, he would stay. Members of George's family, pictured around 1898, are, from left to right, (first row) Sarah Miller Bare, Clory, Annie Bare Fulk holding Nora, Rebecca, and Rev. George H. Fulk; (second row) Otis and Jacob Fulk. (Virginia Ann Fawley Hulvey collection.)

Some family branches moved away. Baltimore, Maryland, and Fredericksburg, Pennsylvania, were popular destinations in the 1920s for farm and factory work. On March 27, 1928, Rev. J. Webster Lantz wrote, "Quite a number [of church members] having moved to Maryland and Pennsylvania in the last five or six years." This truck in the 1920s is packed and ready to go. (Leota Moyers Stultz collection.)

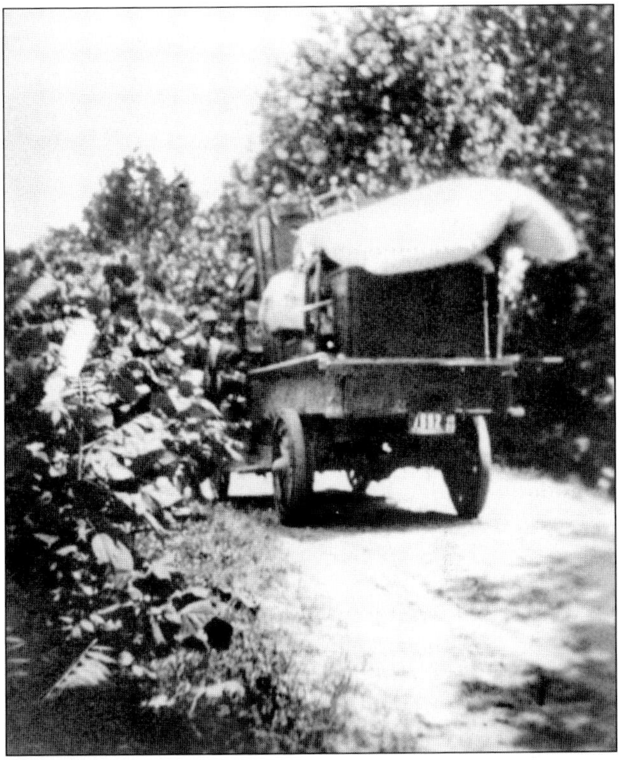

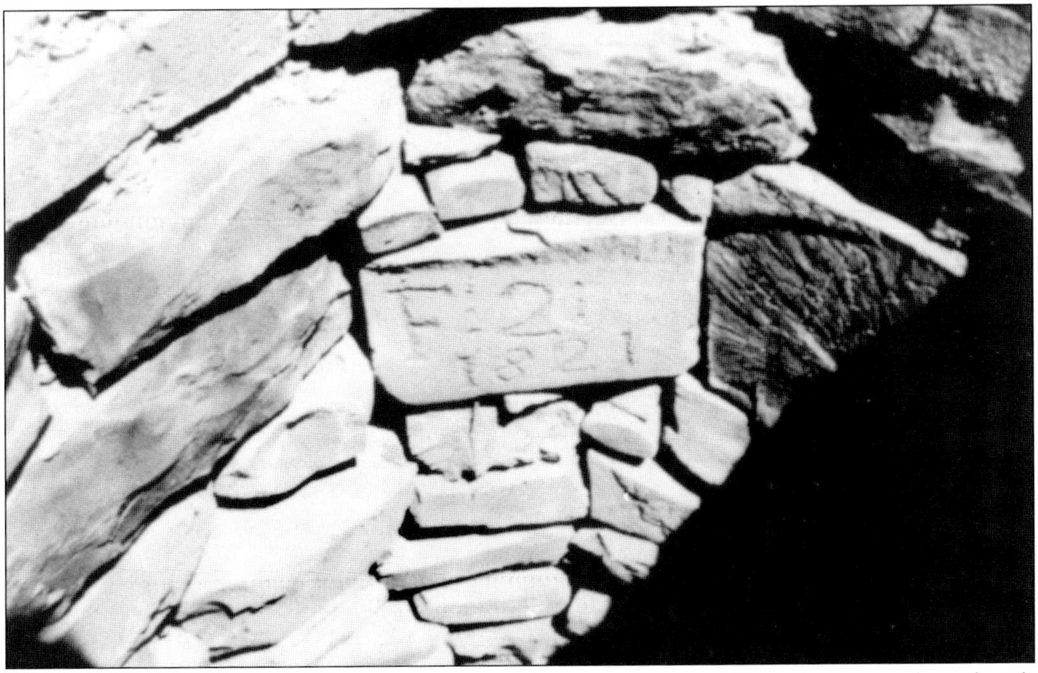

Sometimes our ancestors left mementos for us. The men who dug this well were so pleased with their work that they dated it F 21 1821 (February 21, 1821). The farm is near Trumbo Ford and was in the Riddle-Trumbo-Fawley family for over 100 years. (Carol DeHart, photographer and present owner.)

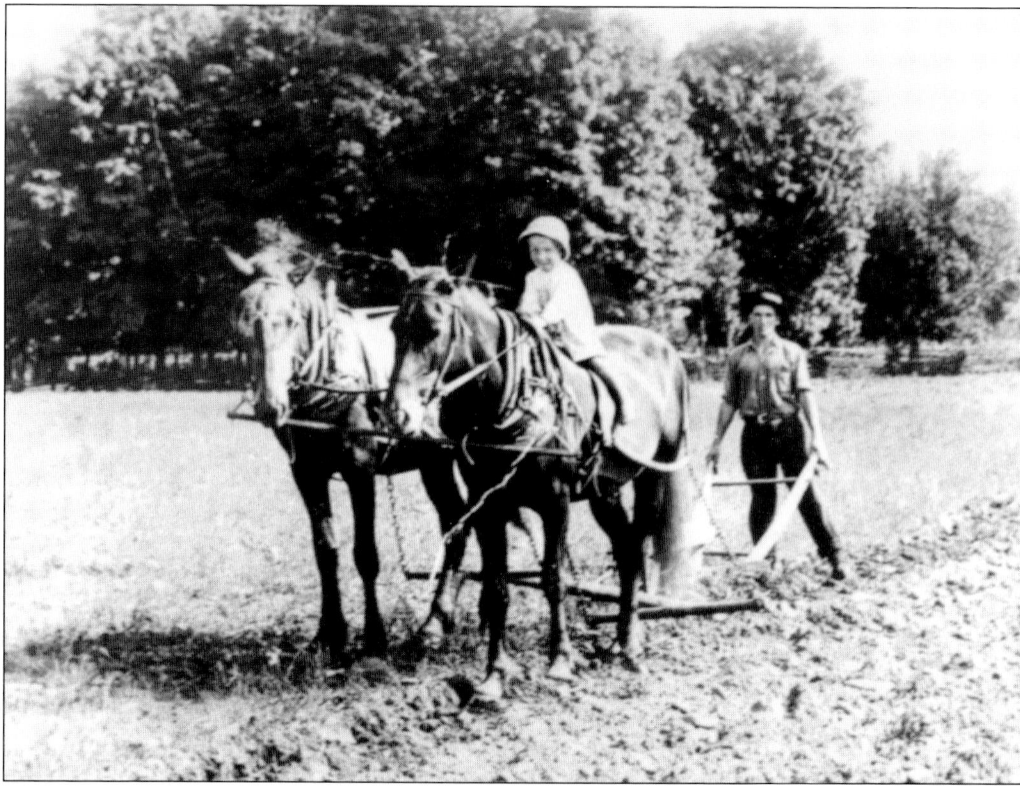

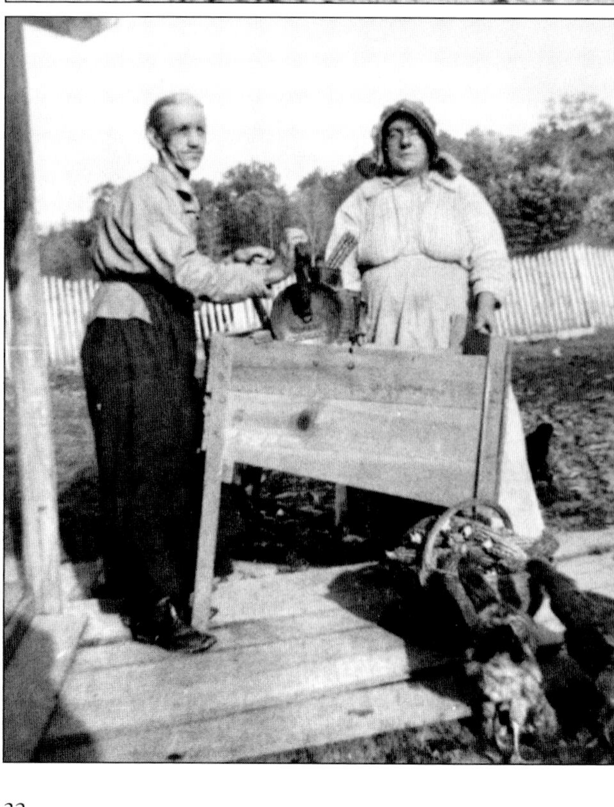

Plowing with horses or mules in the springtime was a common sight before the 1950s. As late as the 1920s, schools operated only from October to April to enable children to help with planting and harvests. Russel J. Whetzel and his youngest brother, Stanley, prepare the field for planting about 1915. (Emma Whetzel Wittig collection.)

Harriet "Hatts" Riddle and neighbor Elizabeth Turner shell dried corn and attract the attention of their chickens. (Velma Turner Cooper collection.)

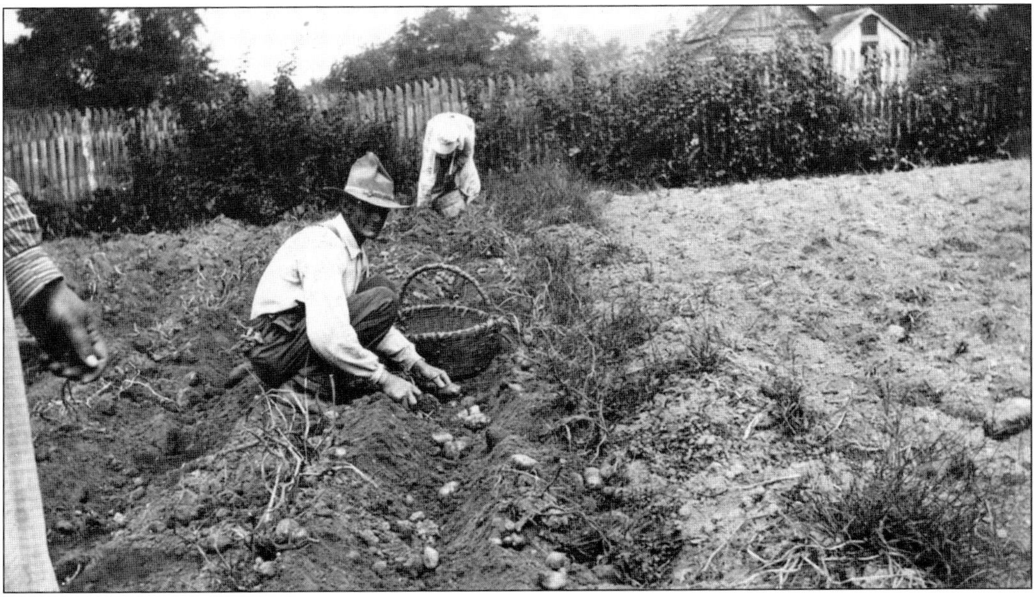

Timothy Ritchie and two unidentified women "make out" potatoes, probably at the Robert and Sarah Trumbo Fawley farm at Fulks Run. The outbuildings in the background have wooden shingles, and the woman at the end of the row is using a wooden bucket to collect her potatoes. (R. Dean Fawley collection.)

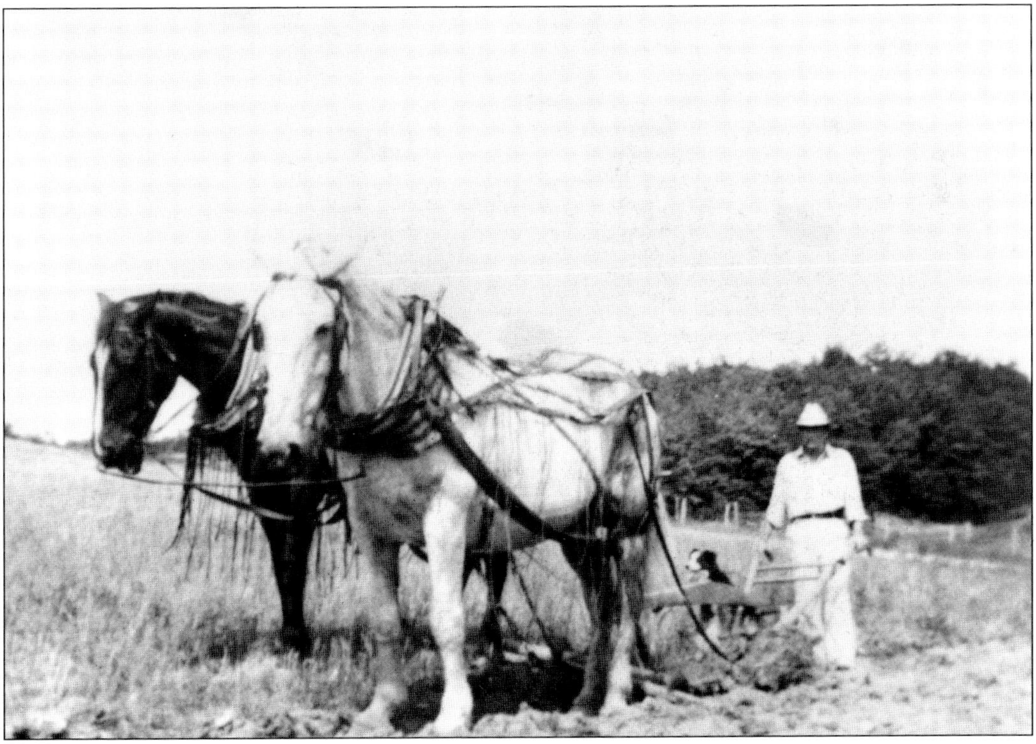

About 1949, Dr. Floyd L. Fulk helped his father, Abram G. Fulk, get ready for spring planting at Fulks Run. Notice the fly straps attached to the harness (early environmentally safe insect repellents). (Dr. Floyd L. Fulk collection.)

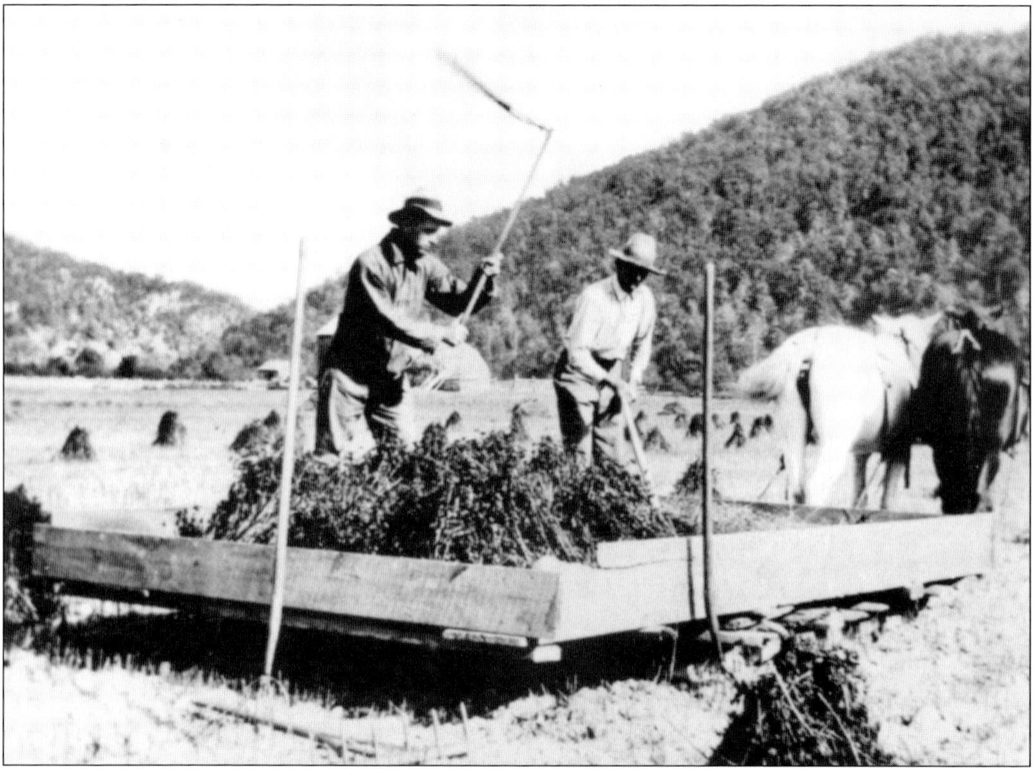

Harold Fawley and John R. Trumbo thresh buckwheat with flails on John's farm, an example of neighbor helping neighbor. The buckwheat had been cut and put into shocks to dry. Notice the handmade wooden rakes beside the threshing platform. Brocks Gap is visible in the background. (Madeline Heatwole Stewart collection.)

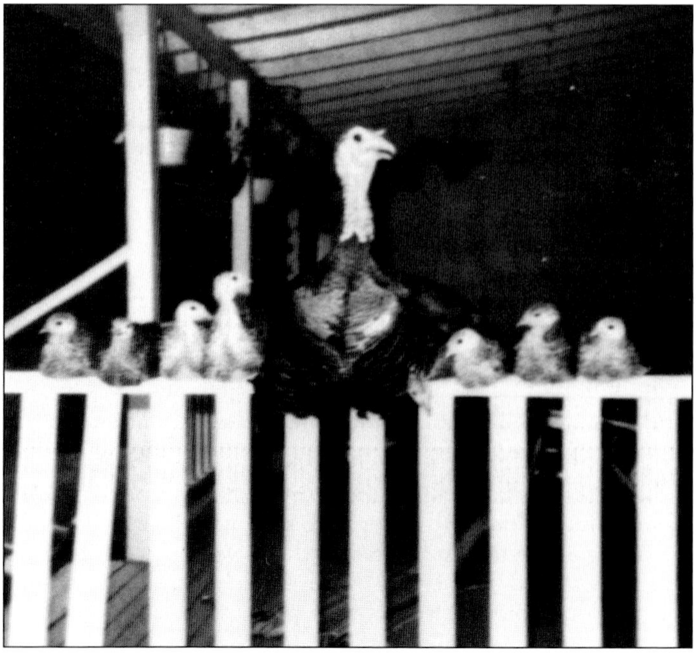

This pet turkey hen and her seven poults enjoy a pleasant evening on the front porch. (Floyd Smith collection.)

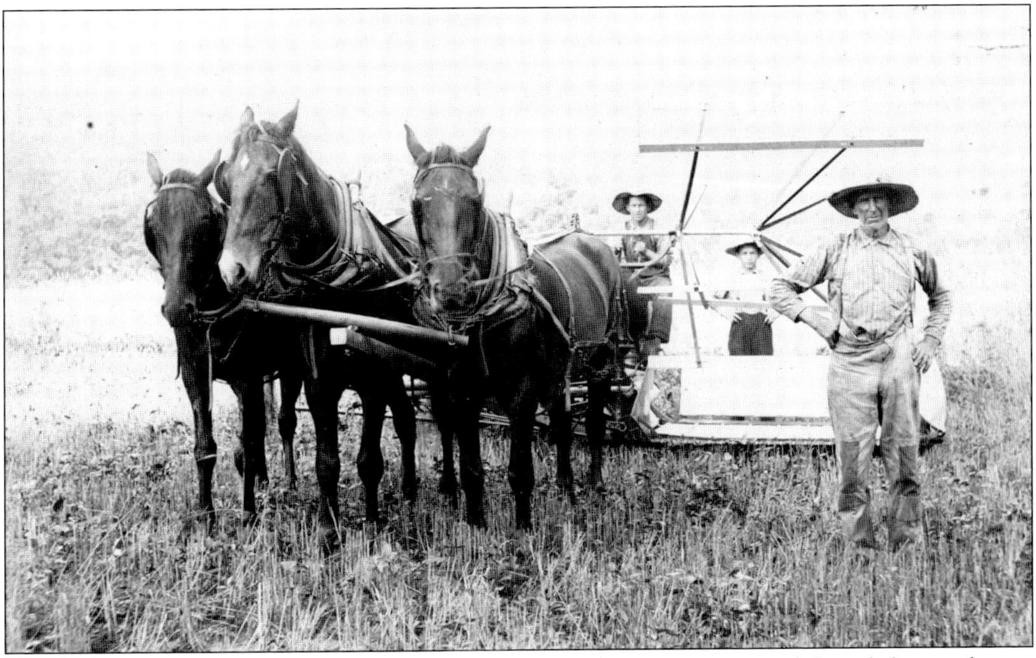

Ahab Dove owned one of the first binders in the Bergton area. Pictured from left to right are horses Moll, Rob, and Pet with W. Hampton "Hamp" Dove, Charlie Riggleman, and Ahab Dove. Ahab was a Confederate veteran and lived near the Bergton store. His daughter Rachel Dove Albrite was a seamstress and may have made his dungarees. (Lena A. Turner collection.)

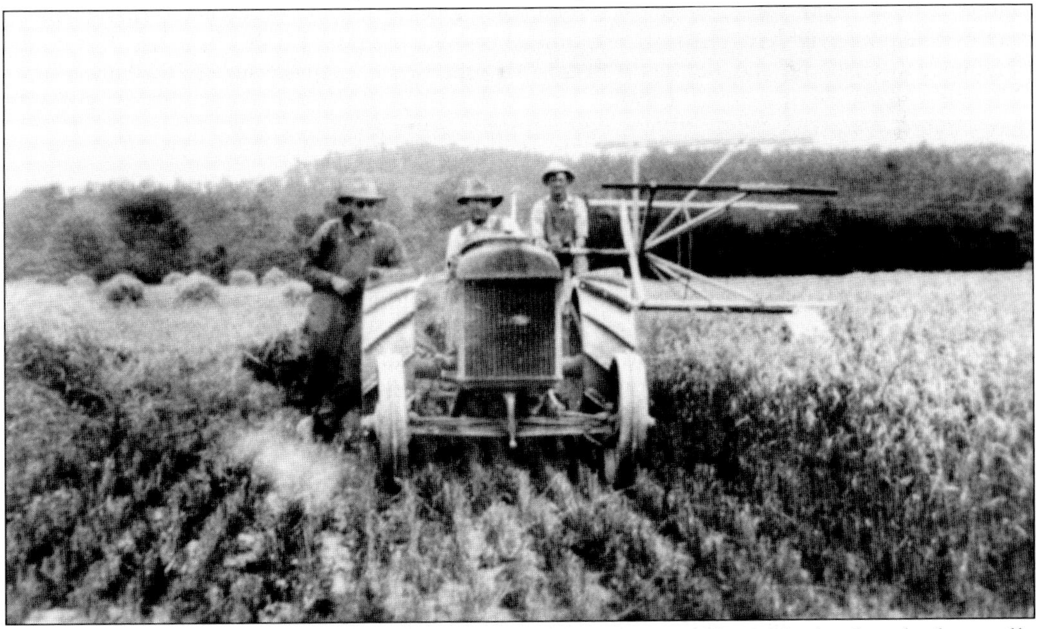

Lloyd G. Turner owned a 1920 four-cylinder Fordson tractor with steel wheels, which usually ran on three cylinders. When harrowing, if the motor died down, the driver had to push in the clutch to rev it up. If the clutch was let out too fast, the front wheels would come off the ground. The workers pictured in this wheat field are unidentified (left), Lloyd Turner (center), and Paul V. "Mick" Miller. (Earl Fulk collection.)

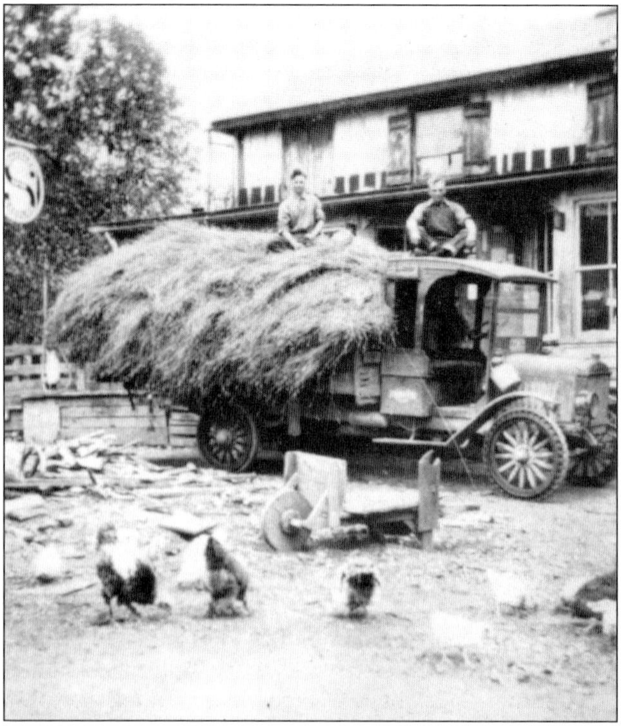

A truck loaded with hay waits at Stultz and Turner's store in Criders. Even though it has no doors, there are roll-down curtains on the window, a bucket to fill the radiator, and large headlights. The driver and passengers sat on wooden supply boxes instead of seats. The chickens are eating around an old wooden wheelbarrow. (Goldie Ketterman Whetzel collection.)

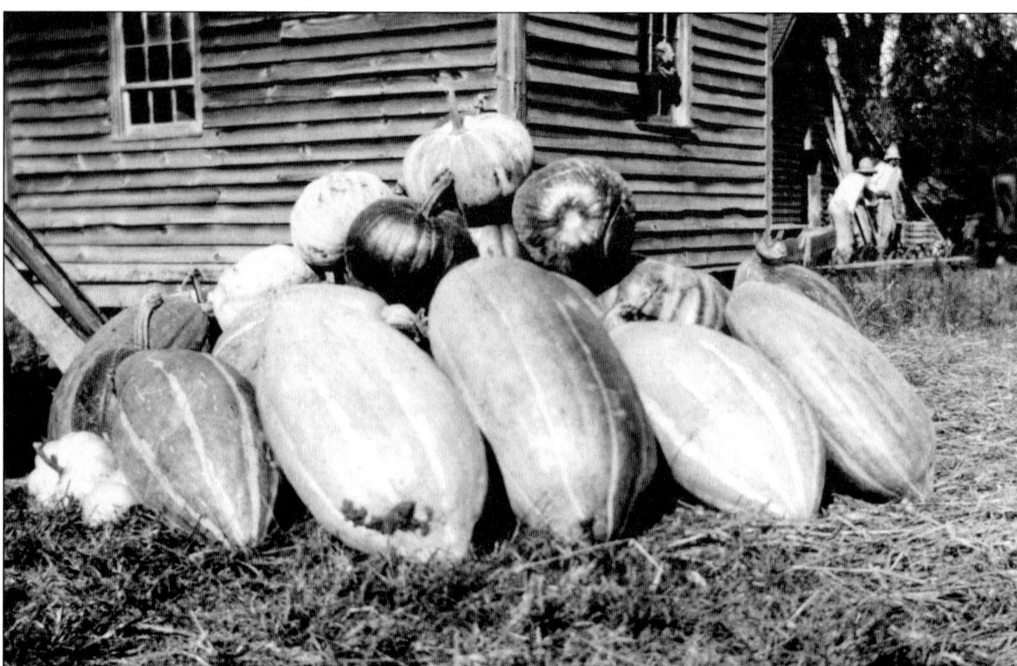

Part of the pumpkin harvest at Elder Daniel Turner's home waits to be stored for the winter about 1918. The four long pumpkins in front are banana pumpkins, a favorite for pies. Some families have saved seeds from year to year from this variety and still grow them today. (Ruth Turner collection.)

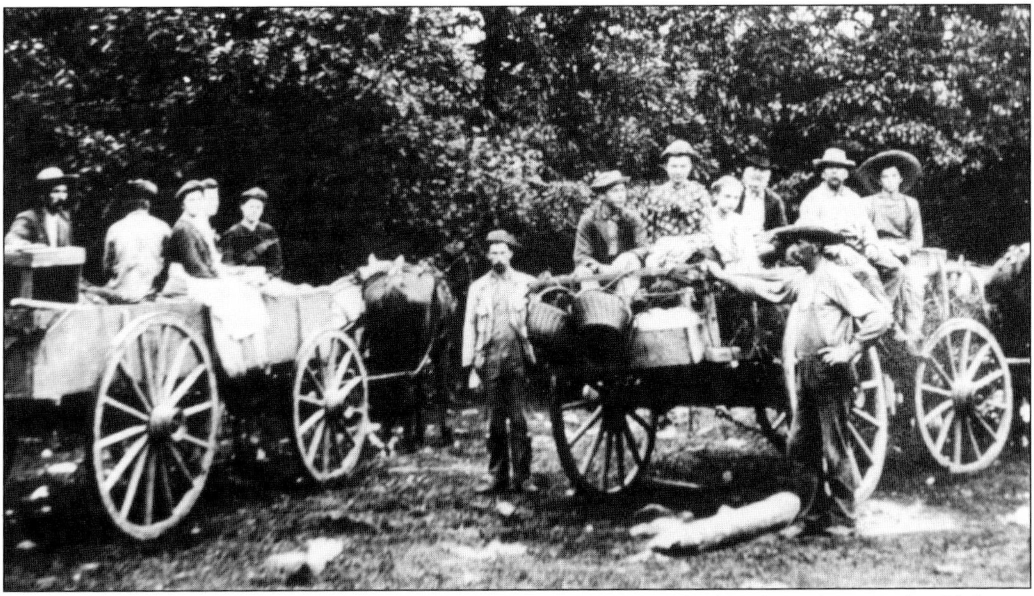

Mountain families gathered nature's bounty. This group is packed and ready to go huckleberry picking in the mountains around 1900. The following are pictured from left to right: Hubert Armentrout, E. P. "Jim" Will, Mag Mauck, Myrtle Fansler, Gertrude Wealty, Will Mauck, John Fansler, Emma Mauck, Effie Weatty, Josiah Turner (black hat), George Mauck (standing), John Will, and Charles Fansler. Josiah was going along to provide fiddle music for the campers. (Lois May Rhodes collection.)

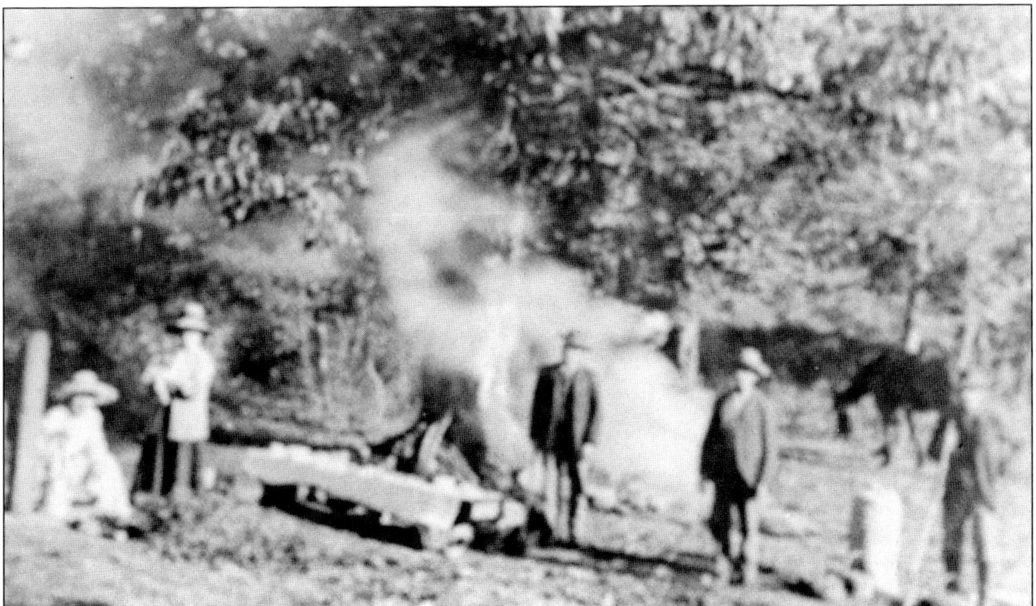

Chestnut trees provided both housing and food until they were killed by blight in the 1920s. Chestnuts were roasted for humans and also fed to the animals. In 1871, Benjamin Trumbo sent a barrel of them to his daughter in Dayton, Illinois. Even though this photograph is not clear, the white sacks full of chestnuts can be seen on the sled and beside the man on the right. (Helen Fulk collection.)

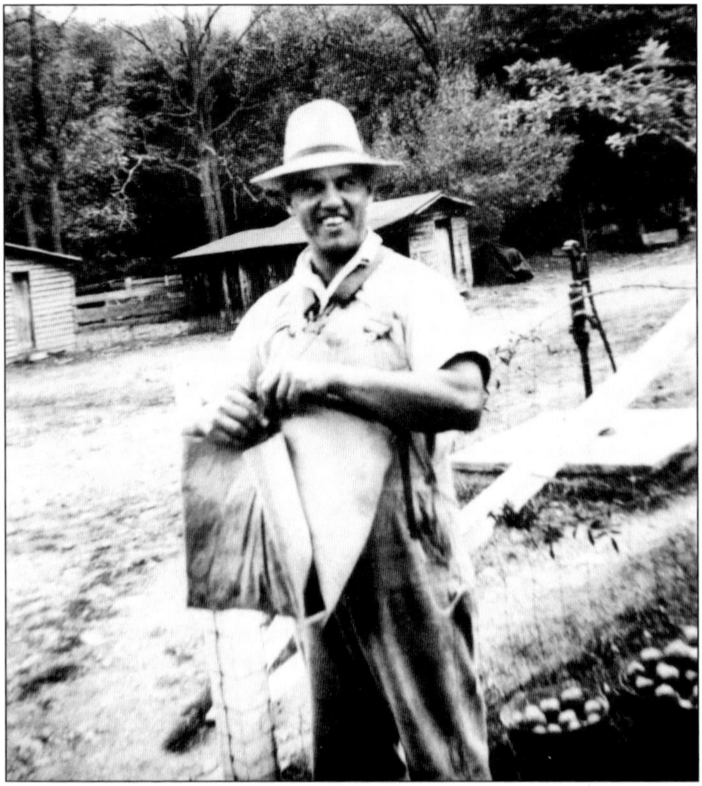

Dorman Ritchie has gathered several bushels of apples and is ready to gather more at his homeplace in Criders. To keep his hands free for picking, he uses an apple-picking bag. The Ritchies sold or traded their excess crop to neighbors. (Thelma Ritchie Bowers collection.)

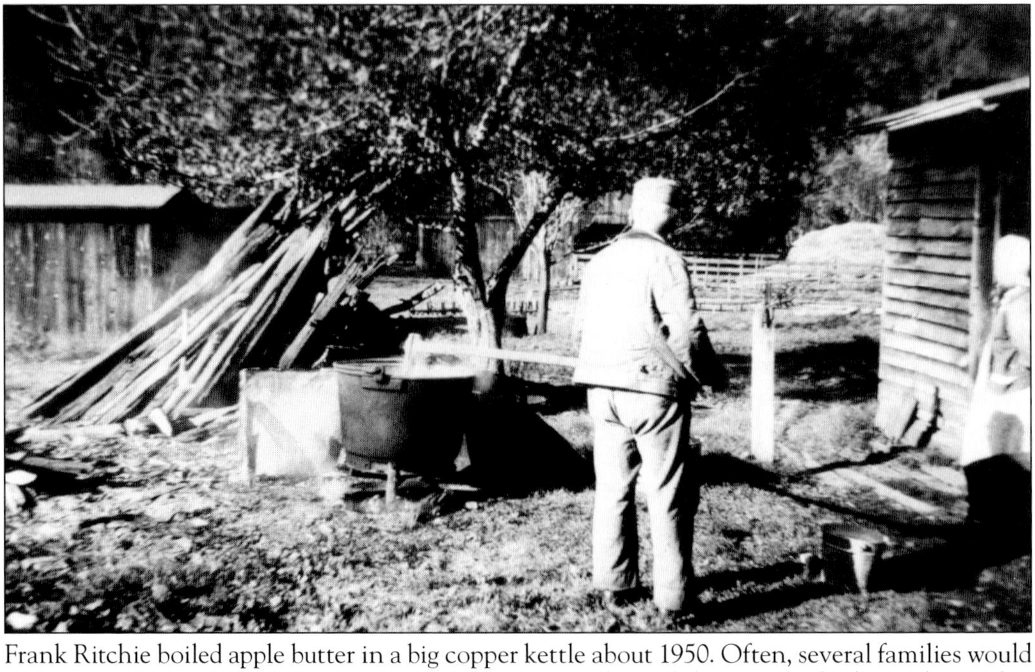

Frank Ritchie boiled apple butter in a big copper kettle about 1950. Often, several families would gather to peel 10 to 12 bushels of apples in the evening and spend the next day boiling cider, apples, sugar, and spices over an open fire. After a day of stirring and tending the fire, 20 gallons of apple butter would be divided among the families who helped. (Thelma Ritchie Bowers collection.)

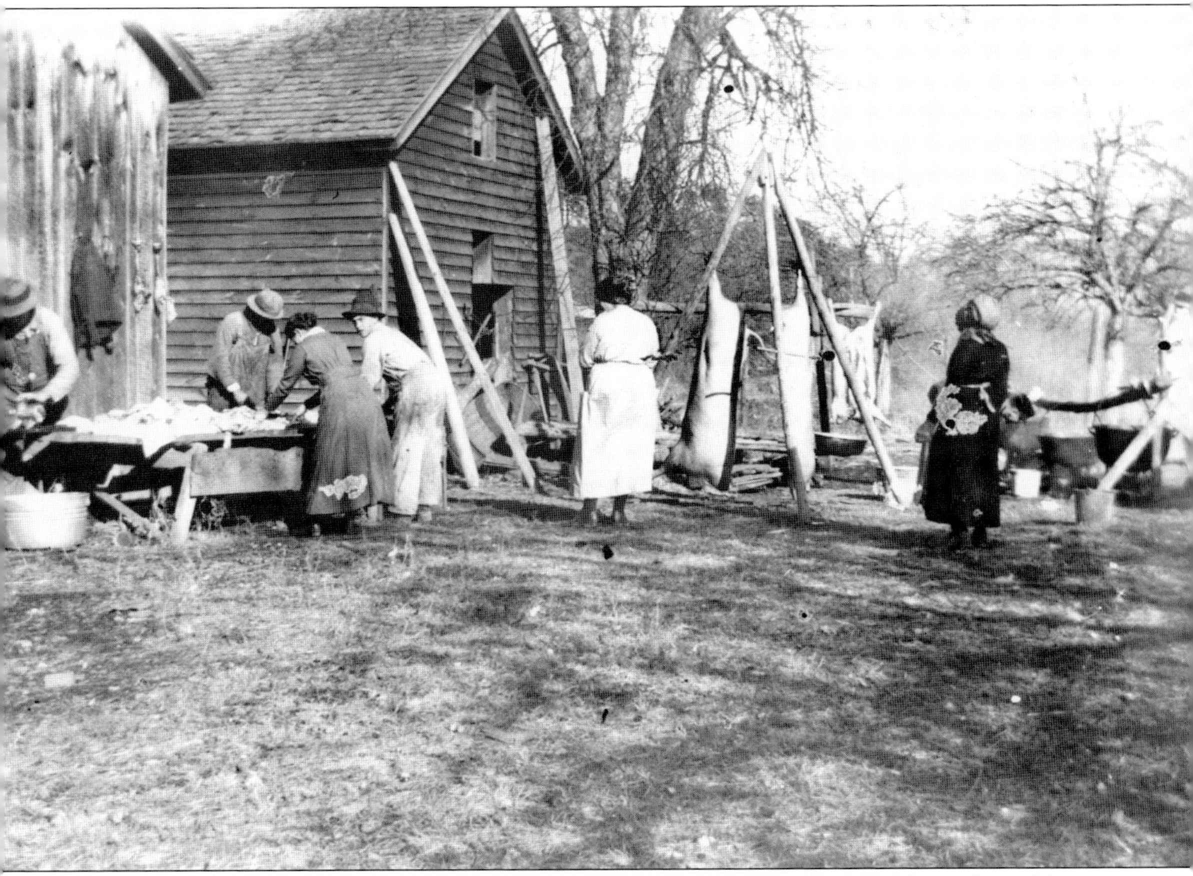

Butchering day was one of the most important days of the year, when family and neighbors gathered to prepare meat for the winter. Imaginative farmers found a way to use every part of the hog except the squeal. Even the pig's tail was used to lighten the hard work of butchering day as workers tried to pin it secretly to the shirttail of an unsuspecting worker. Almost the entire butchering operation is pictured at Elder Daniel Turner's farm about 1918. On the left, the man is grinding sausage and letting it fall into the tub while three others cut meat at the table. A scalding barrel is tipped sideways near the door of the outbuilding. Three hogs are hanging, and the basin under the hog on the right is catching blood and internal organs to keep them clean for "sorting." Three kettles over the fire are ready to cook the lard. It appears to be a warm day because everyone is in shirtsleeves. Hog tails have served their purpose and are nailed to the side of the building. (Ruth A. Turner collection.)

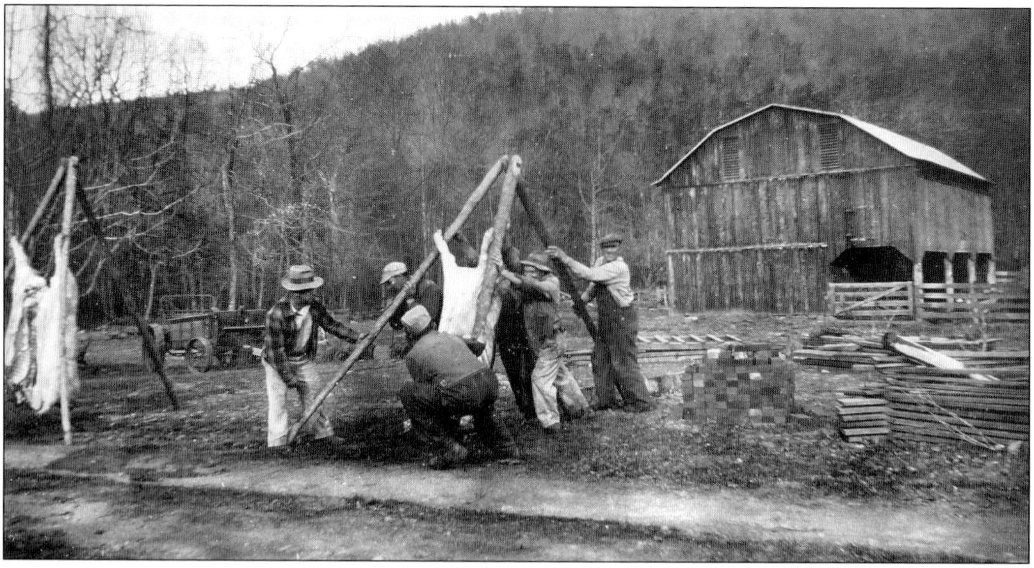

Butchering was heavy work and required cooperation with extended family or neighbors. Six men at Frank Ritchie's about 1940 hoist the hog onto the hog hanger, three poles fastened with a bolt at the top. The hangers were saved from year to year in the smokehouse attic to be ready for the next season's butchering. (Thelma Ritchie Bowers collection.)

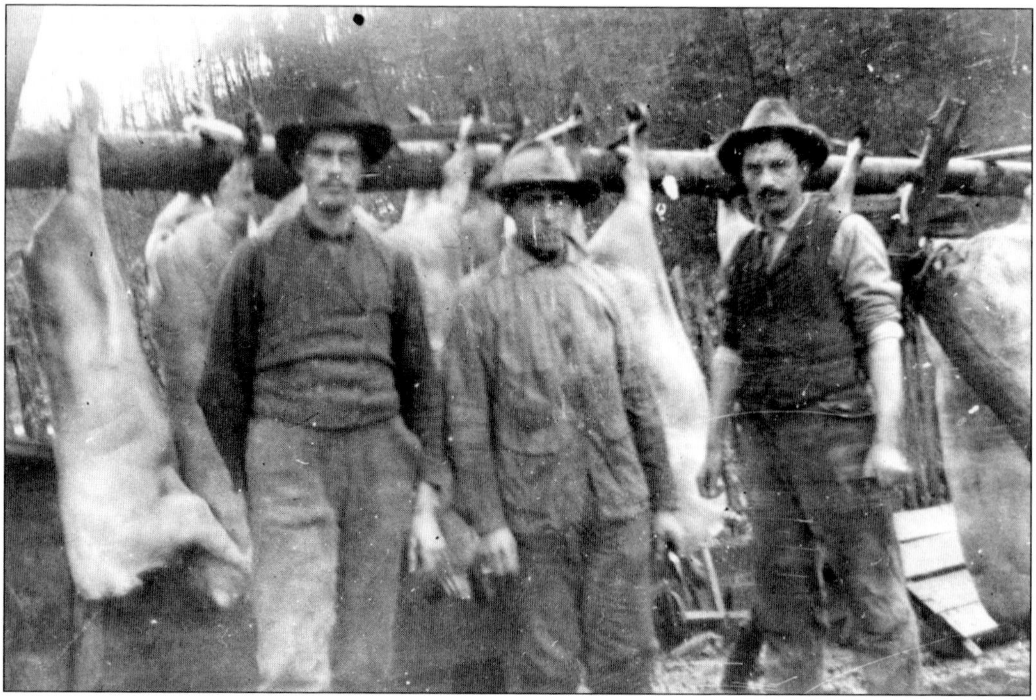

Albert, Jacob "Jake," and William "Bill" Albrite take a break from butchering nine hogs for the family about 1903; the Albrites lived near Bergton. Because lard was a necessity for cooking, families took pride in how fat their hogs were. In the Fulks Run community on January 1, 1885, Uncle Josh Fulk butchered a hog weighing 616 pounds, large enough to be reported in the newspaper. (Mabel Albrite Mathias collection.)

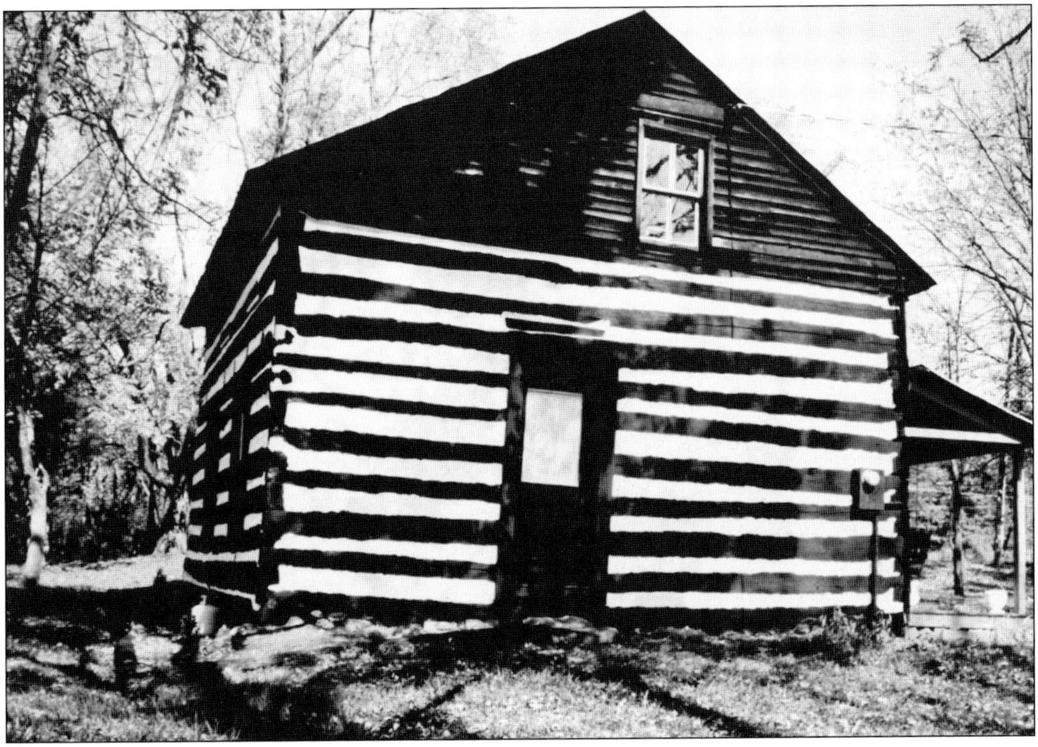

At times, war was part of everyday life. Brocks Gap residents were attacked by Native Americans during the French and Indian War in the 1750s; four people were killed and two were taken prisoner. Fort Hog (or Hogg) at Fulks Run was near Third Hill and had a log building with loopholes surrounded by a stockade. Tradition says that logs from the stockade were used to build this log home.

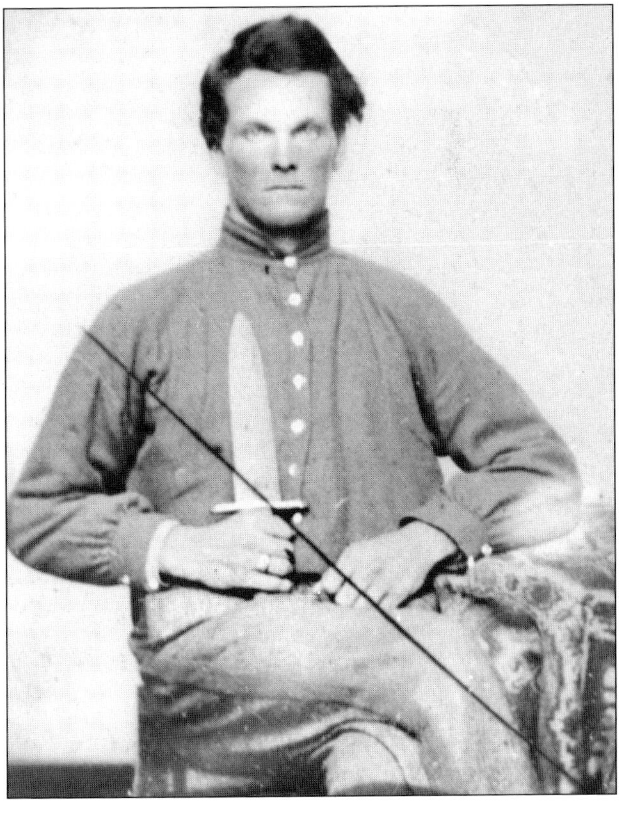

During the Civil War, Adam C. Fulk joined the Brocks Gap Rifles, whose uniforms were of "handsome home-made gray cloth, manufactured by Funkhouser & Bro. . . . at Naked Creek. The plain, unassuming, unpretending home-made gray cloth . . . covers the vigorous and stalwart forms. . . Besides, there is not one of them who can't hit a squirrel's head every crack at a distance of 50 yards." (*Rockingham Register*, May 25, 1860.)

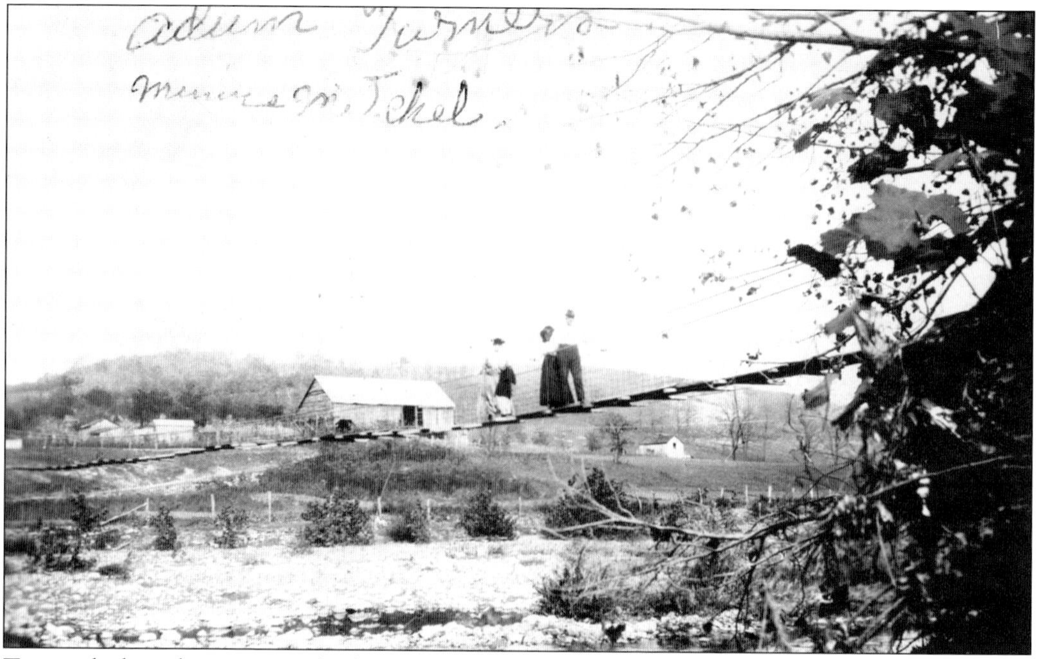

To travel when the water was high, some families built footbridges across the streams, sometimes simply logs with a board nailed on top. There were tall swinging bridges at some fords, such as German River, Riverside, Trumbo Ford, old Fulks Run Elementary, and below Cootes Store. Minnie Turner Mitchell and Adam Turner are pictured on the bridge. (Ruth A. Turner collection.)

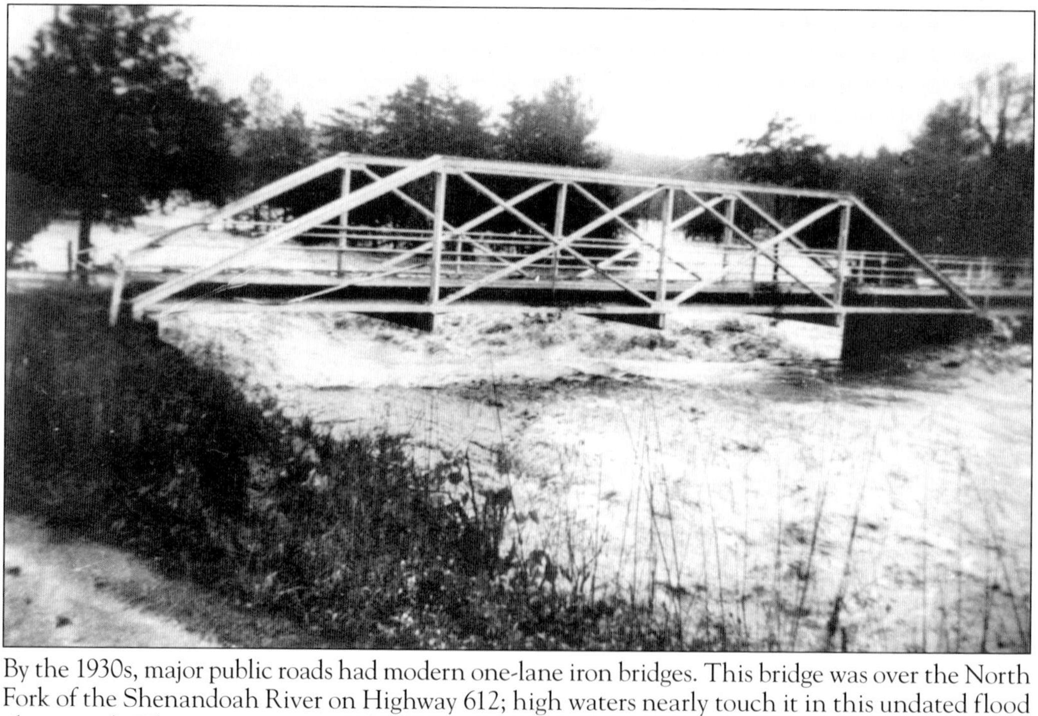

By the 1930s, major public roads had modern one-lane iron bridges. This bridge was over the North Fork of the Shenandoah River on Highway 612; high waters nearly touch it in this undated flood photograph. The present concrete bridge replaced it in 1959, when the road was straightened and widened. (Velma Turner Cooper collection.)

Three

HUNTING

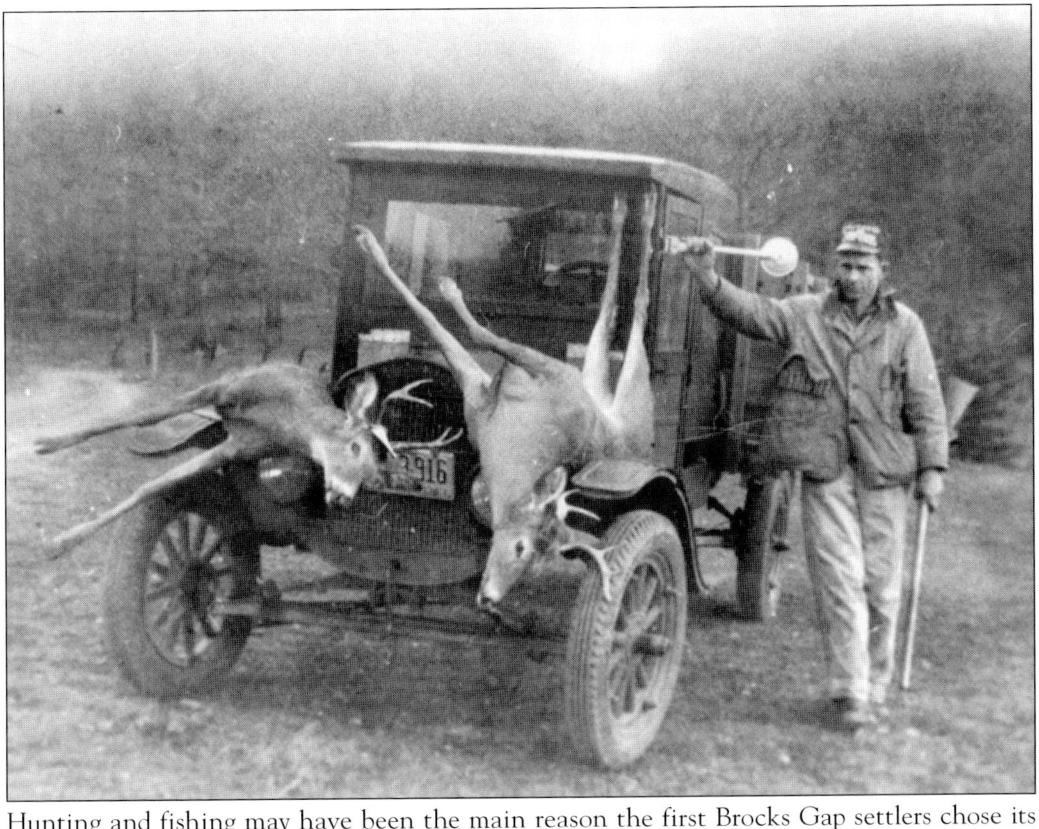

Hunting and fishing may have been the main reason the first Brocks Gap settlers chose its mountain valleys instead of the large fertile bottomlands of the Shenandoah Valley. Ernest C. Fulk displays two nice bucks on a foggy autumn day. (Nova Roadcap Fulk collection.)

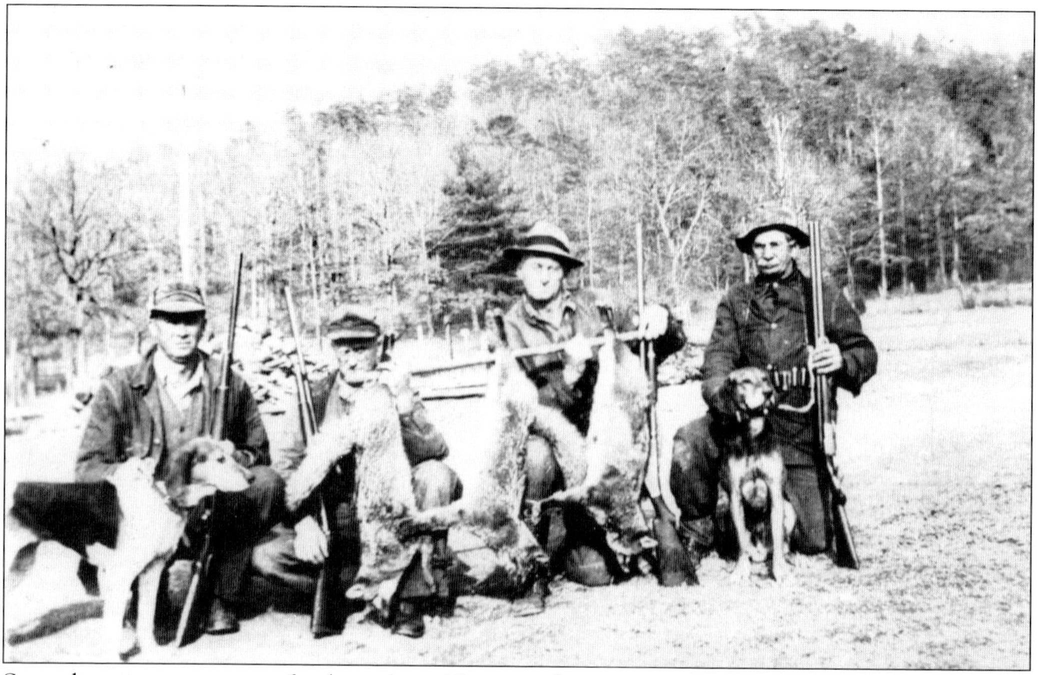

Some hunting was to put food on the table, some hunting was to protect livestock, and some hunting was for fun. Animal skins from hunting and trapping were sold at the local store for extra cash. Benjamin W. "Ben" Fawley, Robert C. Hulvey, Joseph W. "Joe" Fawley, and Mark "Buck" Hulvey pose from left to right with their dogs and three foxes. (Private collection.)

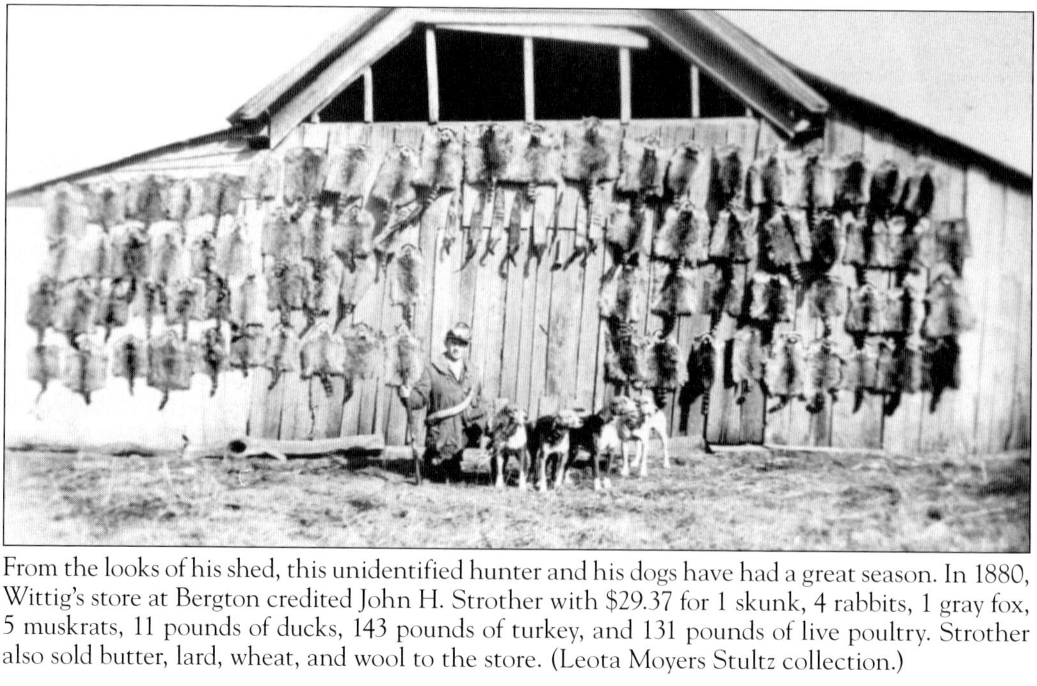

From the looks of his shed, this unidentified hunter and his dogs have had a great season. In 1880, Wittig's store at Bergton credited John H. Strother with $29.37 for 1 skunk, 4 rabbits, 1 gray fox, 5 muskrats, 11 pounds of ducks, 143 pounds of turkey, and 131 pounds of live poultry. Strother also sold butter, lard, wheat, and wool to the store. (Leota Moyers Stultz collection.)

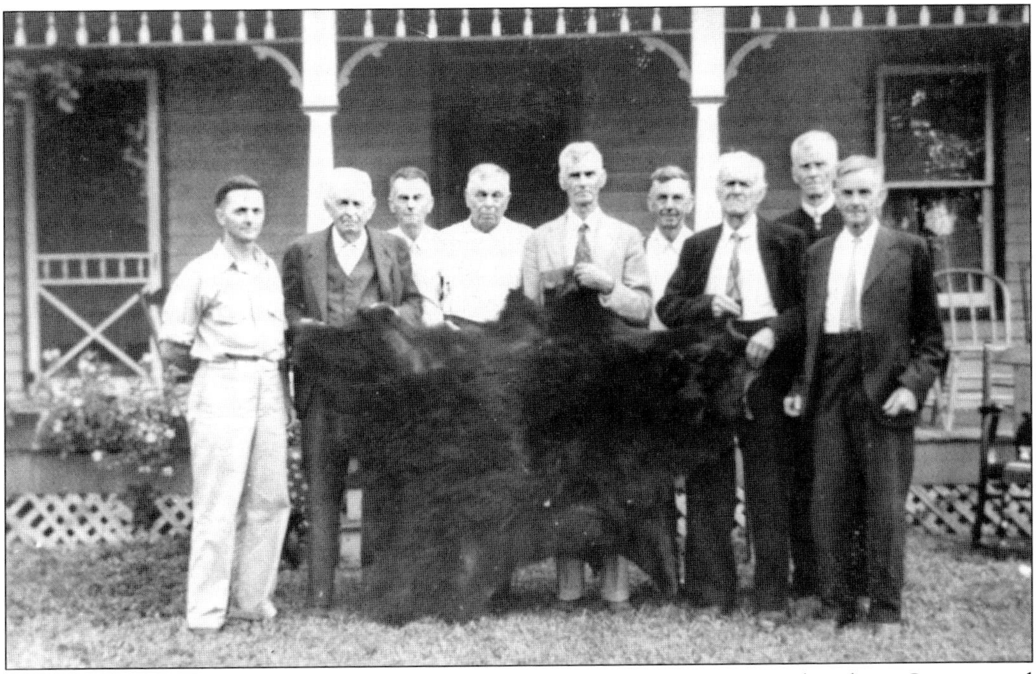

Turner men were "one of the largest and most widely known clans of Rockingham County and counties of West Virginia where they were famous for their bear hunting and valuable packs of bear hounds." The following men are pictured from left to right: (first row) Lewis Crider, Benjamin F. Turner, John Casper Turner, Zack A. Turner, Adam M. Turner, and Charles A. Turner; (second row) George B. Turner, Daniel M. Turner, and James Hopkins Turner. (Turner family collection.)

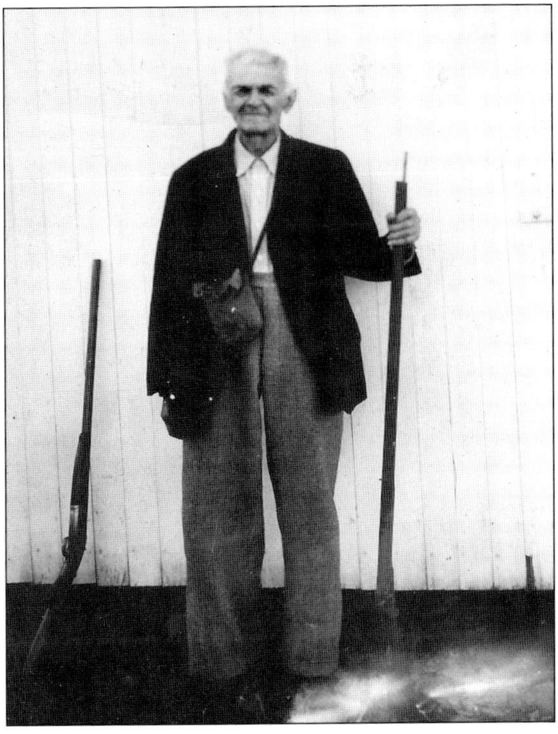

Adam M. Turner killed 158 bears, at least that many deer, and three times that many wildcats during his lifetime (1859–1949). He sold bear hides for up to $20 each. His first kill was made with a muzzle-loading flintlock rifle when he was 13, but his favorite gun was a 16-shot .45-caliber Winchester repeater. Adam also killed bears with an axe and once with a knife. (Carl Fulk collection.)

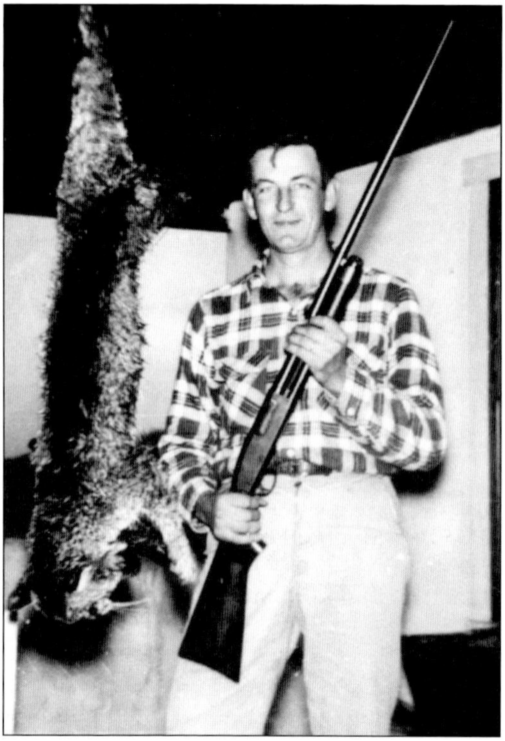

Lloyd Alton Whetzel shows off his bobcat trophy. Lloyd was the son of John William "Will" Whetzel. In earlier times, farmers were free to kill predators that threatened their livestock. For instance, a March 1888 news article reports that Israel Mongold caught (killed) a large bald eagle, which had been playing havoc with his lambs. Its wingspan measured seven feet. (Luther Crider collection.)

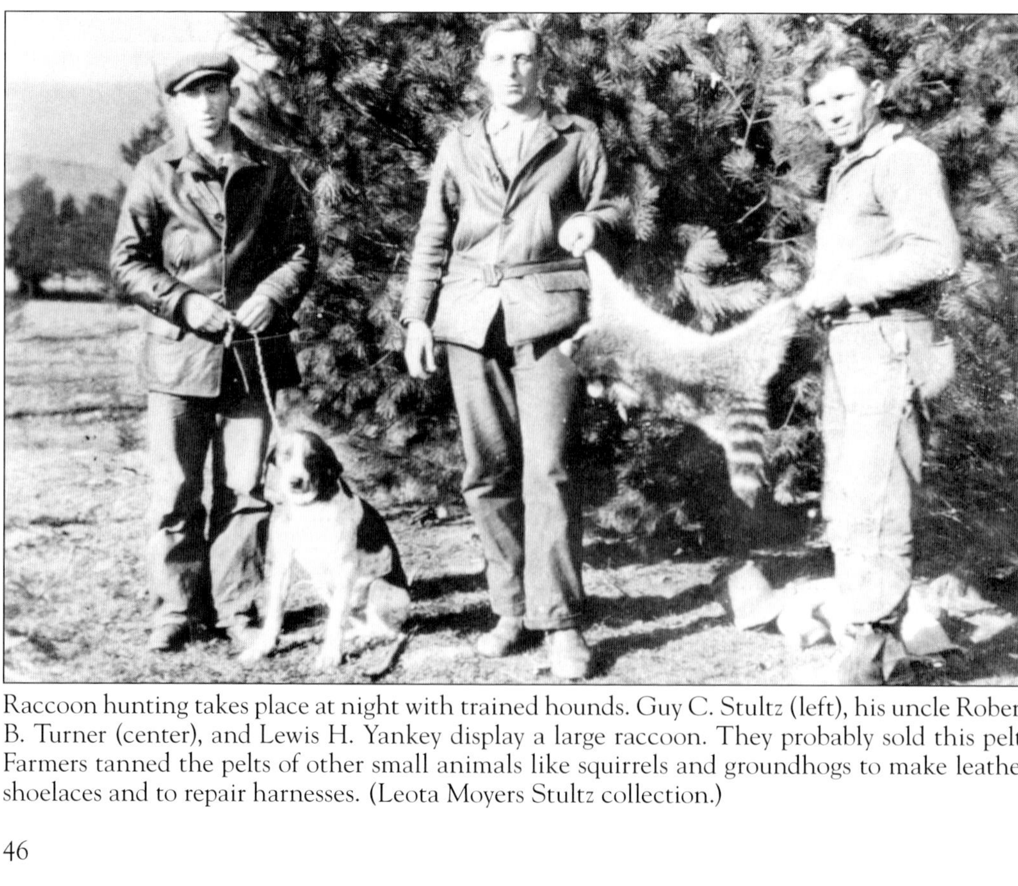

Raccoon hunting takes place at night with trained hounds. Guy C. Stultz (left), his uncle Robert B. Turner (center), and Lewis H. Yankey display a large raccoon. They probably sold this pelt. Farmers tanned the pelts of other small animals like squirrels and groundhogs to make leather shoelaces and to repair harnesses. (Leota Moyers Stultz collection.)

In October 1877, a Brocks Gap hunter stated that while sitting on a log, he killed 100 squirrels and at least 500 more passed by his seat during the day. "It was not a first class day for squirrels, either," the *Rockingham Recorder* reported. Maybe John H. Hess (left) and James J. Custer did not have a first-class day, but they had enough squirrels for dinner in this 1880s photo. (Roy Ritchie collection.)

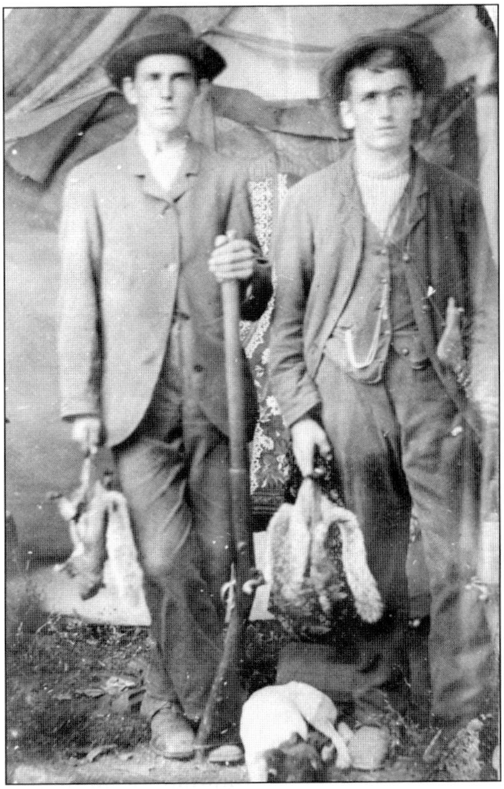

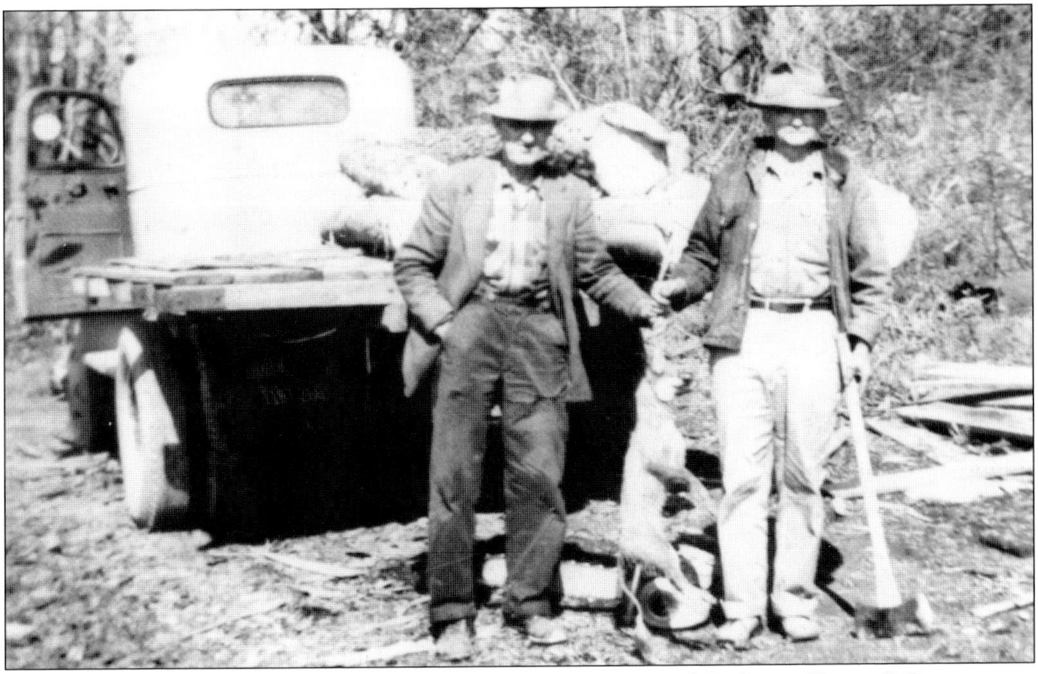

In addition to working their wood, Bernie E. "Bern" Bare and Dulaney "Laney" Custer must have found time for fox hunting. In earlier times, wolves also roamed the mountains and hunters received money from the county for wolf scalps. (Millard D. "Pete" Custer collection.)

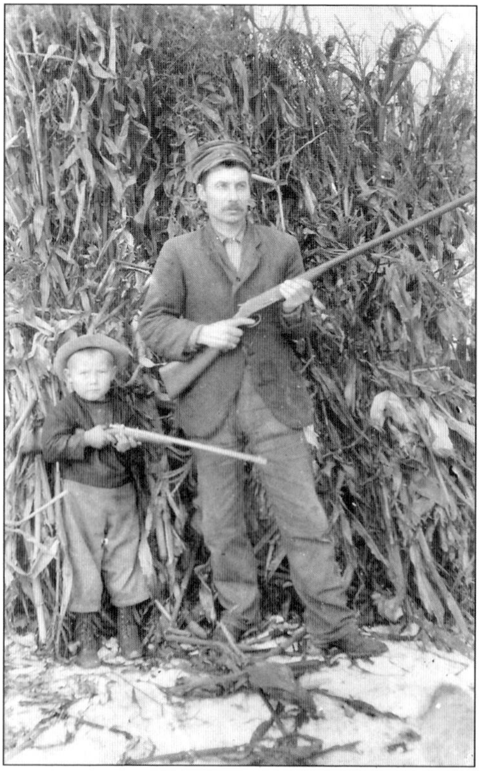

"Hello! Gertie, why don't you come home to help me and Papa hunt rabbits?" asked Davy Dove in this 1914 postcard. Gertie and Davy were children of Abe Van "Seymour" Dove. Families could eat rabbits and sell the pelts or sell the rabbits to country stores for shipment to Baltimore butcher shops. In the 1930s, rabbits were worth 20¢ at A. D. Brenneman's store. (David L. Smith collection.)

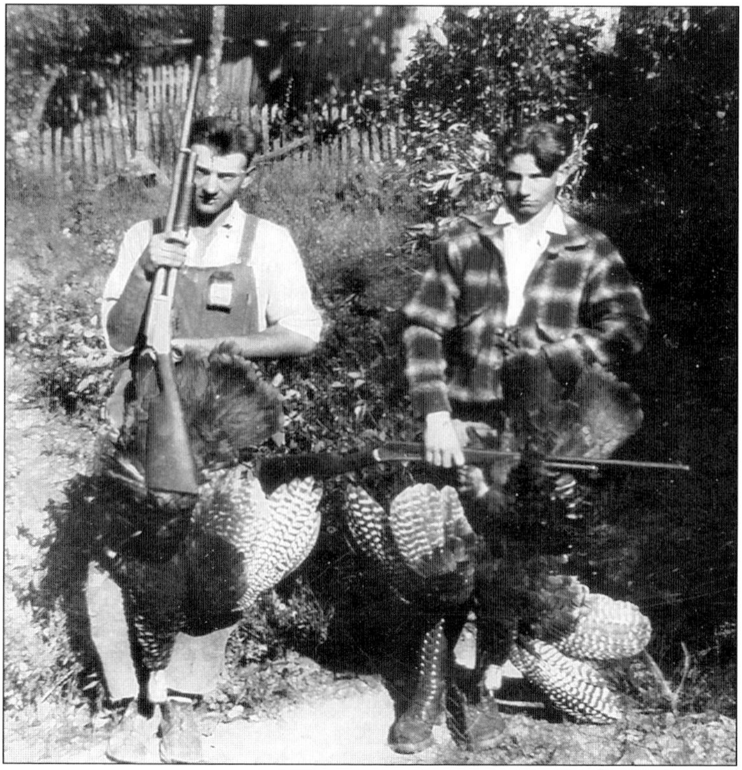

The oldest people in the Gap told historian Lonzo Dove that the first settlers moved there because they wanted to hunt and fish. "No doubt the frequency of the name 'Nimrod' among the first generations of the Dove indicates their characteristics as in the Bible, 'like Nimrod the mighty hunter,' " Lonzo wrote. Dove descendants David L. Smith (left) and Casper Allen Hottinger have their Thanksgiving turkeys. (David L. Smith collection.)

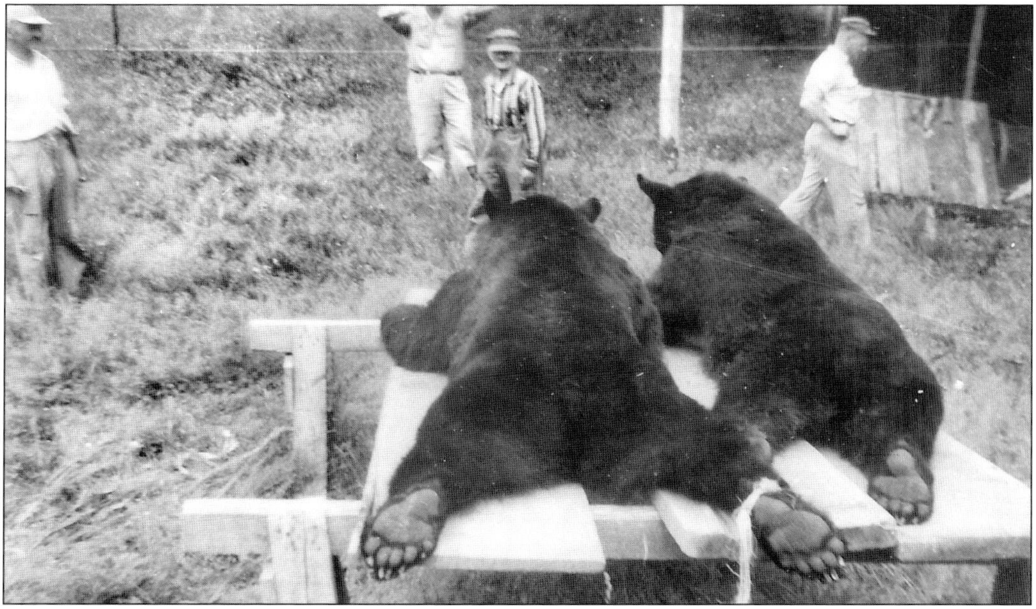

David L. Smith (far left) admires bears killed near the Bennetts Run area, probably in the 1960s. Harvey Smith wrote in an article that David killed a 400-pound bear with his powerful rifle called the "gem of the woods" on the Shenandoah Mountain. The other men are, from left to right, M. Clay Hinkle, Gilliam Mitchel, and Floyd D. Fulk. (David L. Smith collection.)

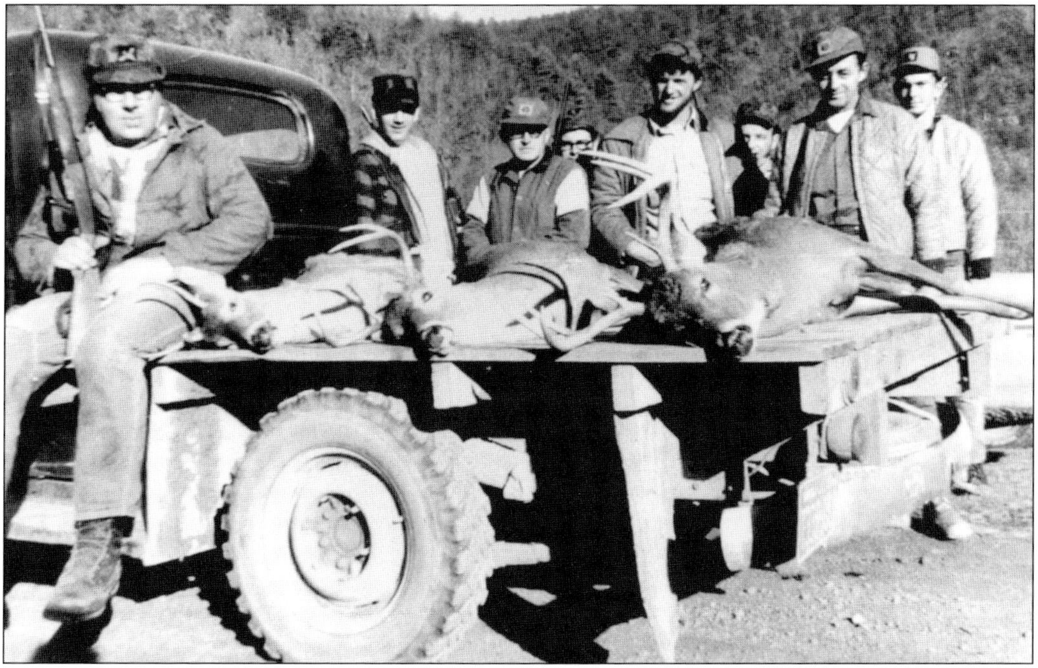

These three bucks were killed on West Mountain near the Bergton Store in the 1950s or early 1960s. Pictured from left to right are Dennis "Moose" Lantz, Lester Mook, Floyd Smith, Roy Stultz, Roger "Eddie" Feddon, Thomas "Bud" Armentrout, Edgar Stultz, and Edgar's son-in-law Rick Miller. Carl Moyer, another hunter, took the photograph of the deer on his truck. The group hunted together and shared the meat. (Floyd A. Smith collection.)

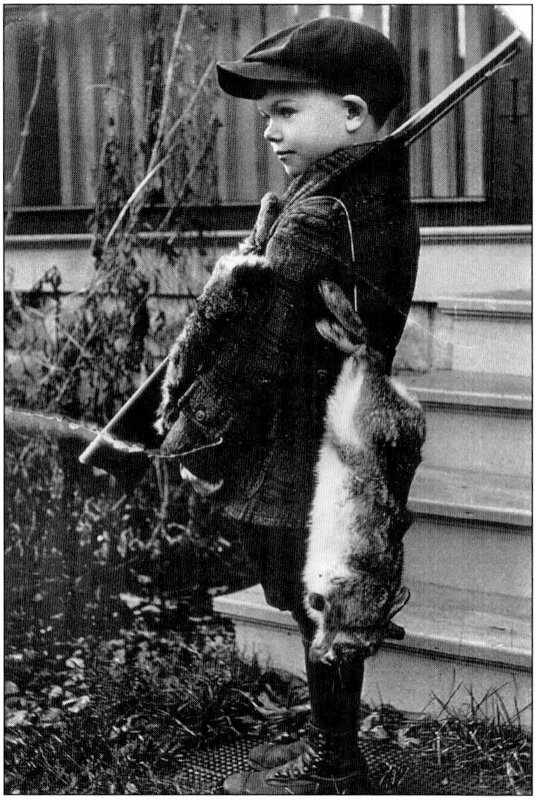

Eston Douglas Yankey, born March 28, 1910, shows that he is skilled with a gun even though he is still in short pants. Men also participated in shooting matches for prizes; an 1886 article reported that "some of the 'old boys' held a shooting match near Jacob Dove's on Saturday last; Sol. Whetzel, Geo. Wittig and Phil. Souders scoring the best shot, captured the mutton." (Shirley Cullers Miller collection.)

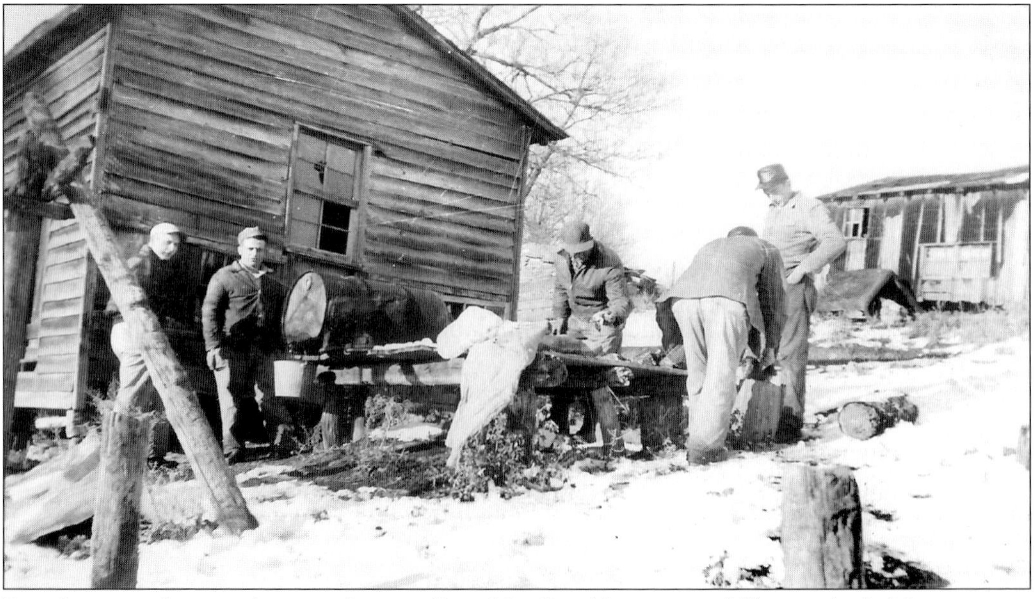

Bear hunters clean and cut up bear at David L. Smith's on top of Shenandoah Mountain in 1960. At the time, Pendleton County, West Virginia, offered a bounty of $25 for each bear killed while pelts were selling for $20 each. Pictured from left to right are Waldo Combs, Norman Cullers, David L. Smith, M. Clay Hinkle, and Matthew E. "Bud" Miller. (Matthew E. "Bud" Miller collection.)

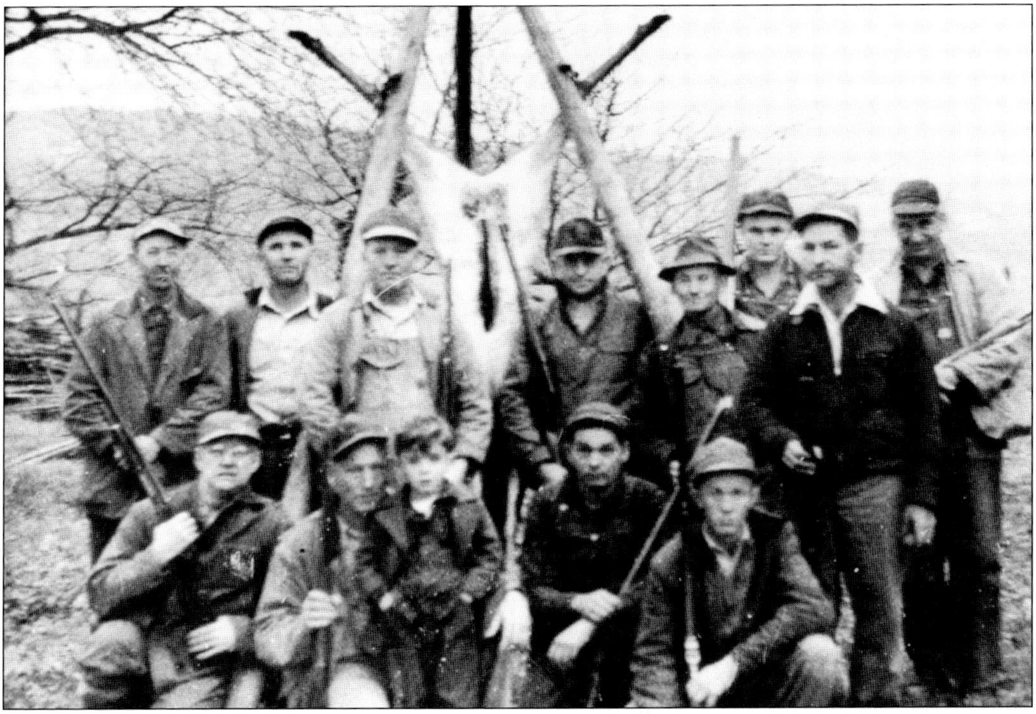

By 1900, deer were gone from Rockingham County because of over-hunting. In the 1920s, deer were restocked in the mountains, and by the mid-1940s, deer hunting had resumed but with strictly enforced limits. The following people are pictured from left to right: (first row) Charles Parks, Maynard Fulk holding Larry Fulk, unidentified, and Robert S. Rhodes; (second row) Olin "Tuck" Rhodes, unidentified, Miles Fulk, Zack M. Turner, Tom Hoover, Everette Brunk, Homer Nesselrodt, and Casper "Cap" Turner. (Lois May Rhodes collection.)

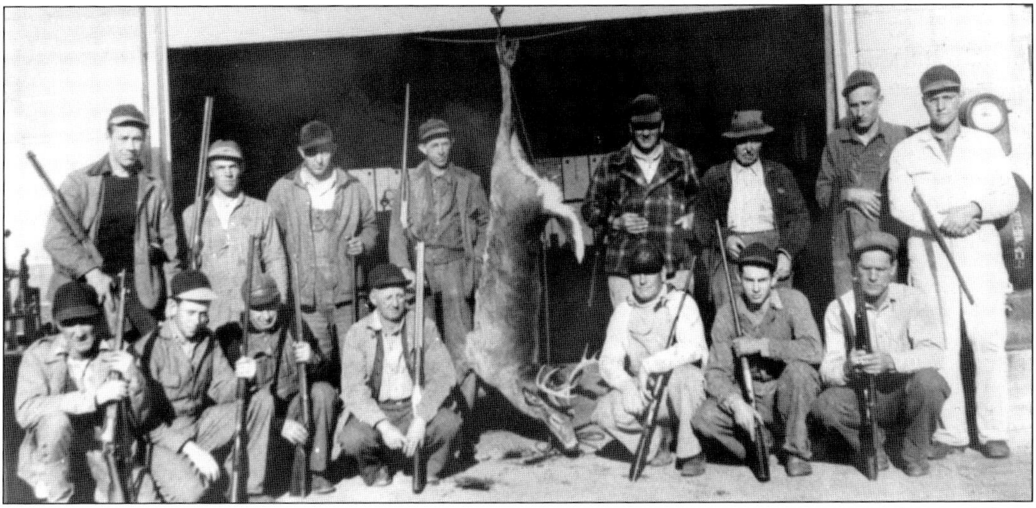

This deer was killed November 16, 1945, at Cootes Store near Brocks Gap. Pictured from left to right are (first row) John Keister, Turner Getz, Casper "Cap" Turner, Willie Tusing, Miles Fulk, John A. Getz, and Doug Simmers; (second row) Gerald Turner, Claude Turner, Ralph Fulk, J. O. "Tuck" Rhodes, Casper "Scrub" Fulk, John Spitzer, Paul Foltz, and Owen Stultz. (Lois May Rhodes collection.)

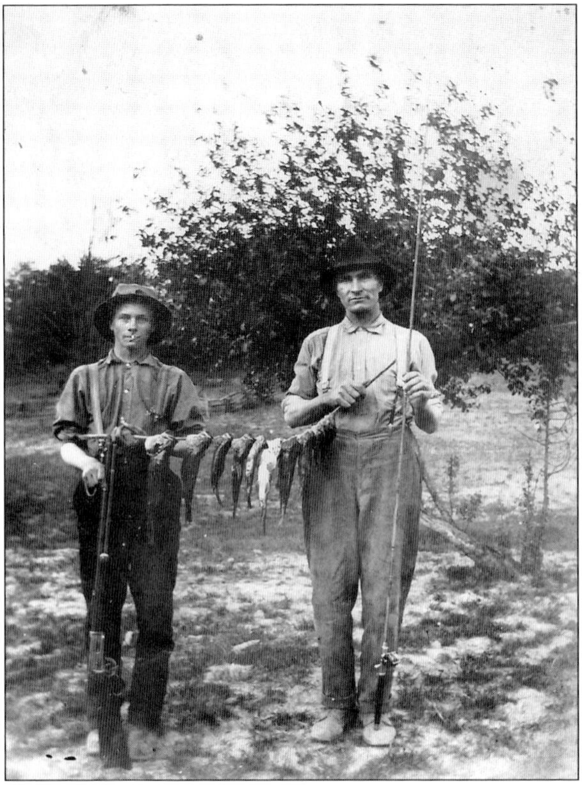

Two men display their day's catch. The man on the right has his fishing rod, but the man on the left has his gun, demonstrating two favorite mountain pastimes—hunting and fishing. (David L. Smith collection.)

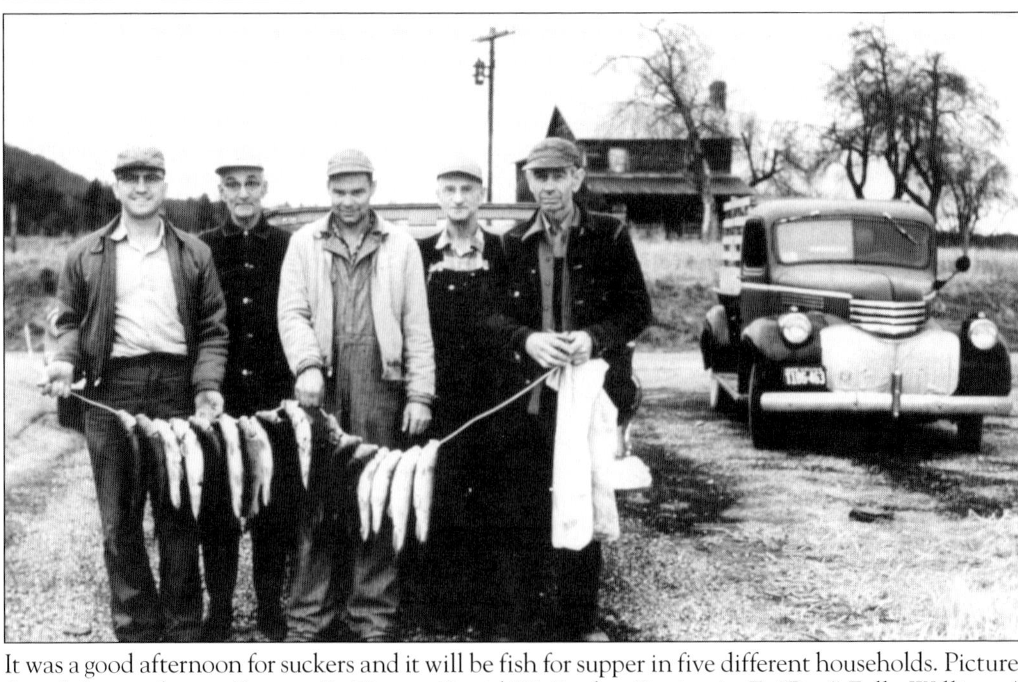

It was a good afternoon for suckers and it will be fish for supper in five different households. Pictured from left to right are Garnett R. Turner, David W. Fawley, Benjamin E. "Ben" Fulk, William A. "Will" Fulk, and Russell L. Turner about 1958. Russell's 1946 Chevrolet truck and George W. Fawley's log home can also be seen in this photo. (Lena Albrite Turner, photographer.)

Four

CHURCHES

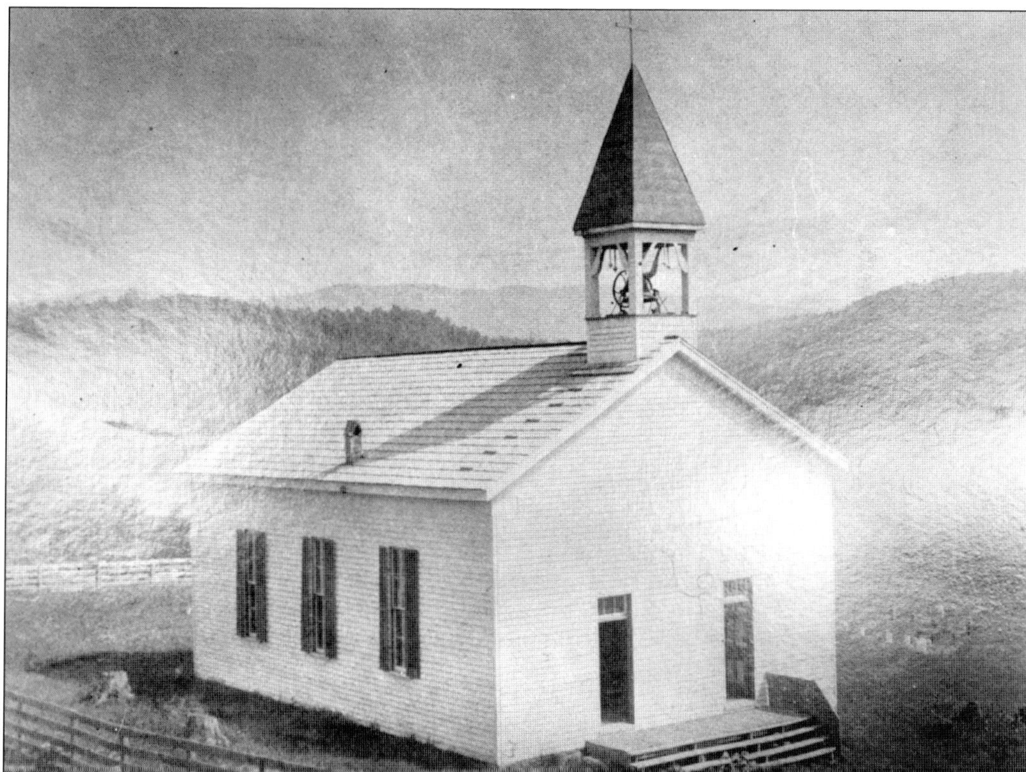

Phanuel's Lutheran Church at Bergton, pictured here about 1890, was an early church. Lutheran minister Rev. Paul Henkel preached in Henry Dove's nearby home in the 1790s. In 1845, Dove's son Jacob wrote a letter of intent giving one acre of land for the church, which also contained a burying ground. A log church was dedicated in 1851, replaced by this frame church on the same site in 1888. (Jennie Cullers collection.)

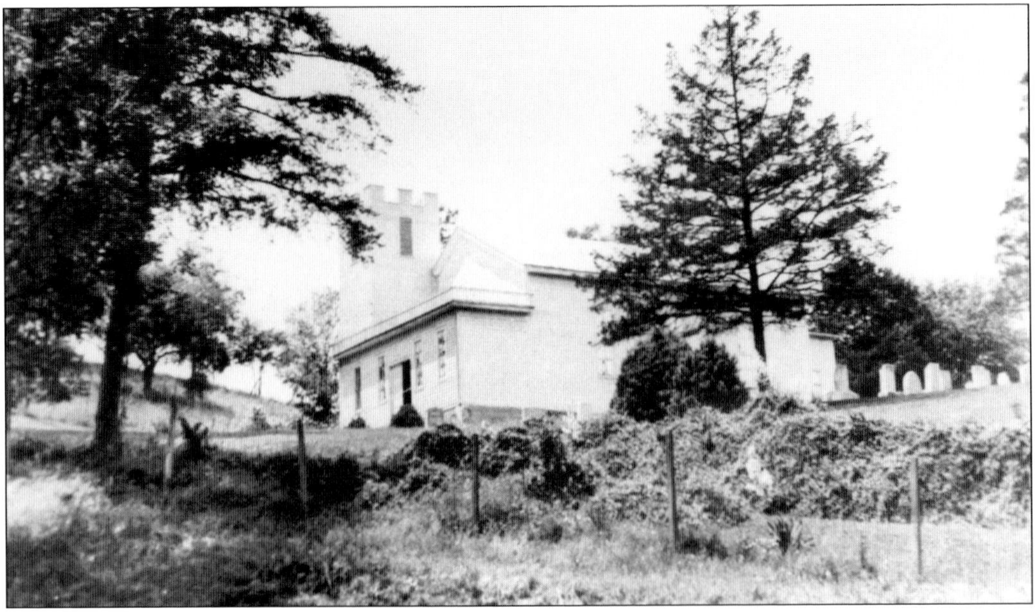

In 1927, Phanuel's Lutheran Church was enlarged and remodeled with a rededication service celebrated on April 29, 1928. At that time, they had 500–600 communicant members. Around 1949, Phanuel's, Bethel, and St. John's Lutheran Churches merged and eventually adopted the name of Martin Luther Evangelical Lutheran Church and built a new brick church and parsonage. (Vita Souder Fulk collection.)

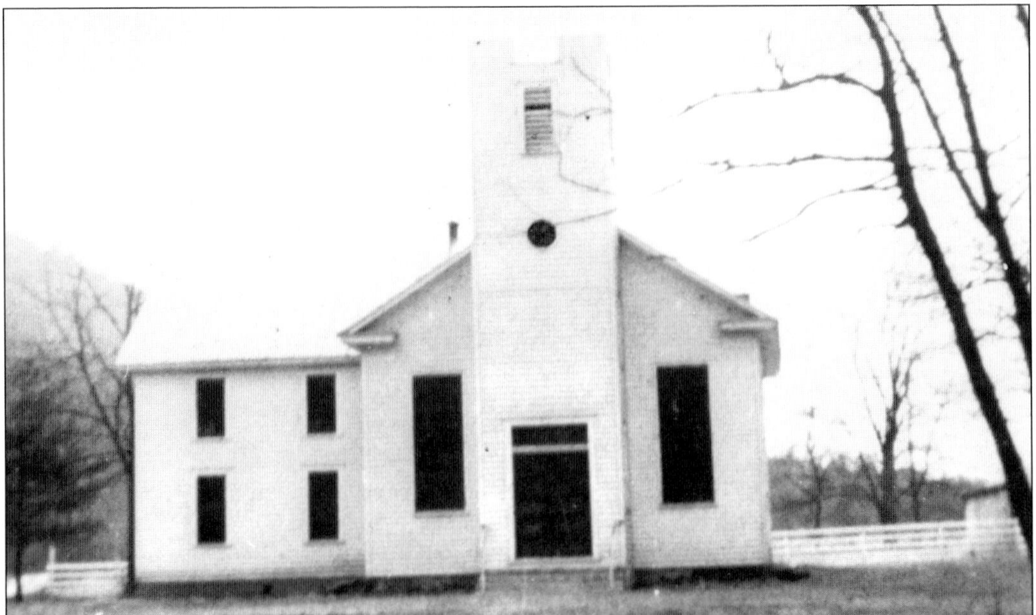

Some members from Phanuel's Church formed Bethel Lutheran Church in 1880. The church was built in 1888 with logs sawed by Frank Souder. Merger talks with Phanuel's Lutheran Church began in 1931 and concluded in 1949 when the congregations worshipped together at Bethel in the winter and at Phanuel's in the summer. The church bell from Bethel is now at Martin Luther Evangelical Lutheran Church. (Warren J. Souder collection.)

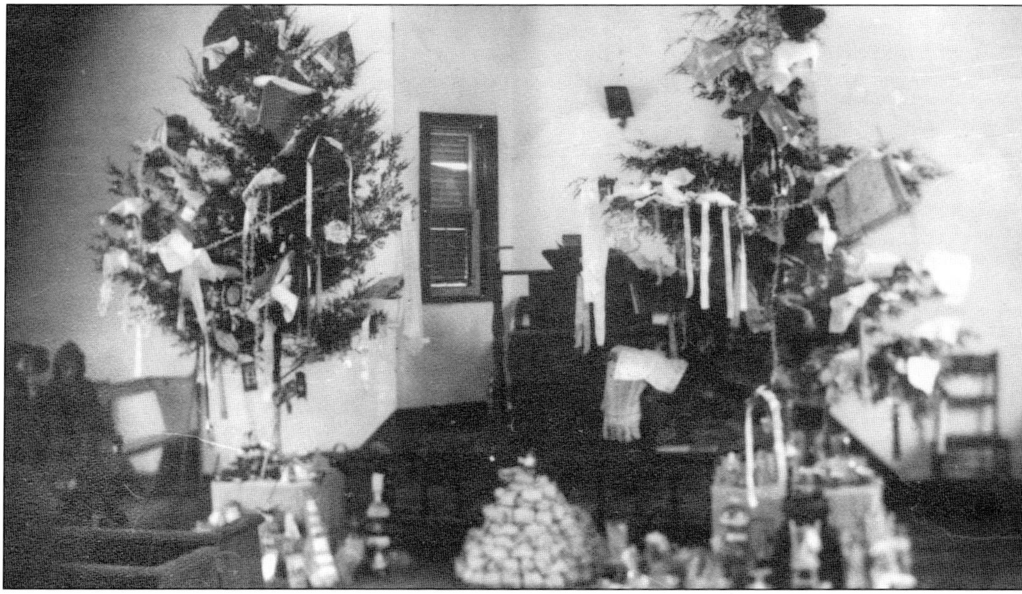

Christmas was celebrated in Bethel Lutheran Church about 1903 with two Christmas trees decorated with hats, scarves, ribbons, and other practical items. Gifts at the foot of the tree include a small doll chair. Two women are just visible on the left. (Mabel Albrite Mathias collection.)

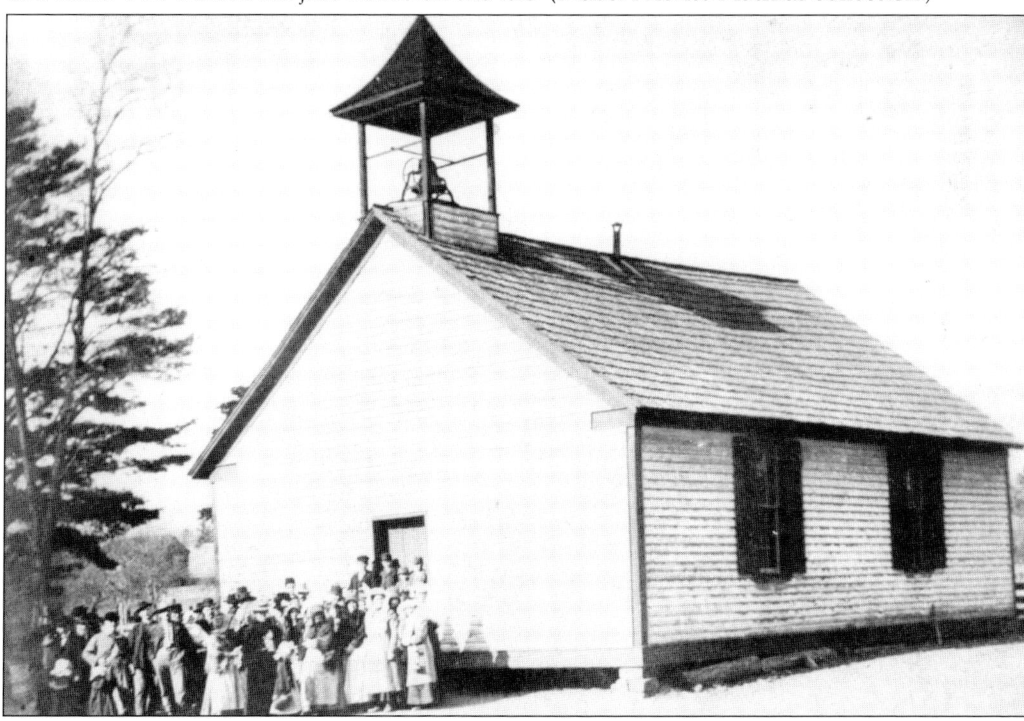

Caplinger United Brethren Church was built in 1858 on land donated by Jacob and Elizabeth Lantz Caplinger. Jacob's father-in-law, Jacob Lantz, is said to have brought the United Brethren faith with him to Brocks Gap. Christian Newcomer, an early United Brethren traveling minister, attended a camp meeting at Jacob Lantz's in Brocks Gap in 1828. The United Brethren later became Evangelical United Brethren and is now United Methodist. (Lona Dove collection.)

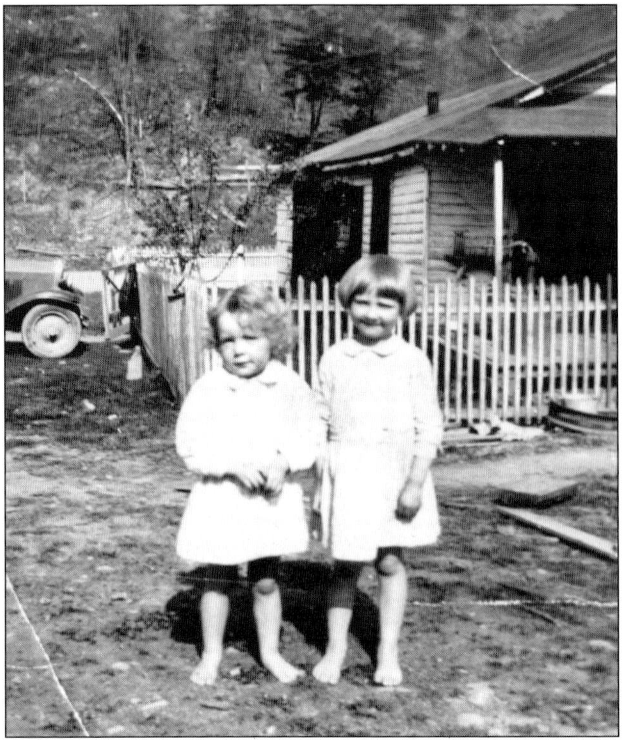

Emma (left) and Helen Whetzel, children of Russel J. Whetzel, stand in front of their home, which had been the building of an Old Order Brethren church on Crab Run Road in Bergton. Rev. J. Webster Lantz preached here on December 5, 1909, and again on July 23, 1910, according to his diary. Sometime before 1930 the church was closed and converted to a home. (Emma Whetzel Wittig collection.)

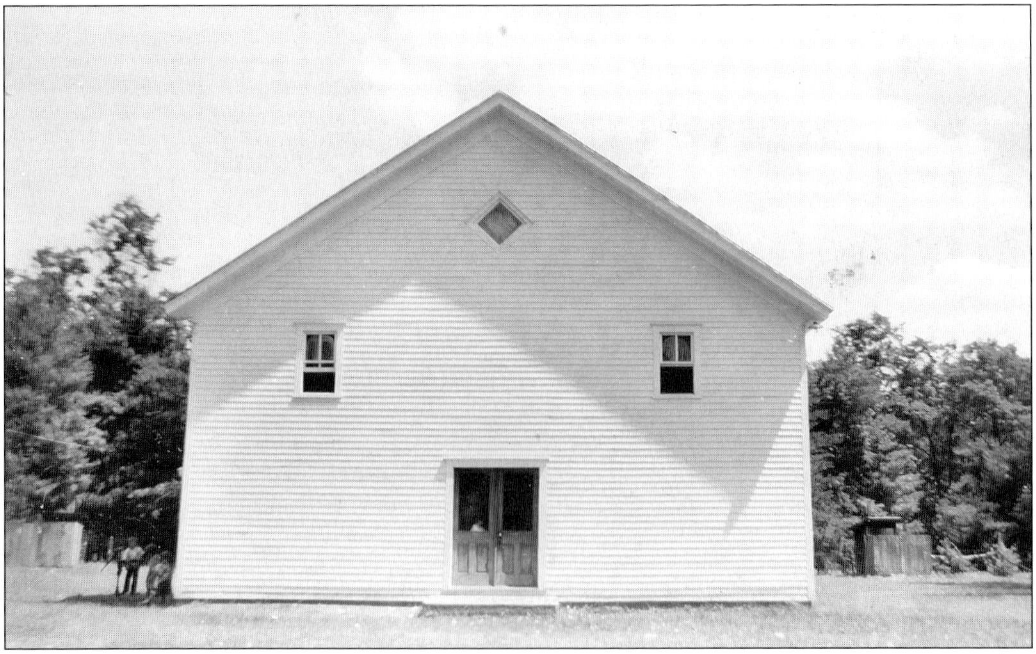

The first Damascus Church of the Brethren was built in 1884 under the influence of F. A. Yankey and others. Rev. Joseph Webster "Web" Lantz wrote that on April 4, 1909, Addison Dove walked from Broadway to Damascus, leaving at midnight in order to attend the 11:00 a.m. service. The new frame church pictured above was dedicated July 22, 1923, and the previous church was converted into a residence. (J. Day Lantz collection.)

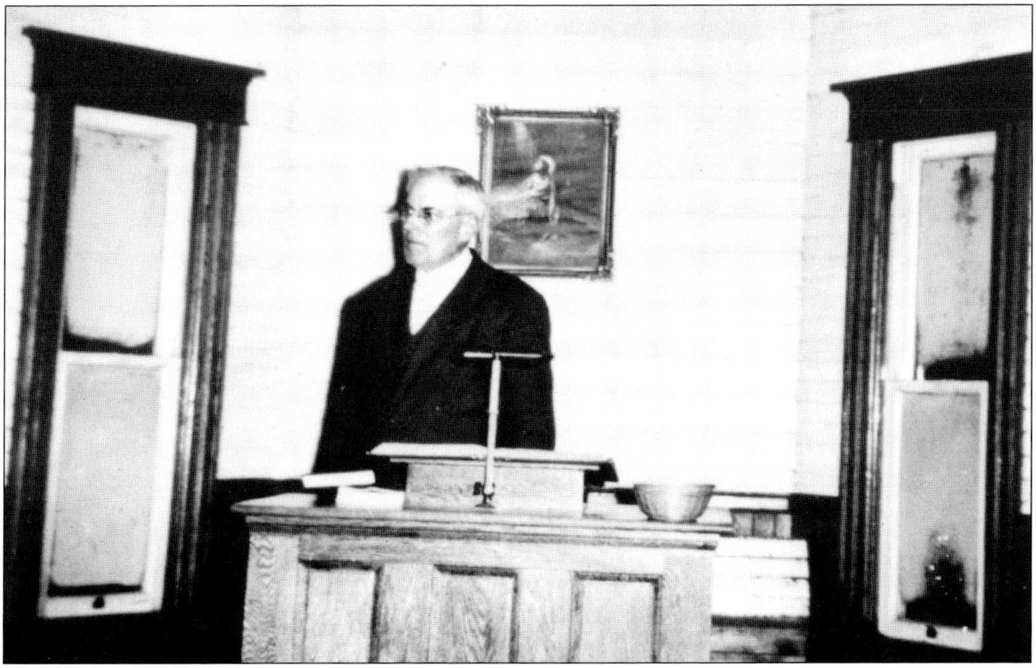

Rev. Web Lantz preached his first sermon at the old Damascus church on January 3, 1909, using Jonah 3:1–2 as his text. His journal records many preaching engagements at schoolhouses and other Brethren churches as well as Damascus. His last sermon was in 1953 and he died May 19, 1953. He is pictured here in the new Damascus church building in the 1940s. (J. Day Lantz collection.)

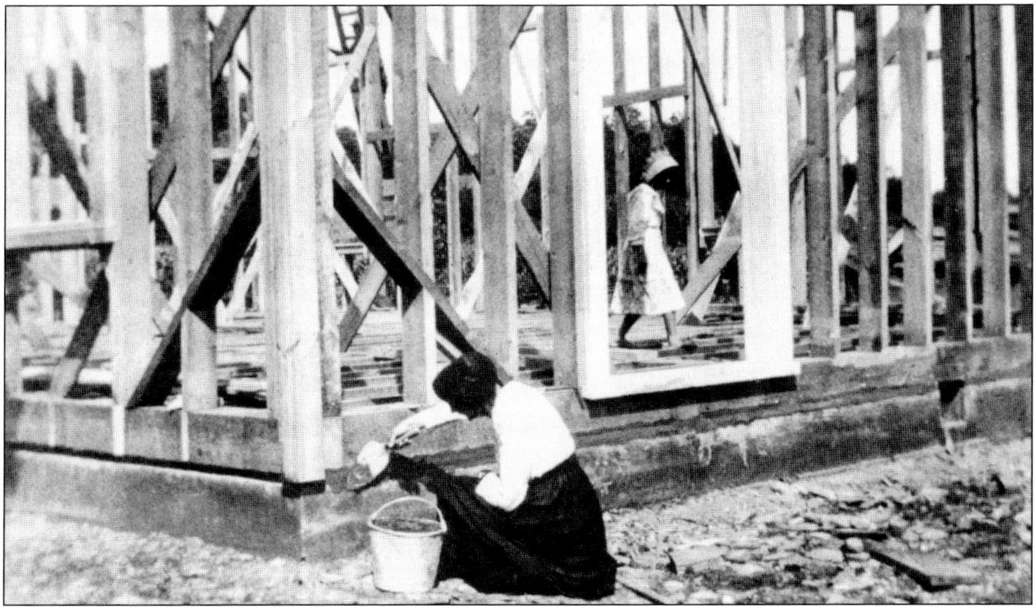

Mennonite ministers began work in the Criders area about 1880–1885, preaching in schoolhouses and in the Caplinger United Brethren Church. In 1922, a frame church was built for the growing congregation of Valley View Mennonite Church. As this photograph shows, all members, including women and children, contributed to the building of their new church. (Thelma Ritchie Bowers collection.)

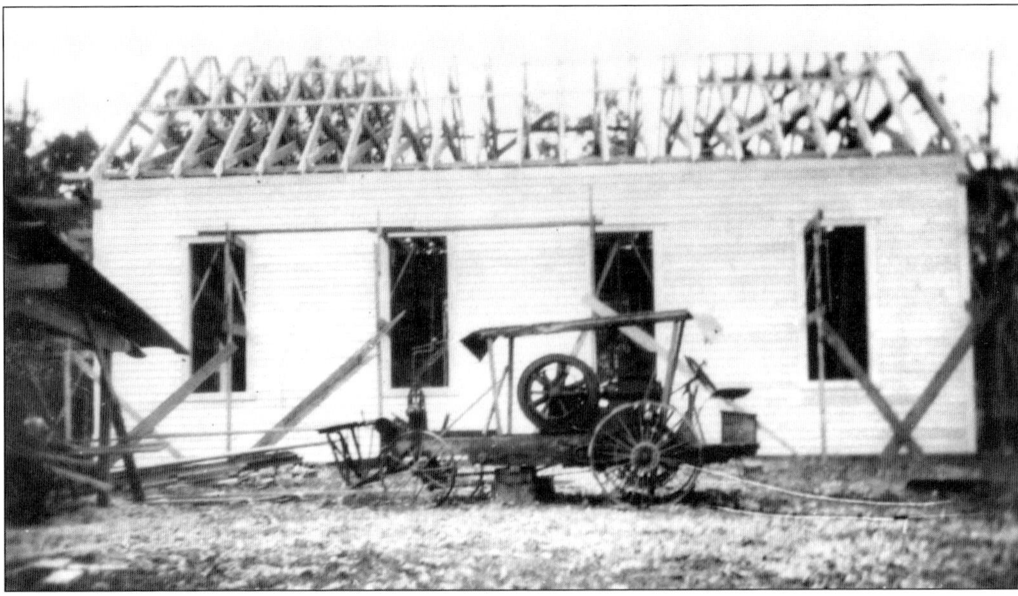

Lawrence Webster "Web" Turner of Fulks Run, one of the carpenters for Valley View Mennonite Church, took this photograph of the church under construction around 1922. The machine is a planing machine. (L. Webster Turner collection.)

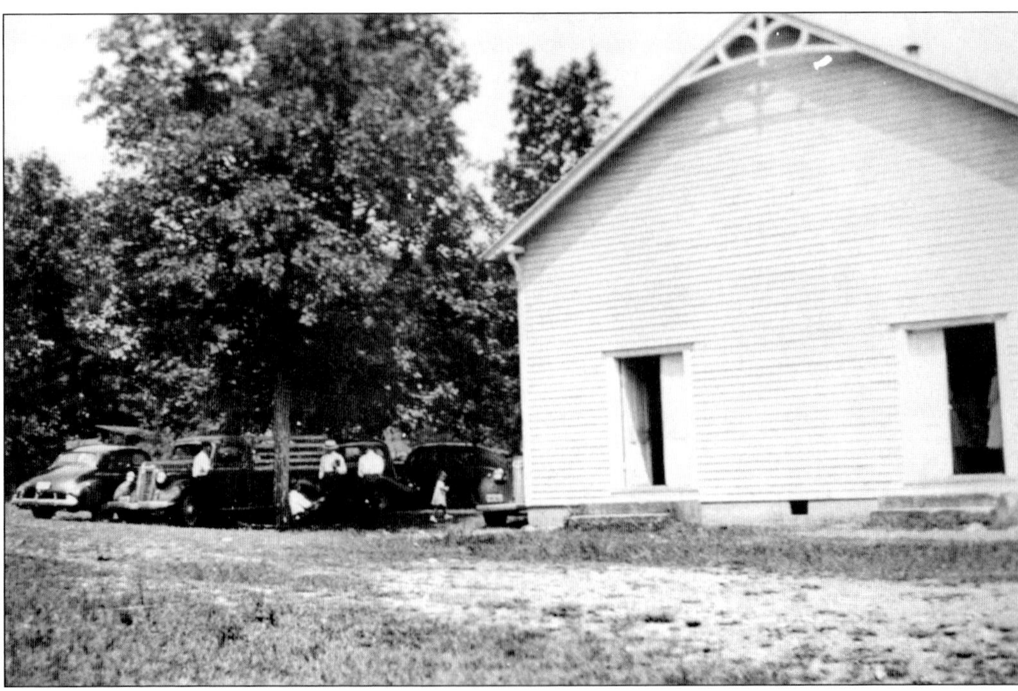

The original Valley View Mennonite Church had the traditional two doors: the right one for women and children and the left one for men. Seating inside was also according to sex. The church was remodeled around 1966 with one front door, and a social hall was added in the 1980s. (Thelma Ritchie Bowers collection.)

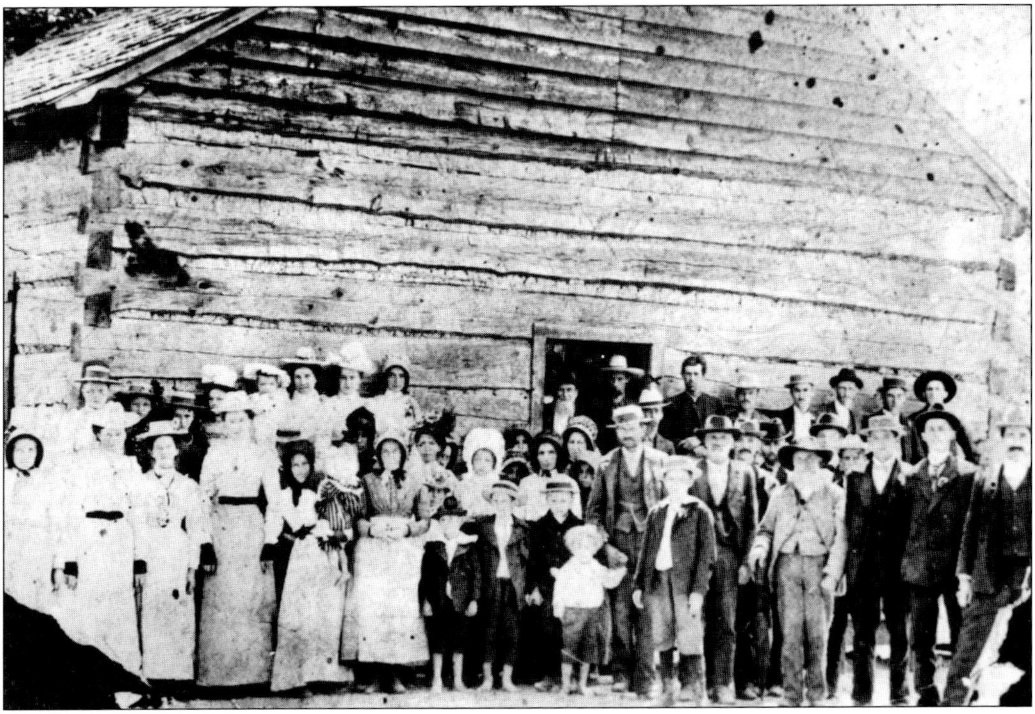

The first Crab Run Church of the Brethren near Bergton was a log structure built by William Stultz, George Moyer, and Abraham Moyer between 1850 and 1871. On March 19, 1911, Rev. J. Webster Lantz preached the last sermon in the log church. It was dismantled and the logs were sawed into framing and used in the present building. (Virginia Fitzwater Souder collection.)

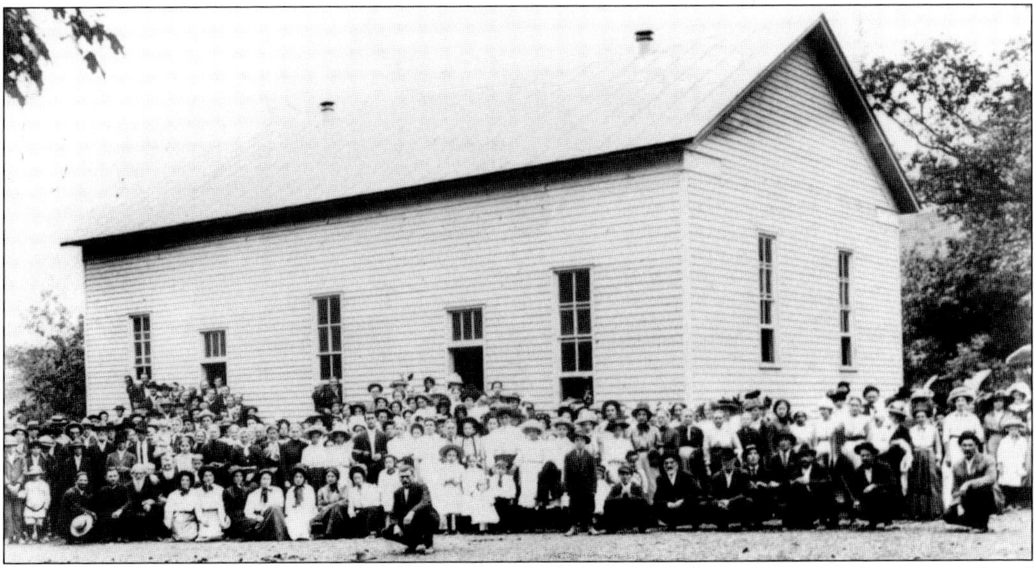

Construction began on the new Crab Run Church on December 9, 1911, and was completed March 16, 1912. J. E. Halterman was head carpenter, and total wages for the project were $46.75 at $1.00 per day. Between 400 and 500 people attended dedication services of the new Crab Run Church of the Brethren on May 26, 1912. It has been enlarged and modernized several times since. (Helen Whetzel Moyers collection.)

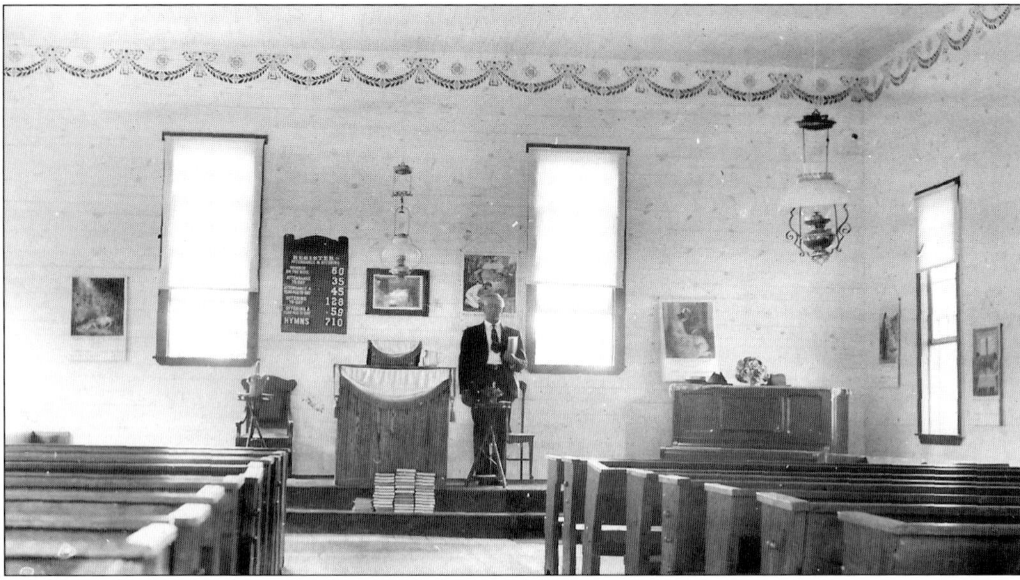

Crab Run Church was decorated with stenciling in the late 1930s or early 1940s. Reverend Stevens is standing on the platform between the piano and pulpit. Hanging kerosene lamps provided light, and two wood stoves, not visible, heated the church. Look closely at the pews—every other one had a back that swiveled to make a table for the Love Feast. (Floyd and Wilma Stultz Smith collection.)

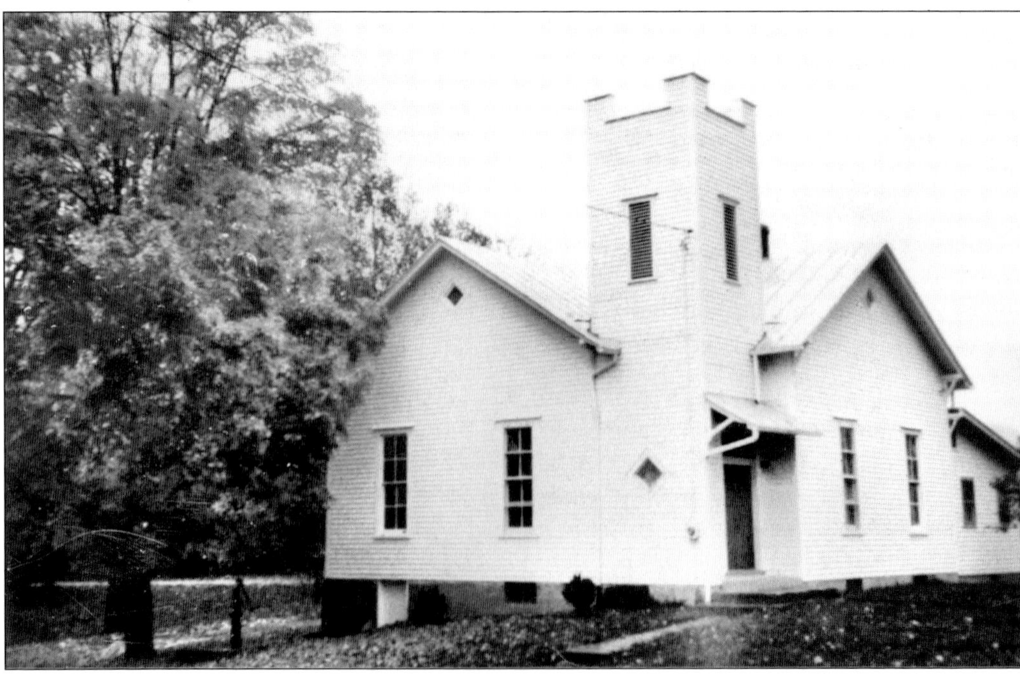

Riverside United Brethren Church near Fulks Run was built in 1921 on land donated by Dorcas Aubrey Brenneman. Brethren and Mennonite ministers also preached here after their regular preaching place, Brake Schoolhouse, was torn down. Marvin Bare took this photograph on October 30, 1985; six days later, the 1985 flood washed the church completely away. Members have rebuilt the church one-half mile west of this site. (Marvin Bare collection.)

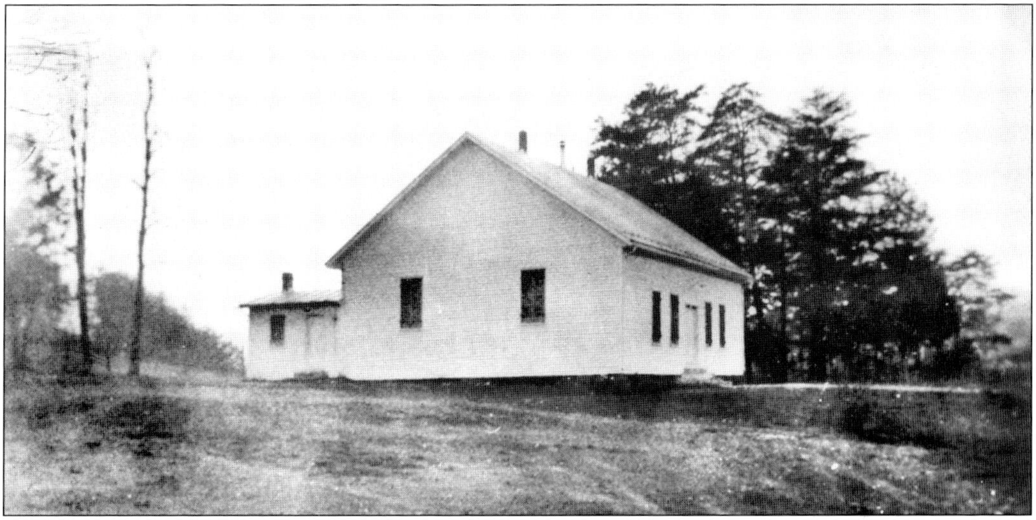

In the mid-1800s, Brethren services were held in Turner, Fulk, Hoover, and Ritchie schools near Fulks Run. The first Mountain Grove Church of the Brethren was built in 1877 with two doors in the front. The building underwent two minor remodelings in 1920 and 1928, and the entrance was changed to one door and two windows. The present brick church replaced this frame building in 1951. (Ava Reedy Dove collection.)

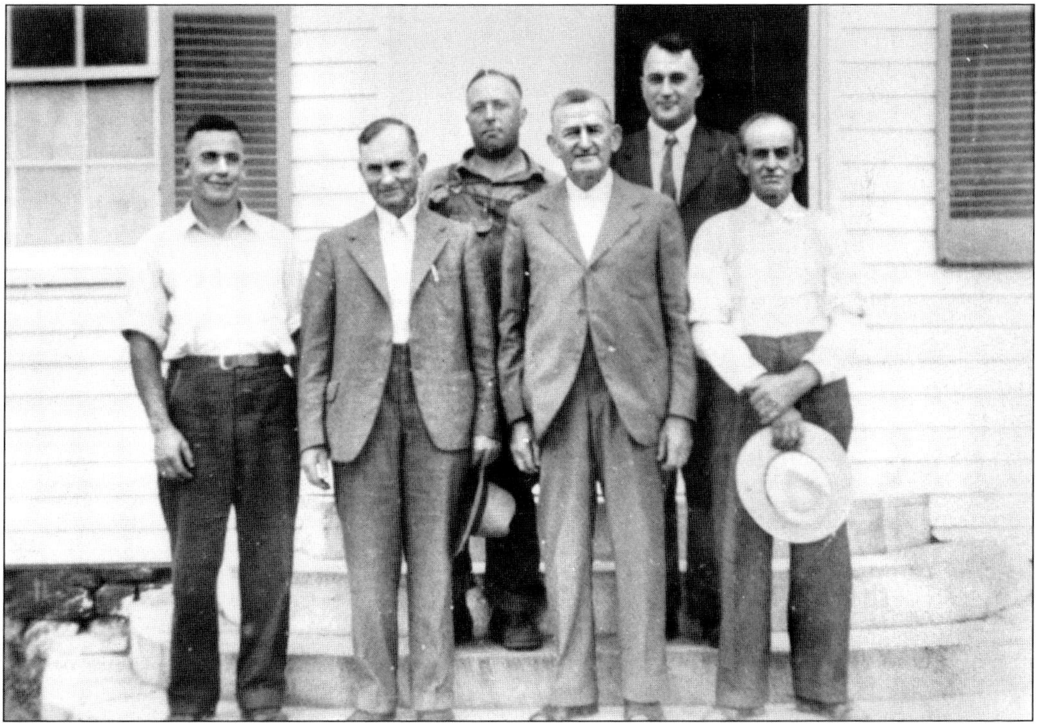

The following leaders of Mountain Grove Church of the Brethren in the early 1950s are pictured from left to right: (first row) Harry Turner, Harold O. Turner, David Huffman, and Frank Trumbo; (second row) Noah Carr and Arnold Wilkins. When the new church was built in 1951, membership was about 240, Harold O. Turner and Arnold Wilkins were ministers, and Harry Turner was a trustee. (Joyce Wilkins Branner collection.)

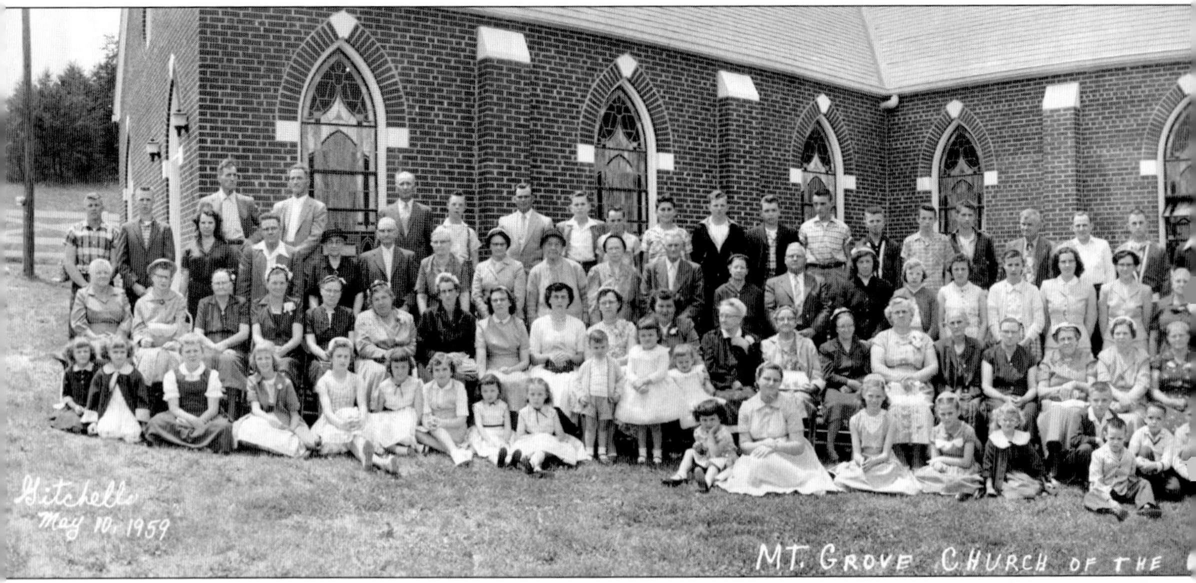

Mount Grove Church of the Brethren members gathered May 10, 1959, for a church portrait. If you look closely, you'll see that two men managed to be on both ends of the photo! The following members are pictured from left to right: (children seated) Brenda Carr Reese, Anna Lou Carr See, Joyce Ann Ritchie Moyers, Dawn Wilkins, Connie Shoemaker, Colleen Fisher, Bonnie Shoemaker, Dixie Fisher, Donna Fisher, unidentified, Shirley Baker, Annetta Flickinger Curry, Joan Hoover, unidentified, Allen Ray Ritchie, Robert "Bobby" Fulk, Stephen Turner, Carl Turner Jr., Terry Ritchie, Junior Wilkins, Daryl B. Ritchie, Jerry Branner, Beverly J. Turner, David Carr, Paul Baker, Danny Carr, Randall May, Carroll Keller, unidentified, Alice Baker, William Baker, Judy Fulk, James Fulk, Danny Slater, and Robert Brady; (children standing) Ronnie Fulk, Sharon Reedy Turner, and Opal Reedy; (ladies seated) Elsie Ritchie, Mrs. Ed Lantz, Minnie Wine, Ruth Wilkins Dettra, Ethel Turner, Cliffie Emswiler, Helen Shoemaker, Anna Belle Fisher, Pauline Fulk, Irene Miller, Retha Reedy, Minnie Fulk, Ida Riggleman, Zona Dove, Katherine Carr, Edith Brady Baker, Herma Roadcap Hoover, Rosa Roadcap Turner, Maida Reedy Fulk Myers, Pauline Ritchie Fulk, Eleanor Fulk Ritchie, Lula Fulk Turner, Hope Fulk Ritchie, Mary Lou Fulk Ritchie, Joyce Branner Wilkins, Edith M. Baker Ryman, Marjorie Carr, Dessel May, Mabel Turner, Marguerite Turner holding Shelia Turner, Rachel Baker, Hilda Fulk, Reba Dare Slater, Margo

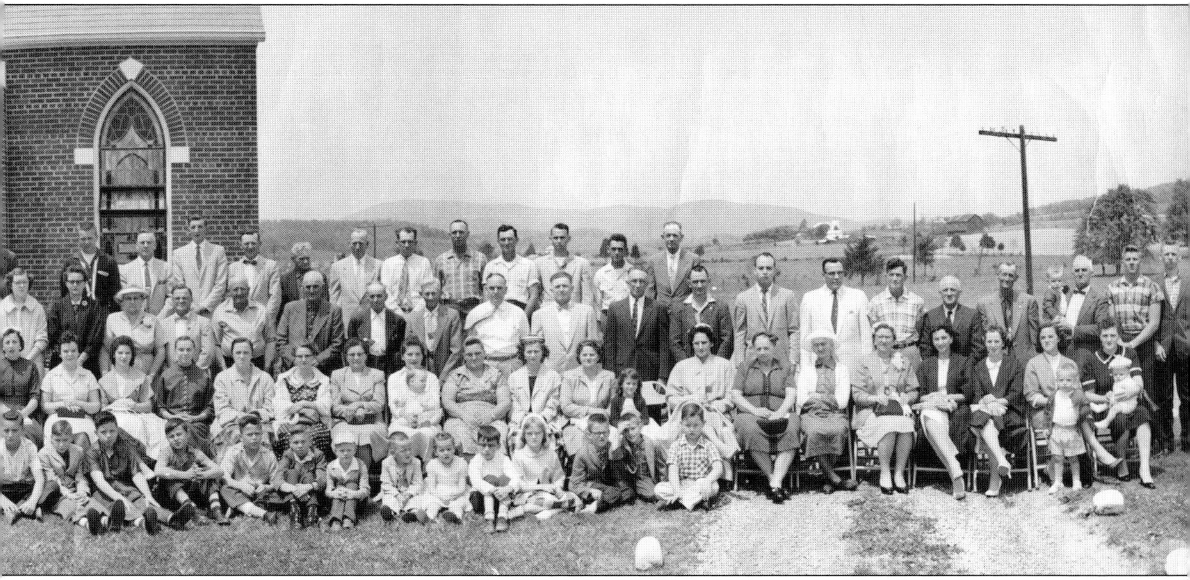

Slater Miller, Vickie C. Slater, Lillie Fulk, Verdie Branner, Naomi Fulk Custer, Phyllis Conley, Kay Wilkins, Joy Fulk Shiflet holding Jerry Shiflet, and Virginia F. Shiflet holding Lyndon Shiflet; (first row, standing) Ray Propst, Richard Fulk, Shirley Fisher, Elbert Dove, Rebecca Miller, Rev. H. O. Turner, Alice Turner, Gussie Turner Custer, Minnie Ritchie, Rosa Ritchie, Isaac Baker, Erma Miller, Blaine Carr, Vada Fulk, Janet Ritchie, Esther Ritchie, Minnie Wilkins, Catherine Comer, Ruth Ritchie, Ruth Sager, Evelyn Branner, Elma Fulk, Jean Turner Fulk, Patsy Turner, Mrs. Reuben Dove, Reuben Dove, Edward Carr, Jacob Fulk, Frank Trumbo, Sidney Wine, Herman Turner, Delmar Ritchie, Benjamin Turner, Delbert Slater, Glade Fulk, Marshall Miller, Matthew Ritchie, Galen Fulk, Robert Hoover, Clory Fulk holding Bart Shiflet, Ray Propst, and Richard Fulk; (second row, standing) Edward Lantz, Olin Lantz, Albert Carr, Tommy Fisher, Garland Reedy, Lester Shoemaker Jr., Jerry Fisher, Johnny Branner, Sammy Fulk, Nelson Turner, Boyd Fulk, Ray Wilkins, Richard Trimble, Delmas Hinkle, Rufus B. Turner, Harry Comer, Biedler Fulk, Raymond Ritchie Jr., David Ritchie, Herman Baker, Gary Custer, Harry Turner, Glen Shiflet, Lynwood Shiflet, Angus W. Dove, Maynard Fulk, Raymond Ritchie, Harrison May, Ernest Branner, Matthew Dove, Carl Turner, and Hoy Turner.

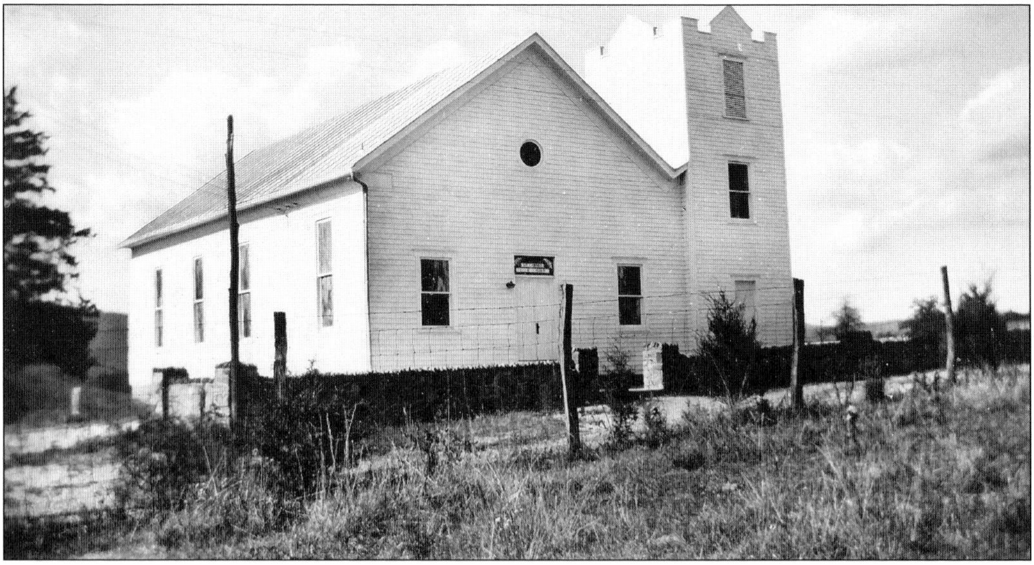

Mount Carmel United Brethren Church near Fulks Run was built about 1877 on land donated by Berryman Custer. The United Brethren used it on the second and fourth Sundays and the Mennonites used it on the first and third Sundays. The church was rebuilt in 1902. In 1950, the front of the church was enlarged and Sunday school rooms, a full basement, and central heating were added. (Ruth A. Turner collection.)

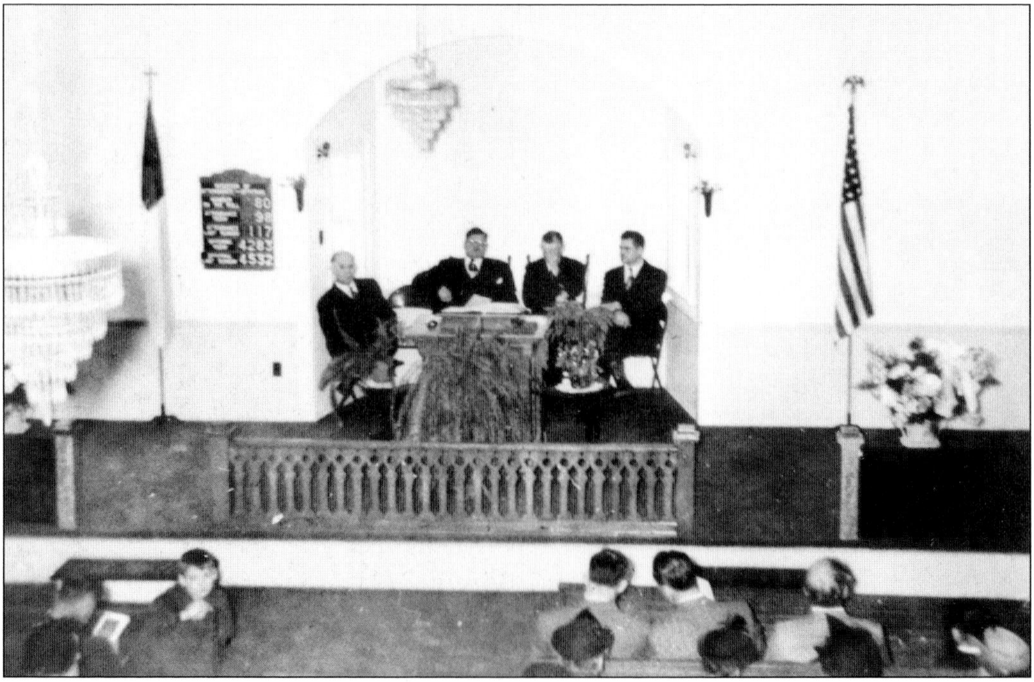

New additions at Mount Carmel were dedicated on December 31, 1950, with preaching by Rev. David F. Glovier and Conference Superintendent Floyd L. Fulk. Ministers pictured on the platform are, from left to right, Rev. Joseph R. Collis, Rev. William E. Wolfe, Rev. Floyd L. Fulk, and Rev. Warren Trumbo. Mount Carmel was the home church of four ministers: Floyd L. Fulk, Warren Trumbo, R. Dean Fawley, and Wilton Thomas. (Velma Turner Cooper collection.)

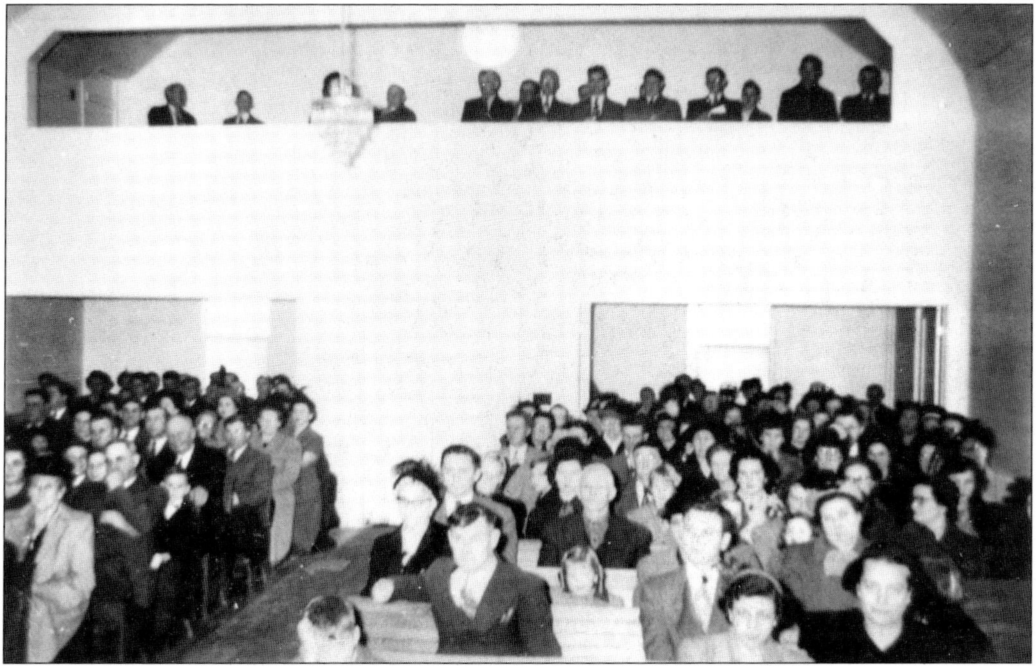

Mount Carmel was crowded on dedication day, with all Sunday school rooms and the balcony in use. Virginia Ann Fawley Hulvey, song leader, and Miriam Hoover, organist, are on the front row to the right. Through denomination mergers, Mount Carmel later became Evangelical United Brethren and, in 1969, United Methodist. (Velma Turner Cooper collection.)

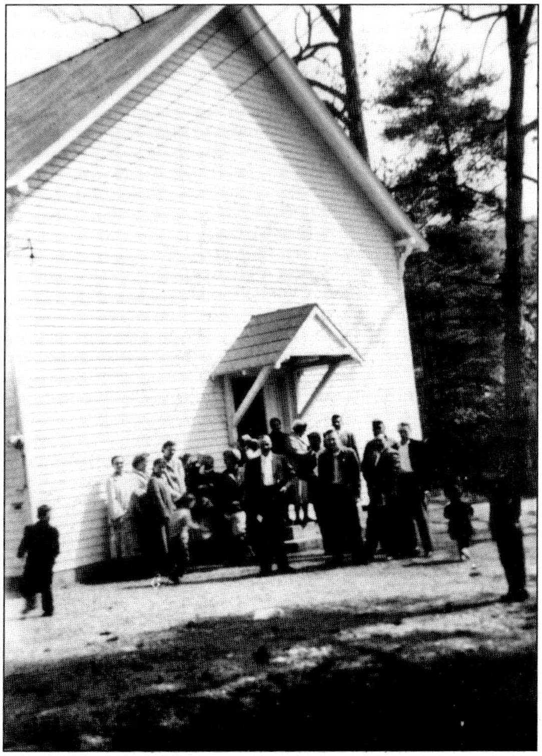

In about 1850, Mennonite Abraham Brenneman moved from Linville to Brocks Gap and, sometime later, Mennonite preaching began in the area. Around 1881, the Mennonites shared the Mount Carmel United Brethren church building. When Mount Carmel passed into the hands of the United Brethren Church, the Mennonites preached in nearby schoolhouses before building Hebron Mennonite Church in 1915 on Shoemaker River. The church has been expanded and modernized in recent years. (Trovillo S. "Bill" Miller collection.)

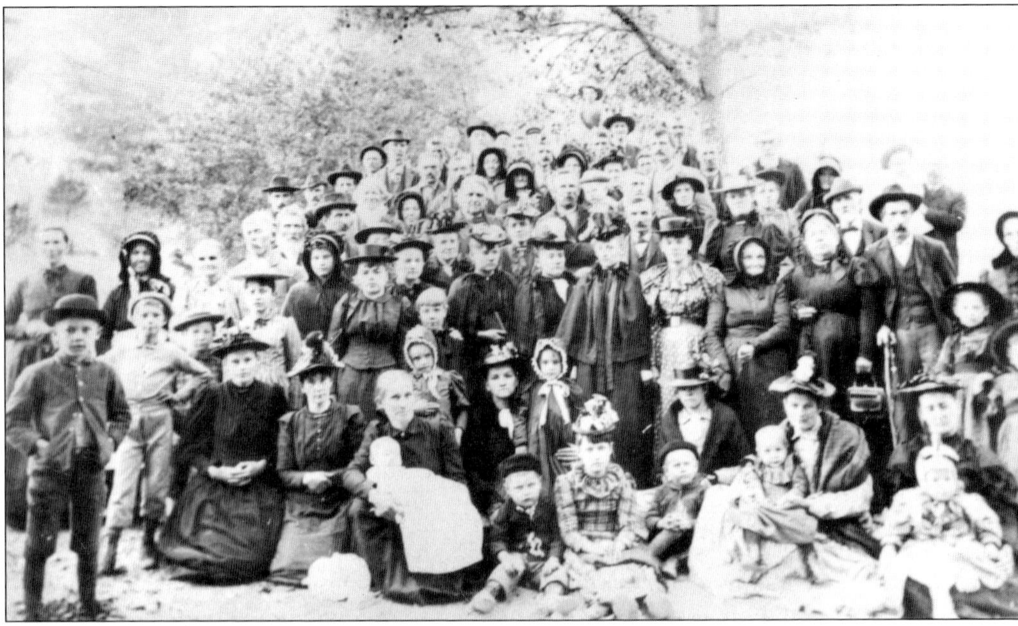

Tunis Old School Primitive Baptist Church was located on Runions Creek. Their church records begin in 1860, but the church was organized before that. The Runion, Tusing, Estep, Biller, Silvius, and Eaton families were among the main families of this church. This photograph was taken about 1895. Some members of the church went west in the 1880s and began the Island Chapel Primitive Baptist Church in Hastings, Indiana. (Reuel Tusing collection.)

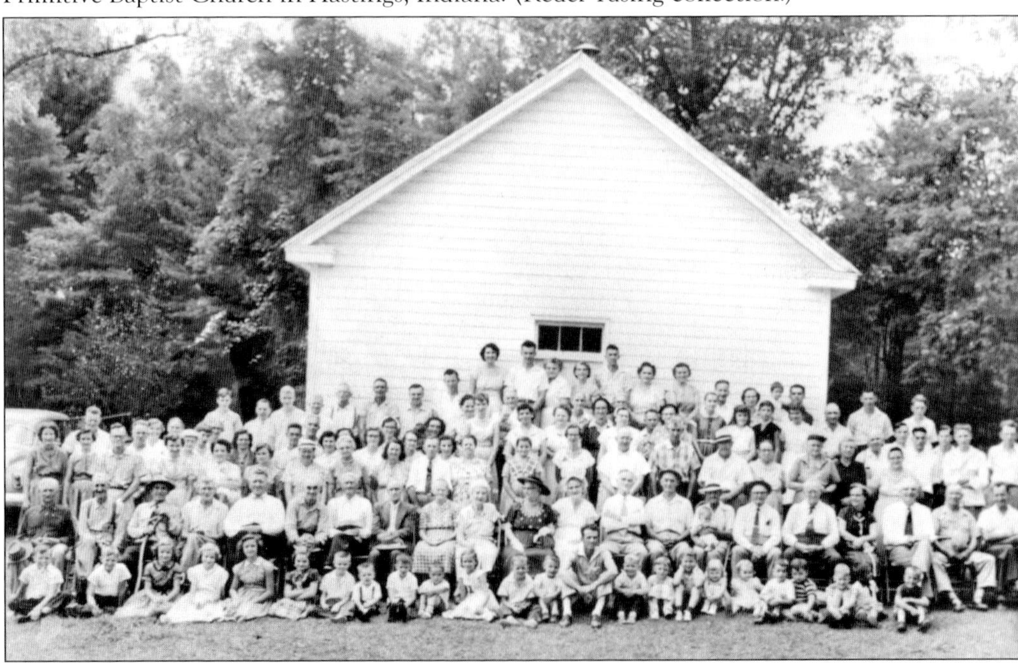

Brethren minister Elder John Kline began preaching in the Ritchie Schoolhouse on Dry River by 1853. The *Brethren Encyclopedia* says the Brethren discontinued preaching there in 1957, although school and family reunions continued to be held at the schoolhouse. The Frank family reunion is the occasion of this gathering in the 1950s. (Ruth Ritchie Baker collection.)

Early mission work in the Hopkins Gap area of Fulks Run by Mennonite preachers began in the 1880s. Gospel Hill Mennonite Church was built in 1908 on Highway 612 and has a church cemetery. Ministers took turns preaching at the church until the 1940s, when one minister became the regular minister for the congregation. The church has been enlarged and modernized in recent times. (Mrs. Branson Conley collection.)

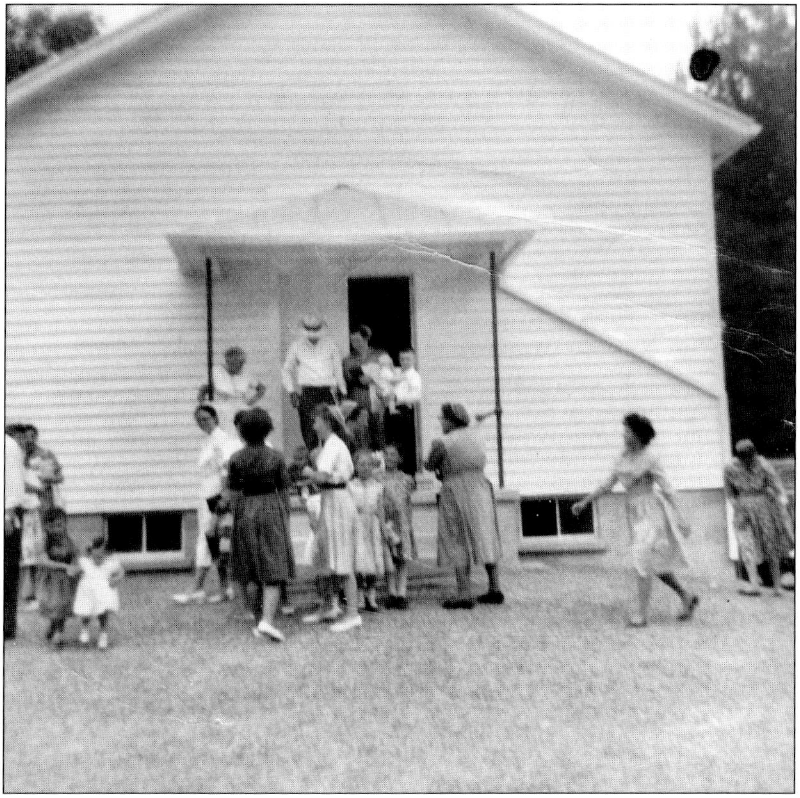

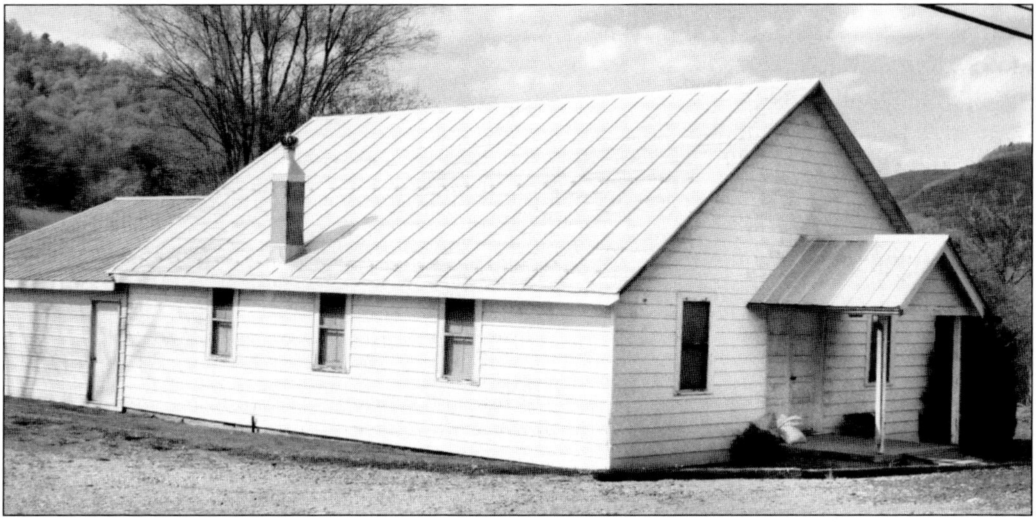

The Pentecostal church at Fulks Run was founded by Thomas J. Marshall (1894–1974). He was a Pentecostal evangelist who married Minnie A. Custer. One of Minnie's brothers, Wade Hampton Custer, was also a Pentecostal evangelist who held tent revivals. Services continued to be held here until about 1980. (Garnett R. Turner, photographer.)

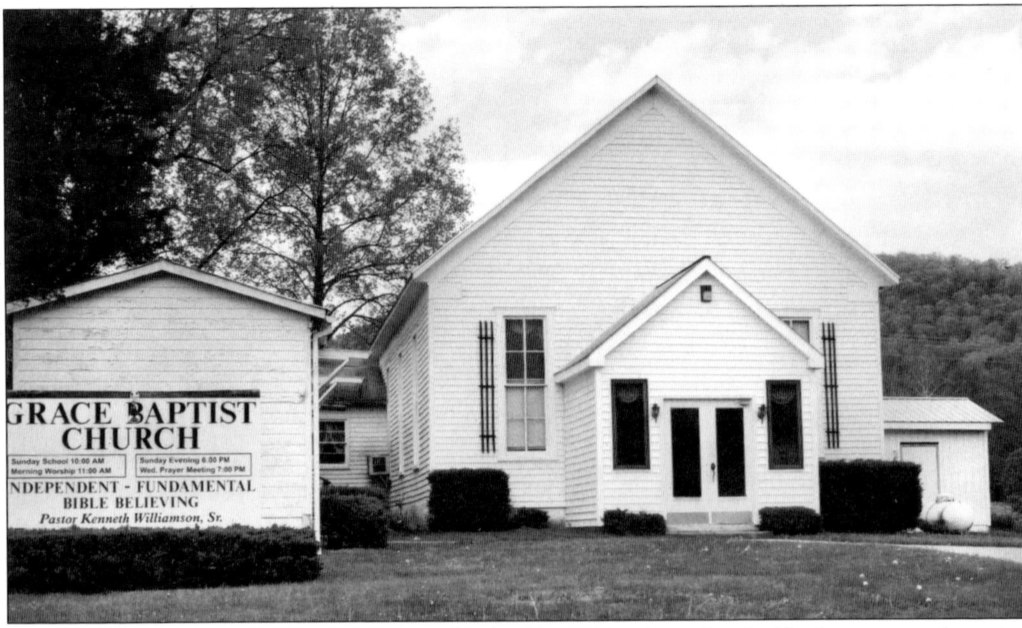

The Baptist Church at Fulks Run was established by 1918, when they held a lawn party featuring sandwiches, soda pop, and chewing gum. When regular services resumed in the 1960s, Pastor James C. "Johnny" Fulk sponsored a youth group called the "Ready Club." Later, the Ready Club building was attached to the church building. (Garnett Turner, photographer.)

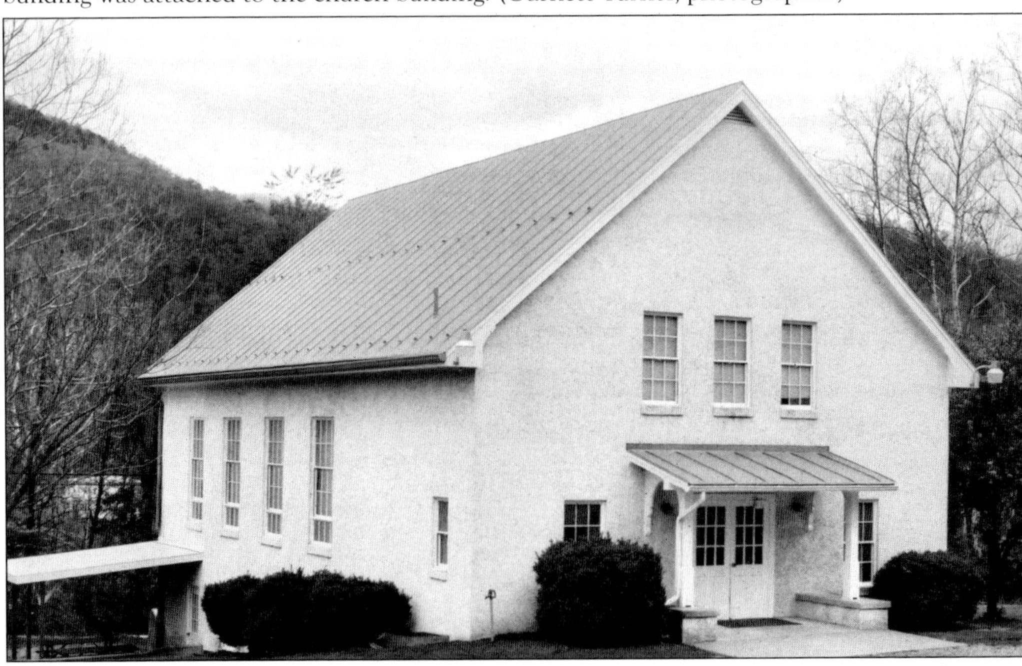

Bethel Mennonite Church began as a Sunday school organized by two Baptist girls under a tree near the present church about 1915. Services moved to an old store building, where shelves were removed to make room for benches. The first church building was built in 1927 and replaced by the present building in 1956. The interior has since been remodeled, but the exterior is original. (Garnett R. Turner, photographer.)

Five

RECREATION

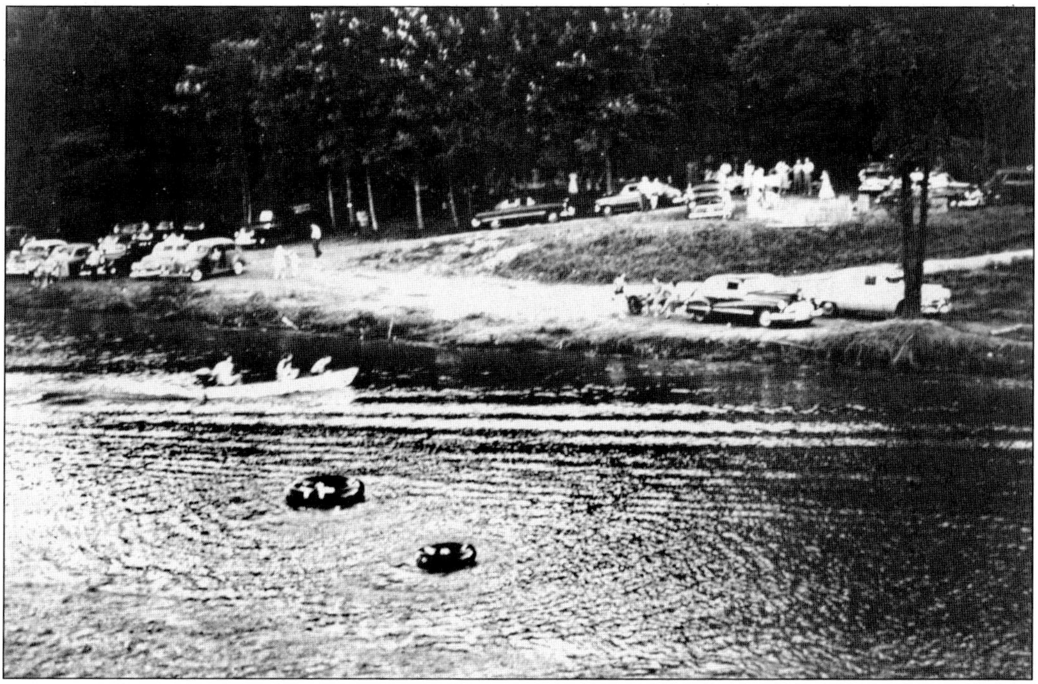

Water sports, from swimming to ice-skating, are popular. This 1951 photograph of Bennie's Beach at Brocks Gap shows people enjoying boating, tubing, and picnicking. Benjamin H. "Bennie" Carr built a block bathhouse just to the right of this photograph; the bathhouse stood until washed away by the 1985 flood. Another photograph from the same day shows several cars parked in the ford while their owners washed them. (Garnett R. Turner, photographer.)

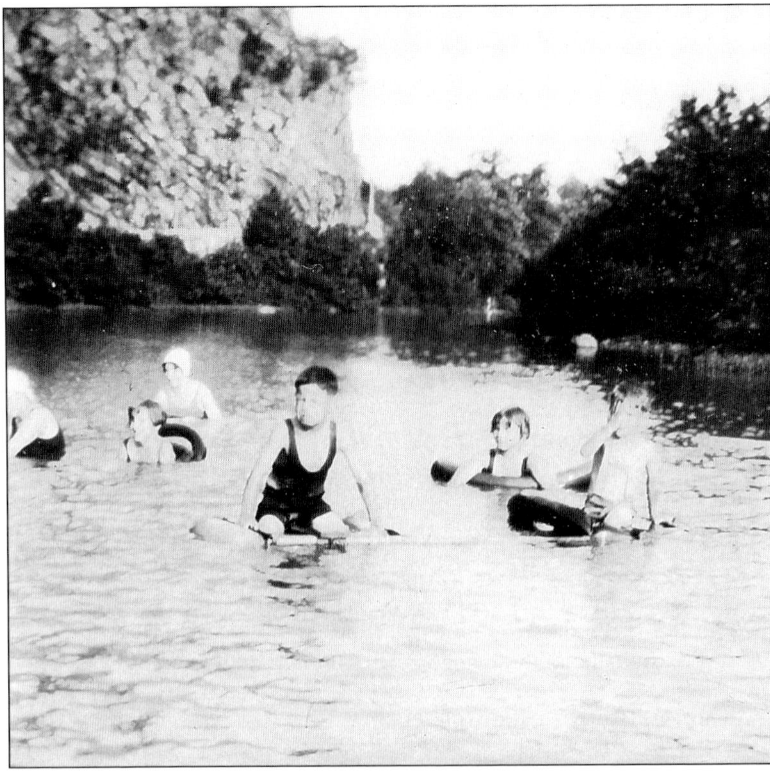

Bennie's Beach at the Gap was a popular swimming hole. Other favorite swimming spots were the Bear Hole, Shoemaker Hole, Mallet Hole, Blue Hole, and Wittig Hole. Starting with the boy on the raft, the three swimmers in front are E. L., Geraldine, and Billy Chapman of Lacey Spring around 1932. Ervin L. Chapman, the children's father, had been a teacher in a Brocks Gap school. (Billy Chapman collection.)

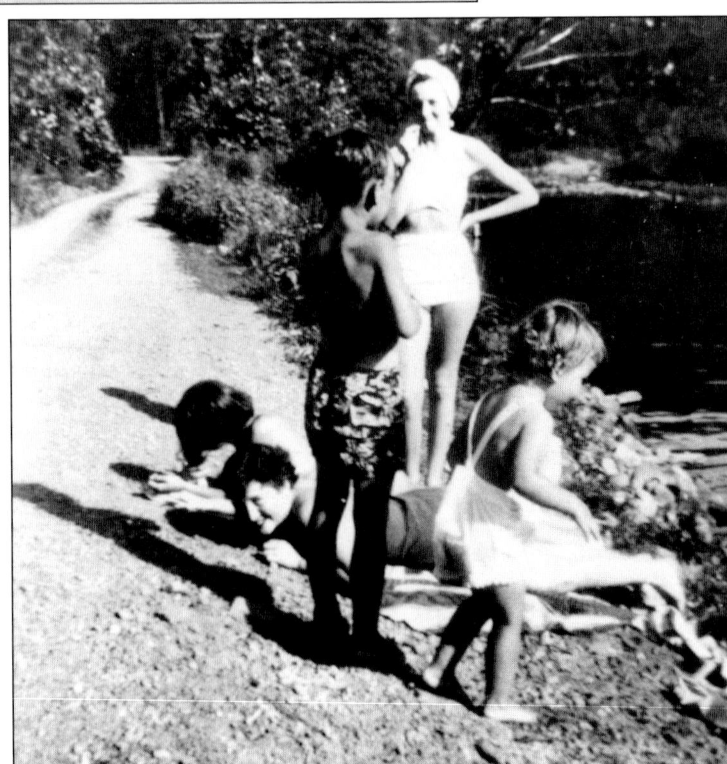

In the 1920s, when Joseph "JoeNat" Fulk took his boy haymakers to Shoemaker Hole to swim, Eunice Thomas and Hazel Bare were already swimming. JoeNat told them to leave and not look back because the haymakers were about to bathe in the nude. If they looked back, he said, they would become a salt pillar like Lot's wife. At right, Howard May's children swim at Trumbo Ford around 1951. (Nancy May Hoover collection.)

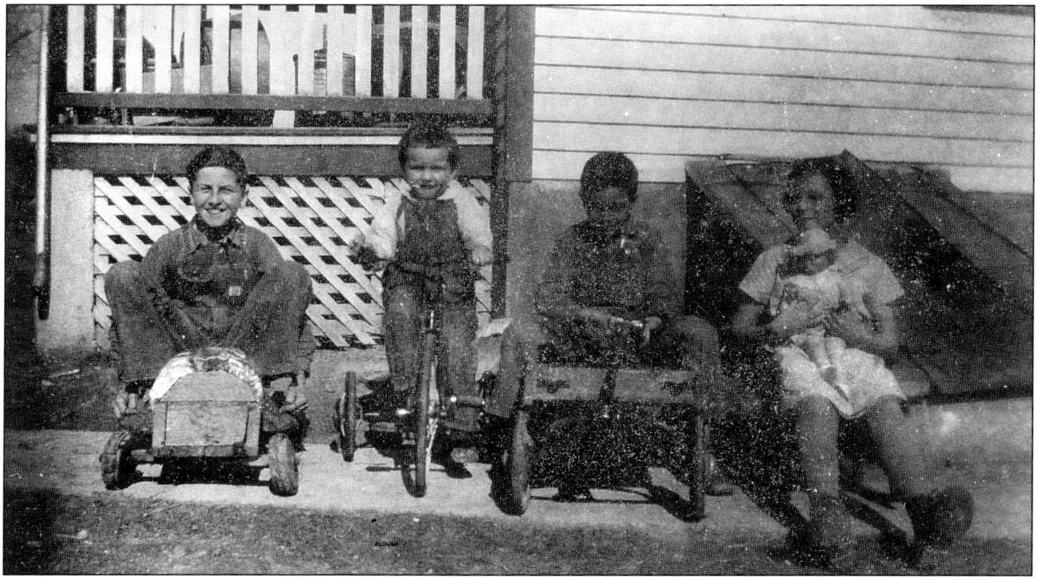

The best toys are not always store-bought. These children in the 1930s made their own wagons, constructing wheels from slices of hickory logs. If available, they put Model T brass bushings in the hubs. Used license plates were their "fenders" to keep burnt oil (used on the axles) from flying on their shirts. Pictured from left to right, Garnett, Miles, and Wayne Turner, and Vada Turner May display some of their creations. (Ruth Turner collection.)

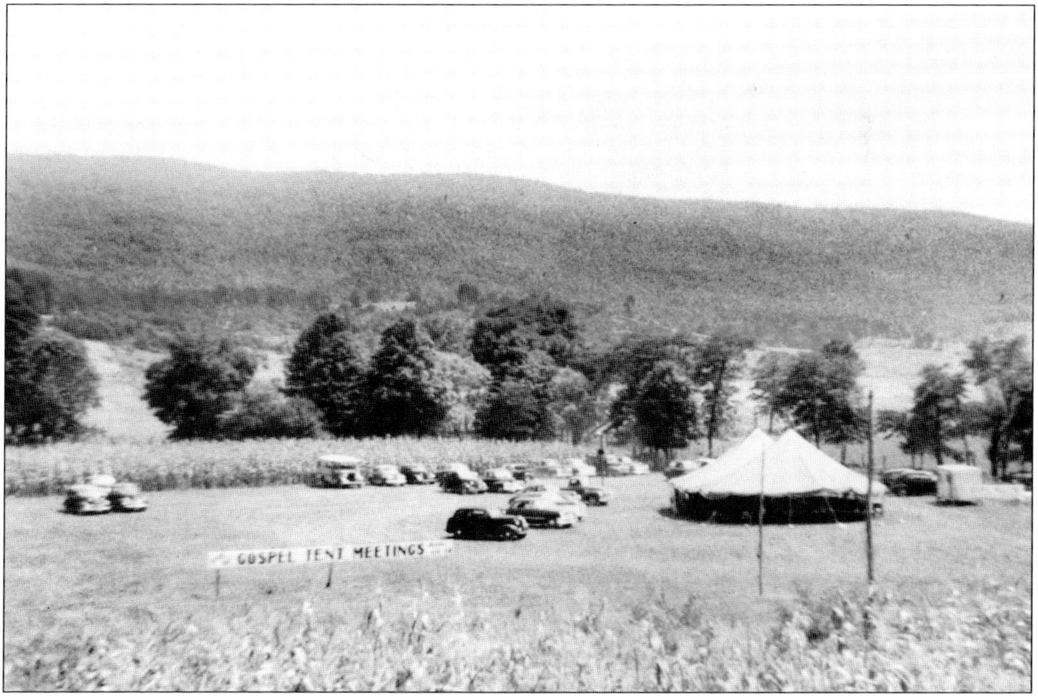

Preaching and singing were excellent reasons for folks young and old to get together to worship and socialize. Sometimes ministers from "away" held gospel tent meetings, but local ministers held regular services and revivals in schoolhouses and, later, in church buildings. Some churches sponsored district meetings with overnight guests from out of the area. (Thelma Ritchie Bowers collection.)

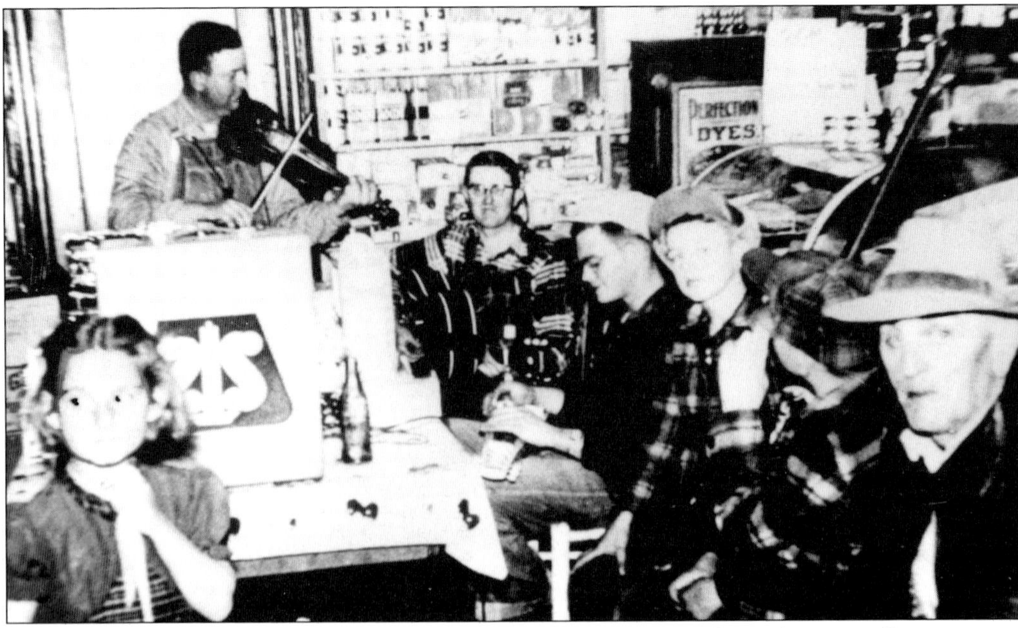

The country store was usually the hub of the community. At Lizzie Custer's store at Genoa around 1953, neighbors gathered to play music after the day's work was over. From left to right, C. Boyd "Cookus" Shoemaker (fiddle), Harrison Fulk (guitar), and Garland Reedy "crack down on it" while two unidentified boys and Jacob "Jake" Fulk listen. The girl is also unidentified. (Vivian Turner Miller collection.)

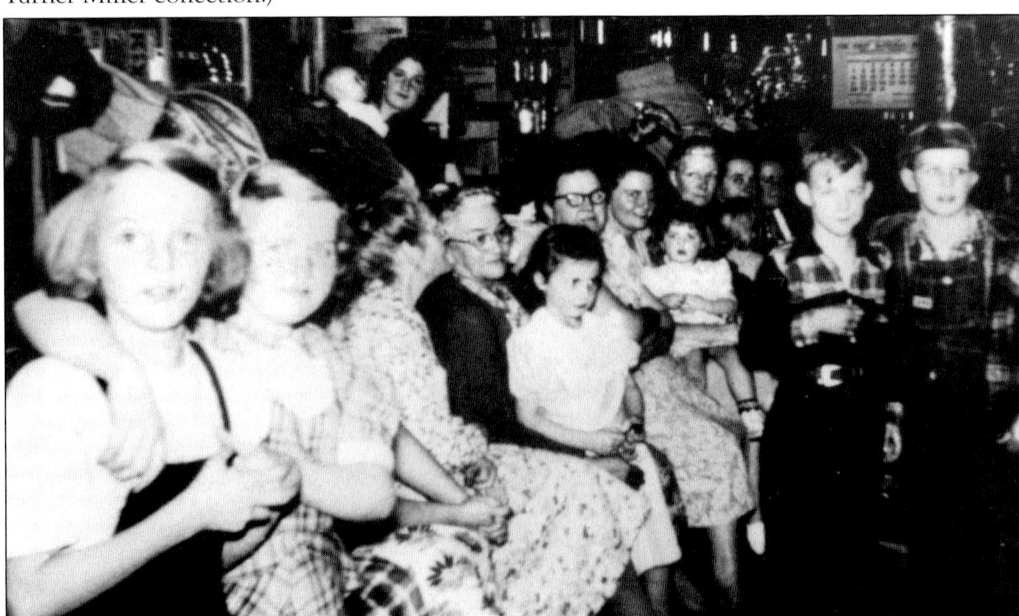

While the men were playing music at Lizzie's store, the women socialized on the other side of the room. From left to right are Kay Wilkins Bowman, Evelyn Fulk Shipe, Bess Turner, Beck Miller holding ? Miller, Helen Phillips (with arms crossed), Naomi Turner Fulk holding Linda Fulk Hopkins, and Nora Fulk. The boys pictured are Roger Phillips (left) and Eugene Phillips (right). Mrs. Porter Miller is standing in back with a baby. (Vivian Turner Miller collection.)

The United States Forestry Services provided paid employment at Cow Knob observation tower during the fire season. The employee lived alone in the tower with only telephone service for companionship. Charles F. Bare, pictured here, was the employee during one fire season. In later years, the tower was a popular destination for autumn picnics. It was torn down in the 1970s. (Kammie Mumbert Bare collection.)

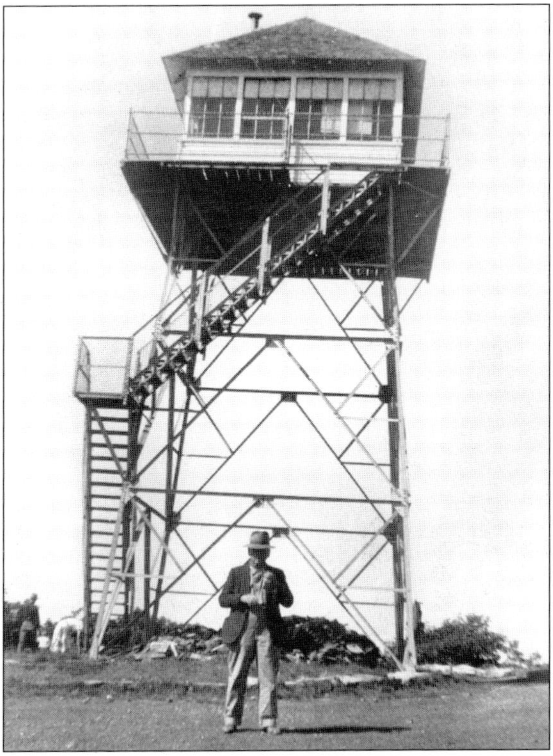

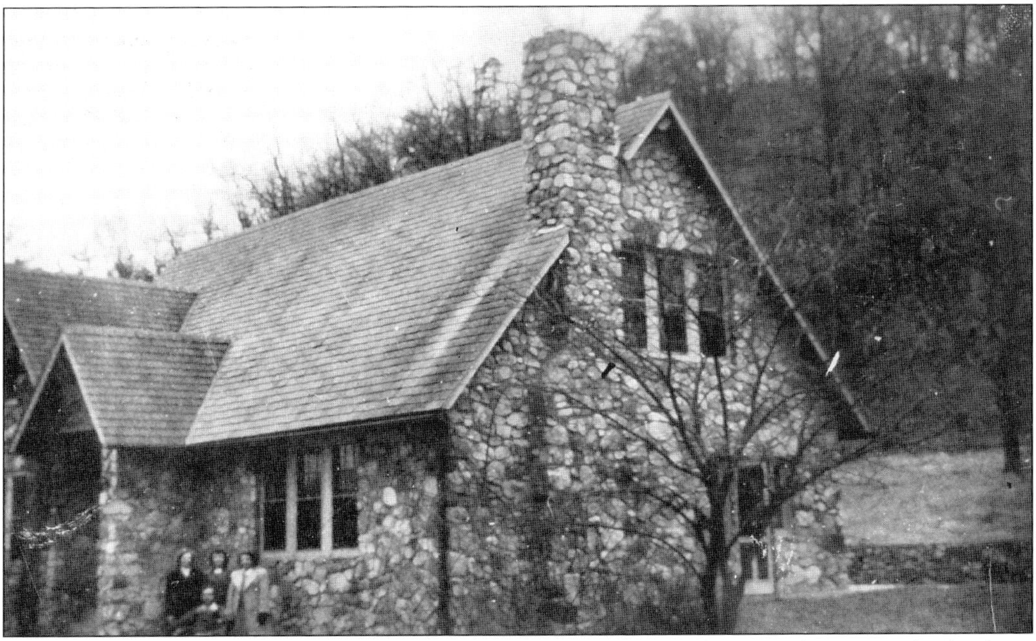

In 1929, Frederick Libbey from New York built a stone house with an outdoor stone bathtub on Church Mountain. The city family did not fit into the community, whose main interests were logging and hunting. His daughter was opposed to cutting trees for their home's road, and a feud developed between Libbey and residents when he killed three valuable hunting dogs that strayed onto his premises. (Ruth A. Turner collection.)

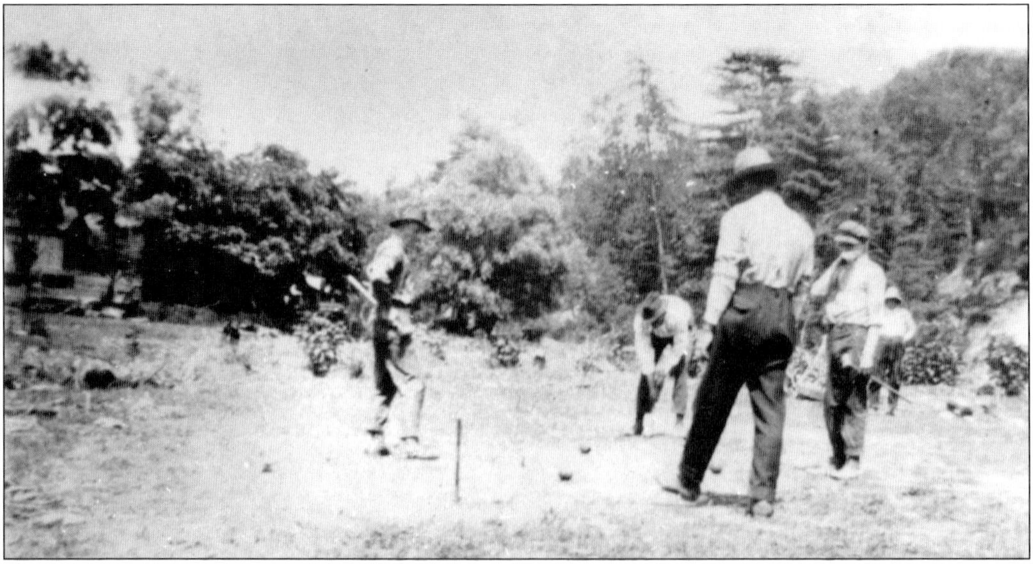

Croquet games continue to be popular in Fulks Run, where a present-day court hosts state tournaments. Pictured in an earlier era, the Robert Miller family plays near the old Dry River road, about 1920. (Matthew E. "Bud" Miller collection.)

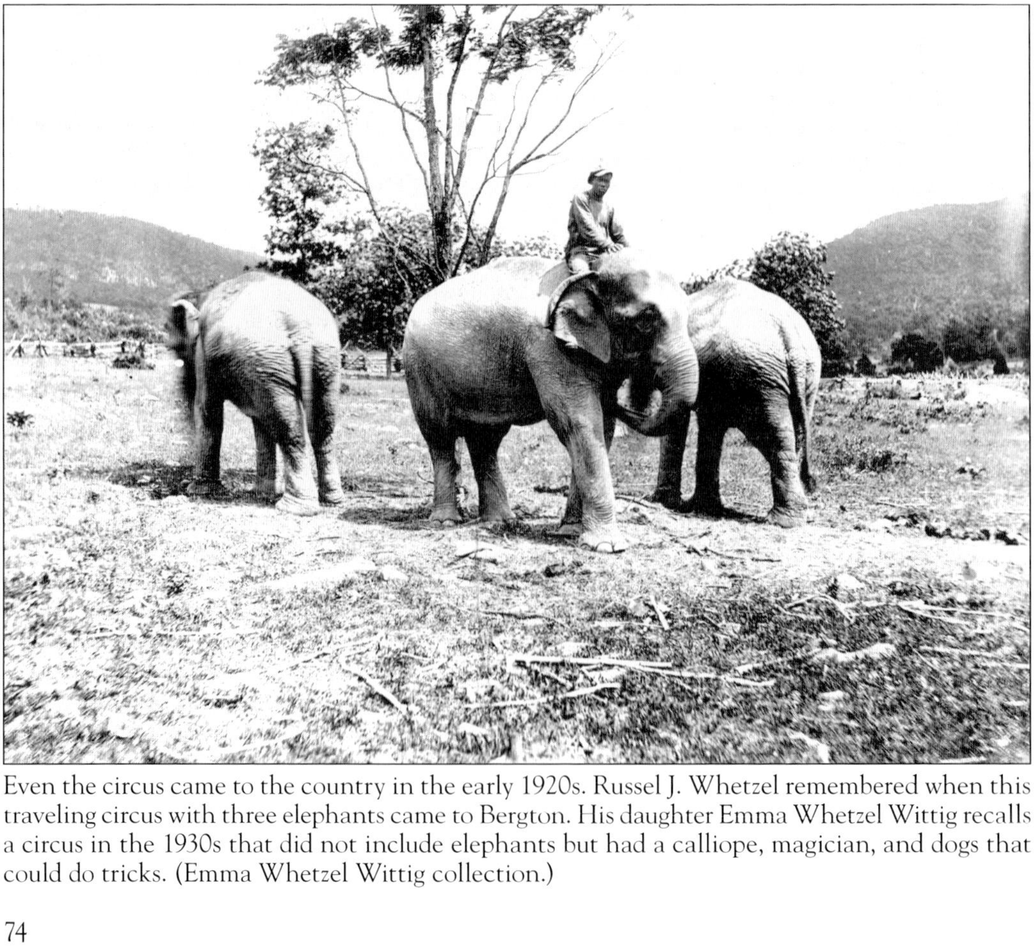

Even the circus came to the country in the early 1920s. Russel J. Whetzel remembered when this traveling circus with three elephants came to Bergton. His daughter Emma Whetzel Wittig recalls a circus in the 1930s that did not include elephants but had a calliope, magician, and dogs that could do tricks. (Emma Whetzel Wittig collection.)

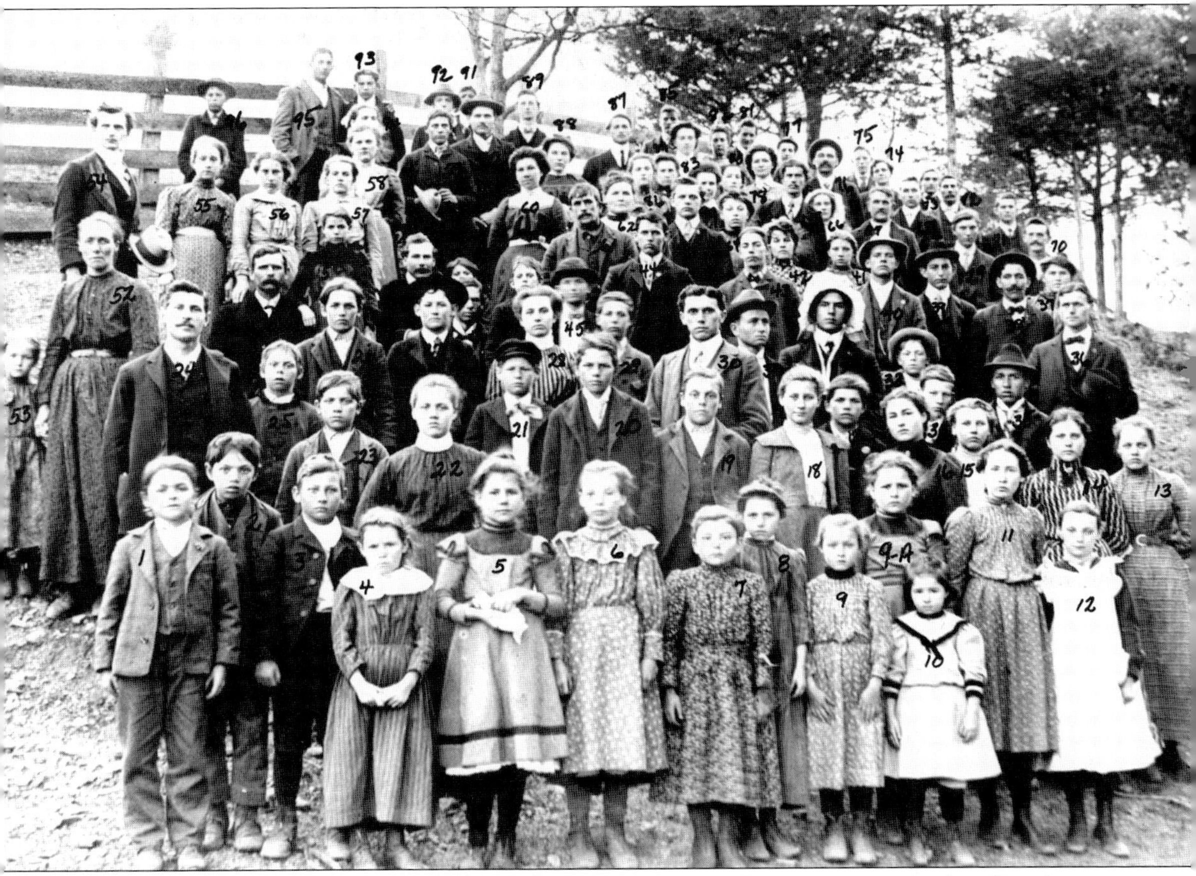

In the spring, many people attended school-closing ceremonies where recitations and spelling bees showed off the scholars' new knowledge. A photographer was on hand to record this Dovesville group about 1900. This photograph identifies the following: (1) Levi "Lee" Dove, (2) unidentified, (3) Allen Wittig, (4) Lula Crider, (5) Minnie Crider Hottinger, (6–9) unidentified, (9A) Mary Crider Dove, (10) Lula Crider Hupp, (11) Ethel Stepp Moyer, (12) unidentified, (13) Susan Whetzel Feathers, (14) Mary Bliss Wittig Caplinger, (15) Pearlie Wittig Fulk, (16) Clara Dove Albrite, (17) unidentified, (18) Ada Wittig May, (19) Adam Whetzel, (20) unidentified, (21) Hamp Dove, (22) Hattie Whetzel, (23–26) unidentified, (27) David R. Crider, (28–29) unidentified, (30) Loy Moyer, (31) Charles Dove, (32) Charles Fitzwater, (33) unidentified, (34) Jesse Wittig, (35) William "Raz" Whetzel, (36) Casper Moyer, (37–38) unidentified, (39) Ed Fink, (40–42) unidentified, (43) Charles Souder, (44) Grant Souder, (45) Casper Hottinger, (46–48) unidentified, (49) James Dove, (50) unidentified, (51) Sam Wittig, (52–53) unidentified, (54) Arthur Moyer, (55) Lelia or Hannah Albrite, (56) Effie Souder, (57) Lucinda Souder, (58) Ida Moyer, (59) Grover Souder, (60–61) unidentified, (62) Martha Wittig Crider, (63) Grover Moyer, (64) unidentified, (65) Albert Albrite, (66) unidentified, (67) Ike Moyer, (68) Luther Turner, (69) unidentified, (70) Vannie Moyer, (71–75) unidentified, (76) Seymour May, (77) unidentified, (78) Delia May, (79) Rachel Dove Albrite, (80–81) unidentified, (82) Wade Hampton Souder, (83–88) unidentified, (89) Samuel A. Crider, (90–92) unidentified, (93) Jacob R. Albrite, and (94–96) unidentified. (Lennis Moyers Garber collection.)

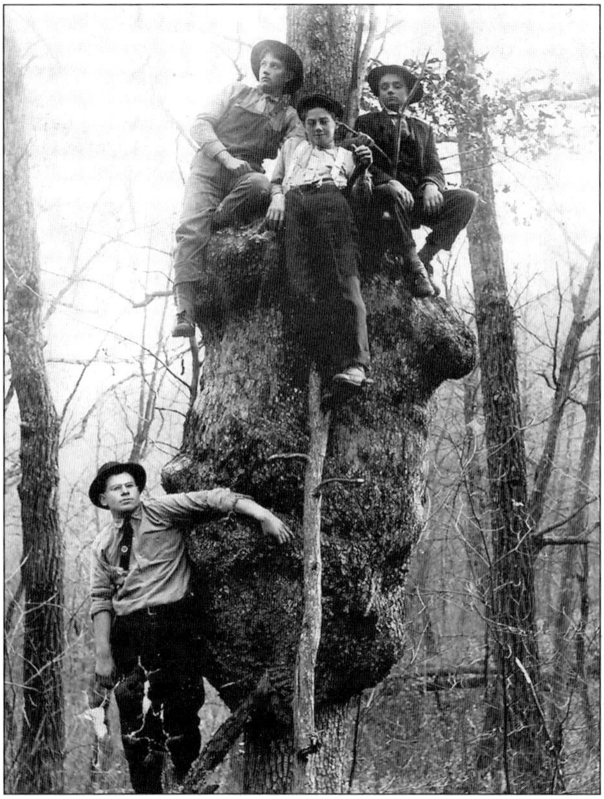

Oddities in nature were an attraction for hikers and picnickers. In 1913, this tree that looks like a snake swallowing a rat was a famous place to visit. The young man pictured on the tree branch at bottom left is Angus Walter "Tommy" Dove. From left to right in the treetop are William Franklin Hupp, Edward "Oscar" Hottinger, and Jonas "Walter" Hottinger. (Shirley Cullers Miller collection.)

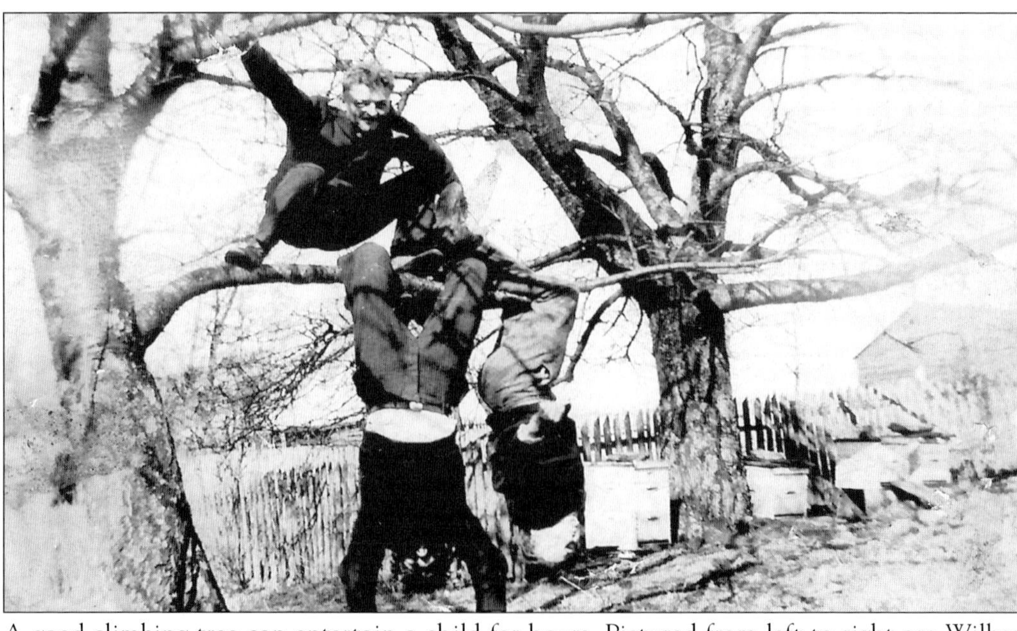

A good climbing tree can entertain a child for hours. Pictured from left to right are Wilbert "Jim" Whetzel, William "Ray" Cullers, and Ralph "Woodrow" Smith, who have "cooned" the black cherry tree and proceeded to do some tricks from the limbs. This photograph was taken at Lorenzo E. Whetzel's home about 1943. (Shirley Cullers Miller collection.)

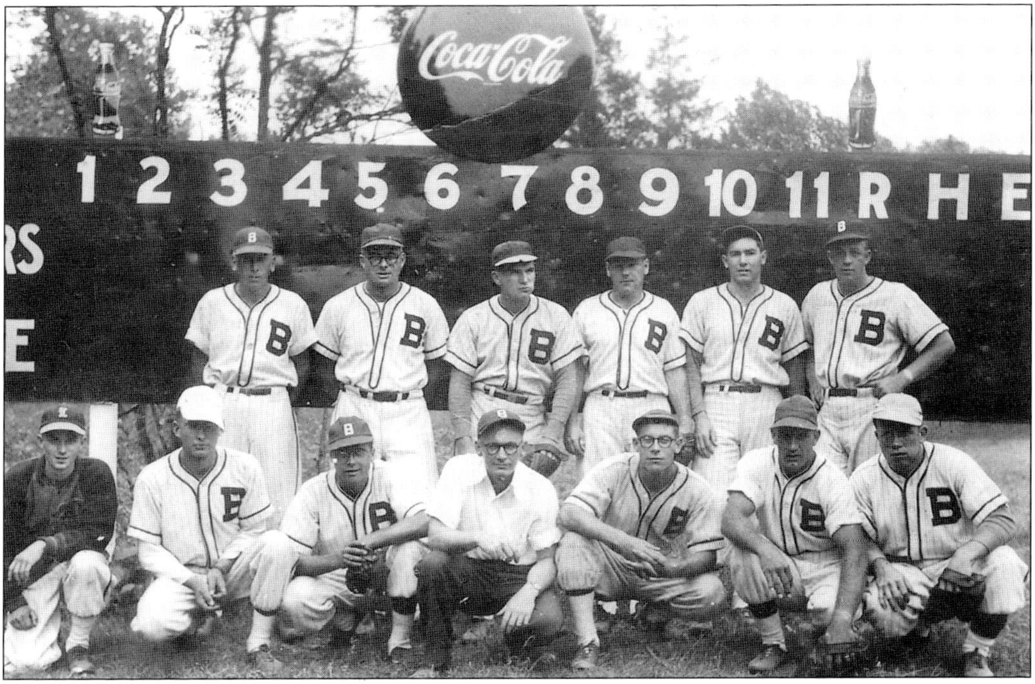

Woodrow Brown organized and managed the first Bergton baseball team to play in an organized league. In the late 1940s and 1950s, Bergton was the team to beat. Pictured from left to right about 1950 are (first row) John Long, Ivan Lantz, Earl Lantz, Woodrow Brown, Day Lantz, Jim Strickler, and Charlie Rodeffer; (second row) Lawrence Moyer, Lloyd Lantz, Jack Mason, Howard Arehart, Roy Billhimer, and Lloyd Whetzel. (Susan Brown collection.)

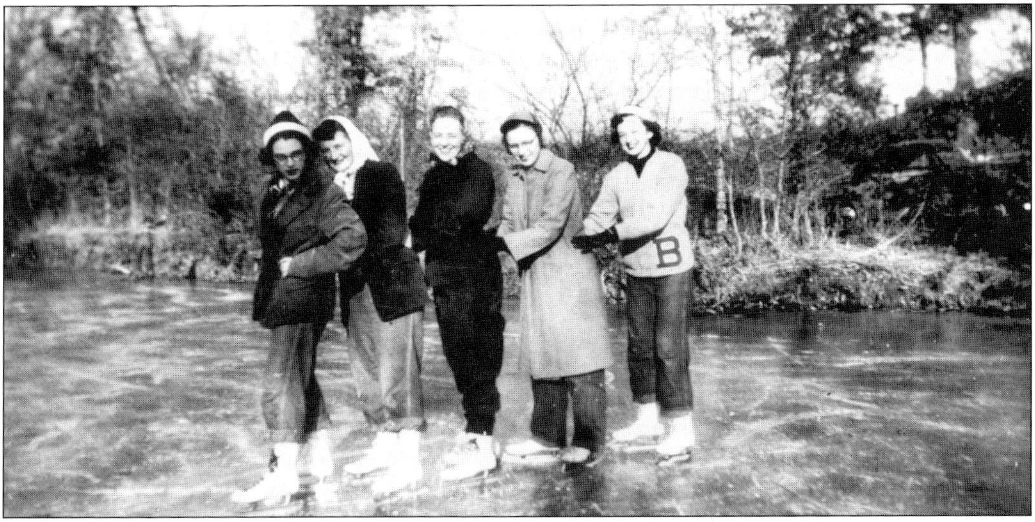

Phoebe May Orebaugh, Lois May Rhodes, Goldie Turner May, Ruby Will, and Nancy May Hoover skated on a pond at Runions Creek in 1950. Another popular spot was a large pond behind Luther Turner's mill at Fulks Run. On Sunday afternoons, 40 to 50 skaters would build a big bonfire and skate regardless of the temperature. The shady location allowed skating until late spring. (Lois May Rhodes collection.)

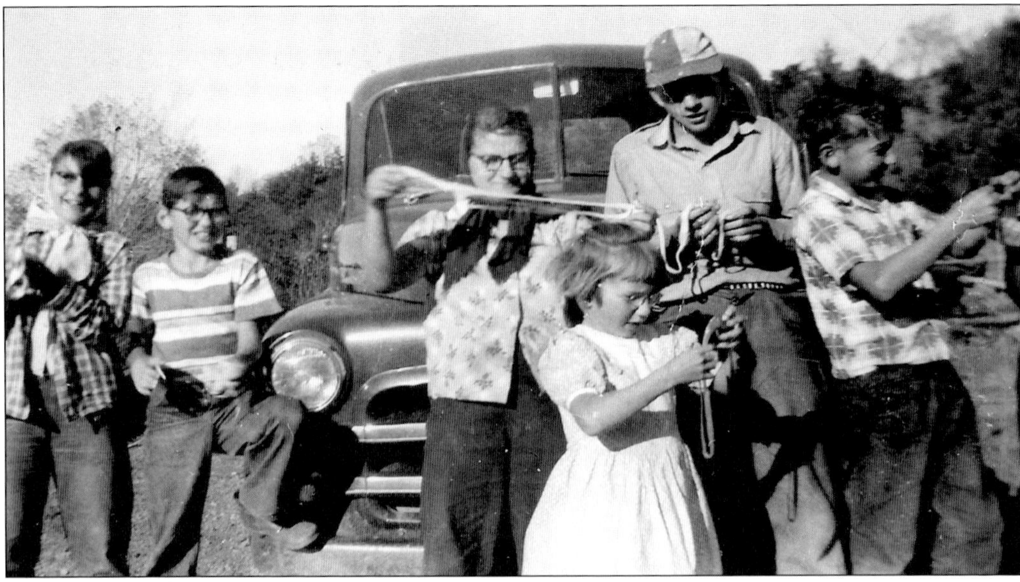

"Many hands make light work," and when taffy is involved, it is sweet work. These children at the Shenandoah Mountain's Mount Pleasant School paired up to pull taffy in 1953. Pictured from left to right are Vada Cullers, Franklin Crider, Violet Cullers, Linda Smith, Leo Smith, and Carl "Wendell" Smith. (Violet Cullers Yankey collection.)

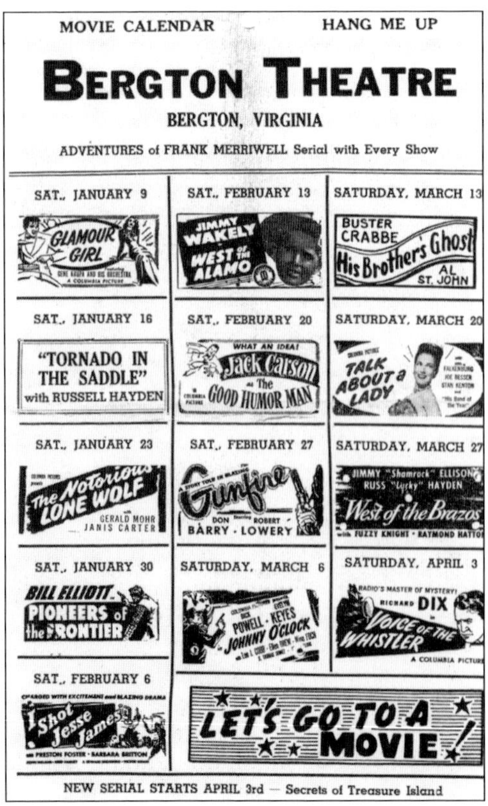

MOVIE CALENDAR HANG ME UP

BERGTON THEATRE

BERGTON, VIRGINIA

ADVENTURES of FRANK MERRIWELL Serial with Every Show

SAT., JANUARY 9 GLAMOUR GIRL	SAT., FEBRUARY 13 JIMMY WAKELY WEST of the ALAMO	SATURDAY, MARCH 13 BUSTER CRABBE His Brother's Ghost AL ST. JOHN
SAT., JANUARY 16 "TORNADO IN THE SADDLE" with RUSSELL HAYDEN	SAT., FEBRUARY 20 WHAT AN IDEA! Jack Carson as The GOOD HUMOR MAN	SATURDAY, MARCH 20 TALK ABOUT a LADY
SAT., JANUARY 23 The Notorious LONE WOLF GERALD MOHR JANIS CARTER	SAT., FEBRUARY 27 Gunfire DON BARRY · ROBERT LOWERY	SATURDAY, MARCH 27 JIMMY "Shamrock" ELLISON RUSS "Lucky" HAYDEN West of the Brazos
SAT., JANUARY 30 BILL ELLIOTT PIONEERS of the FRONTIER	SATURDAY, MARCH 6 DICK POWELL · KEYES JOHNNY O'CLOCK	SATURDAY, APRIL 3 RADIO'S MASTER OF MYSTERY! RICHARD DIX VOICE OF THE WHISTLER A COLUMBIA PICTURE
SAT., FEBRUARY 6 I Shot Jesse James PRESTON FOSTER · BARBARA BRITTON	LET'S GO TO A MOVIE!	

NEW SERIAL STARTS APRIL 3rd — Secrets of Treasure Island

In the early 1950s, Russel J. "R.J." Whetzel operated a movie theater on Saturday nights in the building next to the present-day Bergton Post Office. They even ran serials, including *The Adventures of Frank Merriwell*. Stuart Whetzel ran the movie projector. The theater had a variety of seats, such as benches and davenports, and a popcorn machine. This undated program is from Susan Brown and Emma Whetzel Wittig.

"Idle hands are the Devil's workshop" is a familiar old saying. Whittling wood was a way to keep hands busy while talking with friends or resting. Some men whittled objects, while others just whittled a big stick into a smaller stick. (David L. Smith collection.)

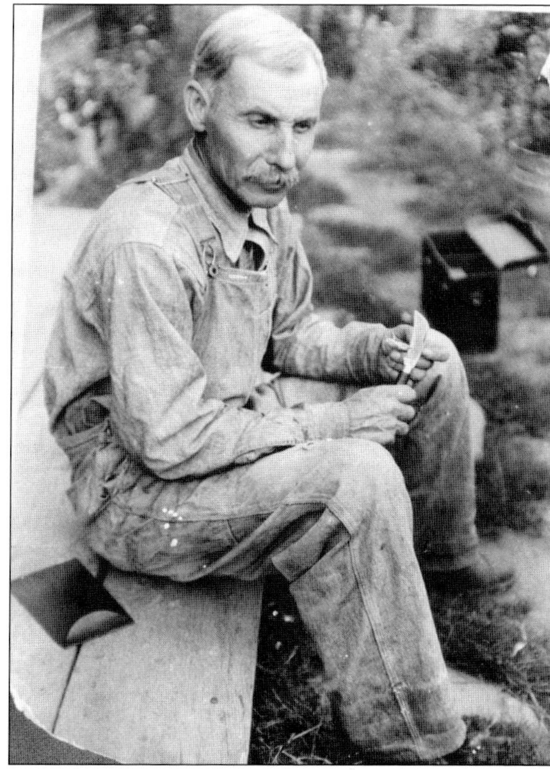

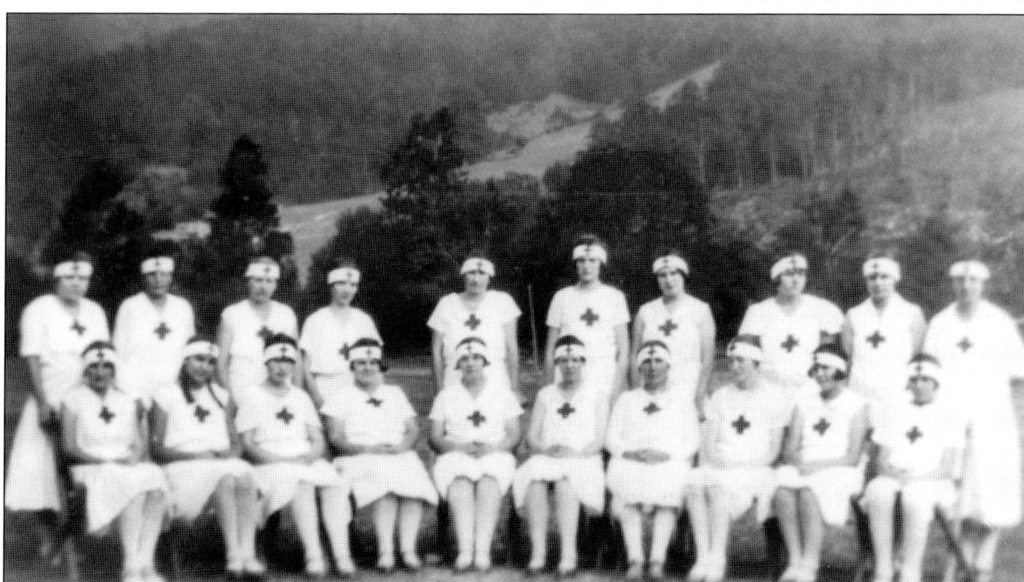

These Red Cross First Aid class graduates were from the Bergton area. The following are pictured from left to right: (first row) Vita Souder Fulk, Pauline Whetzel, unidentified, Sally Wittig, Minnie Wittig, Edith Whetzel, Dottie Dove, Sadie Whetzel, and two unidentified people; (second row) Lena Hottinger, Ida Whetzel, Lelia Dove ?, Cora Whetzel Vaughn, Mae Turner Hottinger, Anne Lee Wittig Lantz, Lennis Moyer Garber, Nora Dove ?, Mabel Albrite Mathias, and Gertrude Souder. (Emma Whetzel Wittig collection.)

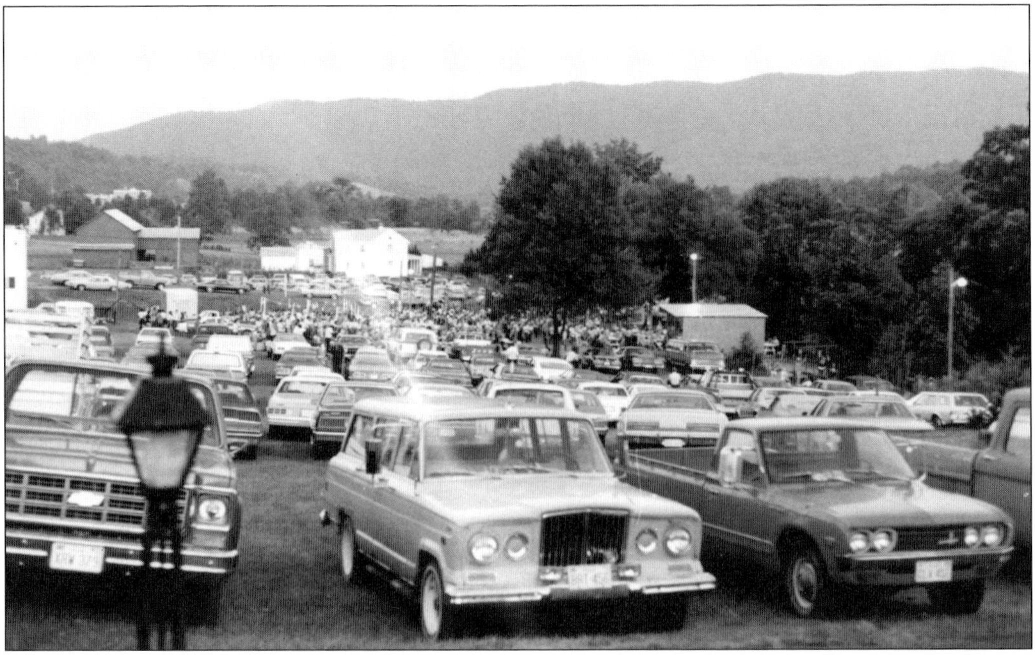

In 1958, the Fulks Run Ruritan Club held its first Lawn Party, featuring cakewalks and local musicians. Thirty-one parties took place behind Fulks Run Grocery. The 1983 party, shown here, was one of the last ones on this site. In 1989, the Ruritans held the first party at their new 55-acre park, which includes picnic shelters, horseshoe pitching pits, ball fields, and bathrooms. (Pat Turner Ritchie, photographer.)

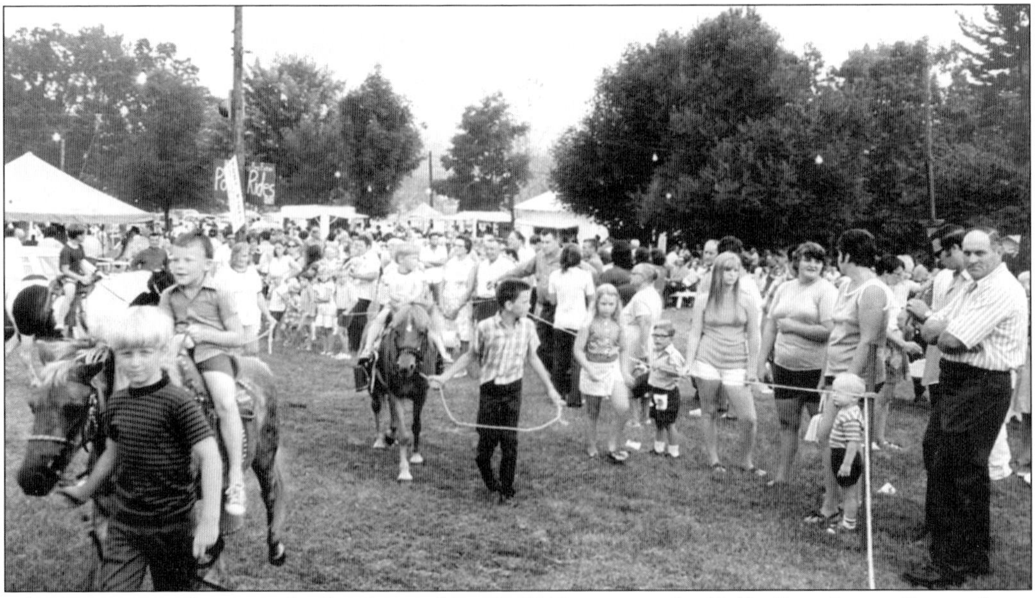

Children enjoyed pony rides by Granvil J. "Red" Turner at the Fulks Run Lawn Party about 1970. In earlier times, churches held lawn parties as fund-raisers. In 1918, 13-year-old Goldie Turner Hoover wrote, "There was a lawn party over at the Baptist Church Saturday night and believe me we had some time. Cake, ice cream, pop, chewing gum, sandwiches, and so forth." (Granvil J. Turner collection.)

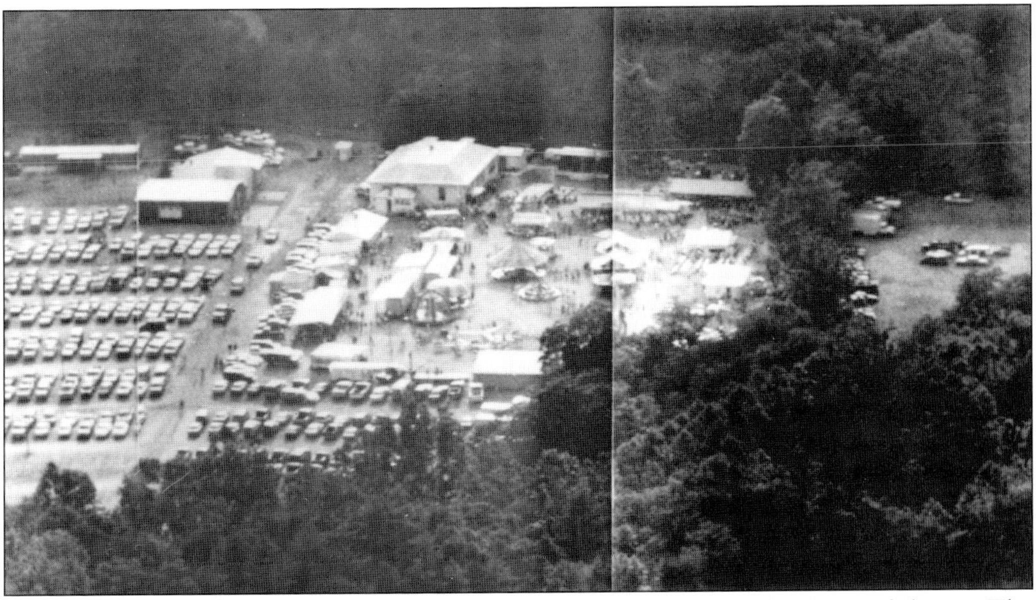

"The biggest little fair anywhere" began in 1951 at Bergton as a one-day farm exhibition. The festival had livestock and gardening exhibits and food for purchase; admission was 25¢. Since then, the Bergton Fair has expanded to five days and draws crowds from several states. This aerial photograph shows the old Bergton School on the fairgrounds and cars parked in the adjoining fields. (Susan Brown collection.)

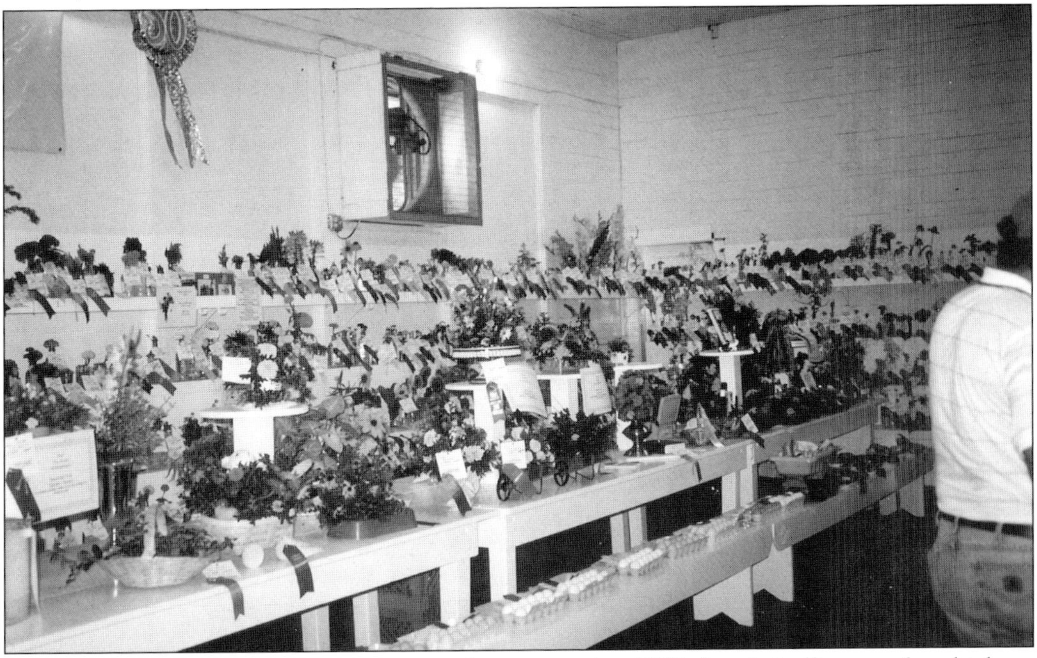

Livestock exhibits at the Bergton Fair were discontinued in 1977 after dwindling to a few chickens and rabbits. The present-day fair awards ribbons and prize money for garden produce, flowers, handicraft items, and baked goods. Young folks have always used the fair as an opportunity to socialize with others. For older people, it is a community reunion, drawing former residents who come home annually for the fair. (Susan Brown collection.)

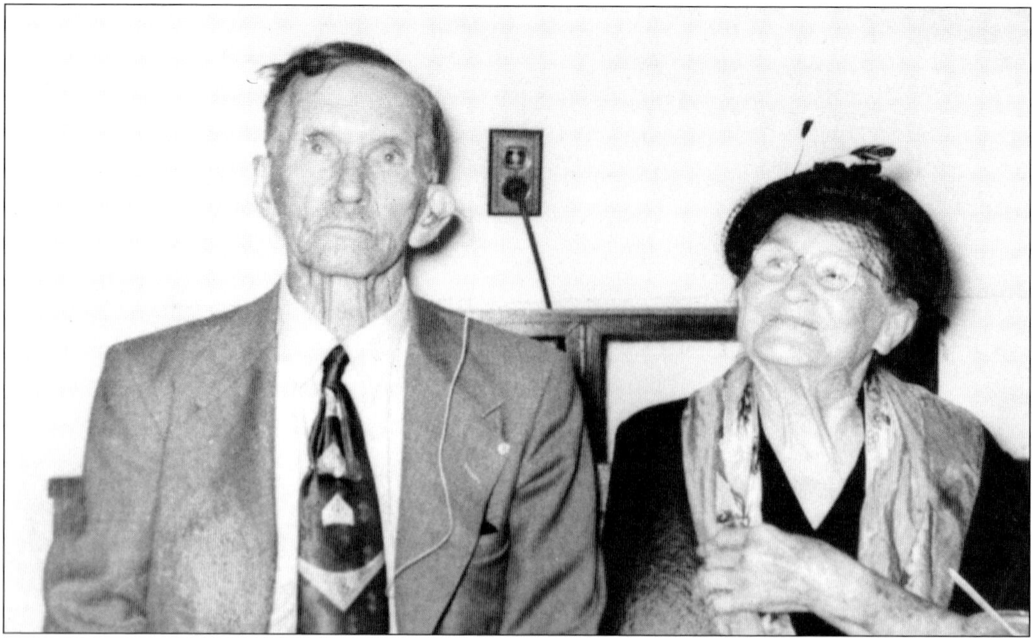

Adam R. Shickle (1865–1956) was a music teacher, walking to as many as 10 households per day to give pump organ lessons for 25¢ each. After spending the night in the homes of his distant students, he returned by a different route and gave more lessons. Several of his pupils went on to become pianists for their churches. Adam and his wife, Fannie, were married 59 years. (Garnett R. Turner collection.)

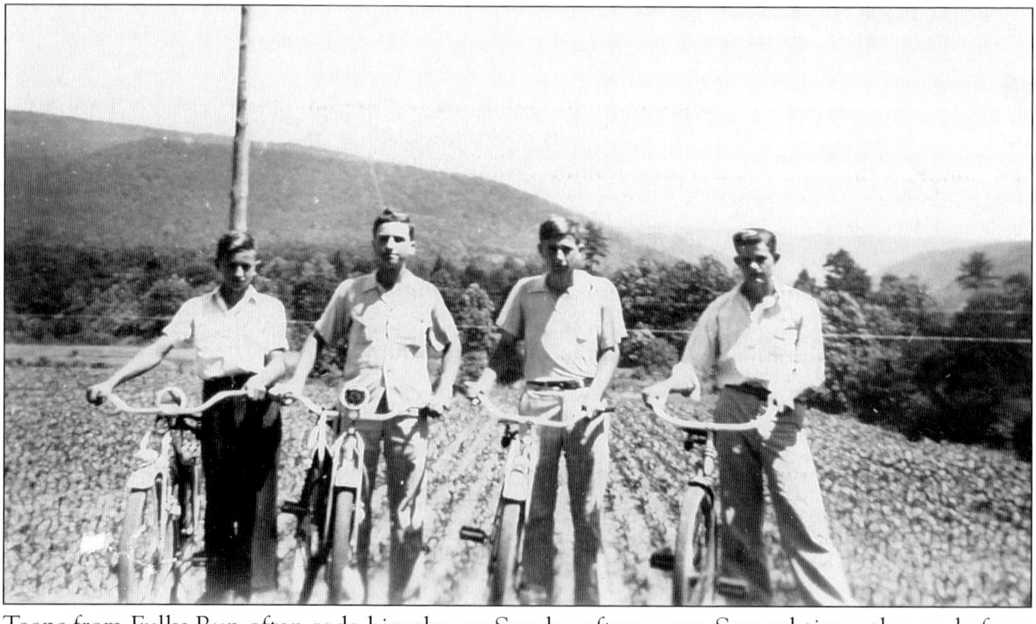

Teens from Fulks Run often rode bicycles on Sunday afternoons. Several times they rode from Fulks Run to Lost City, West Virginia, and back; one Sunday afternoon, they rode to Mount Jackson and back. This group, in about 1940, includes, from left to right, William "Tuck" Roadcap, Garnett Turner, Merlin Turner, and Warren Trumbo in a cornfield near Mathias, West Virginia. (Ruth A. Turner collection.)

Six

Logging

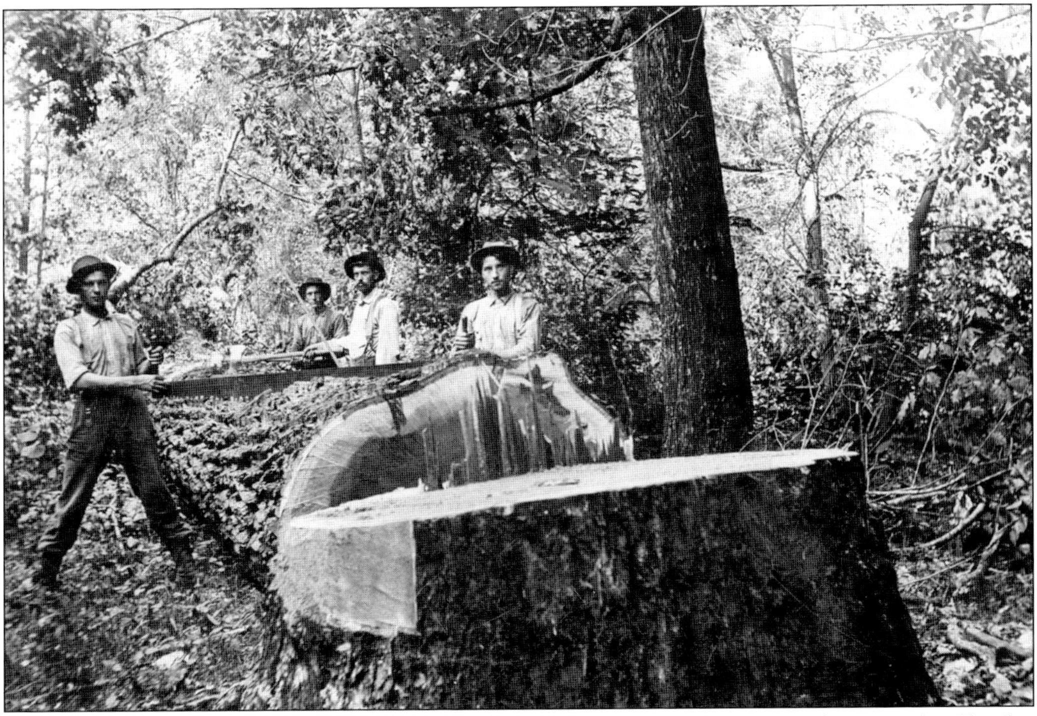

Forests furnished families with shelter, warmth, and cash. In this 1910 photograph, Charles Albrite, John Feathers, Albert Albrite, and Samuel Zirk work with tools that earlier generations would have easily recognized—crosscut saw and ax. By then, steam-powered sawmills had been in use for 30 or more years, and trees could easily be cut into lumber and hauled in wagons to Broadway for local sales or for shipment on the railroad. (Private collection.)

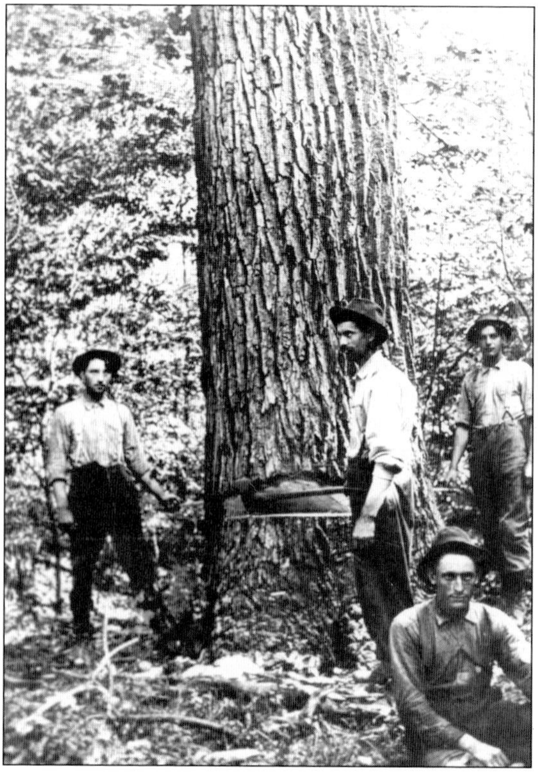

When a man's work was really a man's work—From left to right, Sam Zirk, Albert Albrite, Charlie Albrite, and John Feathers (seated) saw a tree in 1910. Earlier, George Fawley (1764–1815) operated a water-powered sawmill at Fulks Run, and Richard Custer Jr. (1788–1857) had one on Dry River before 1850. (Private collection.)

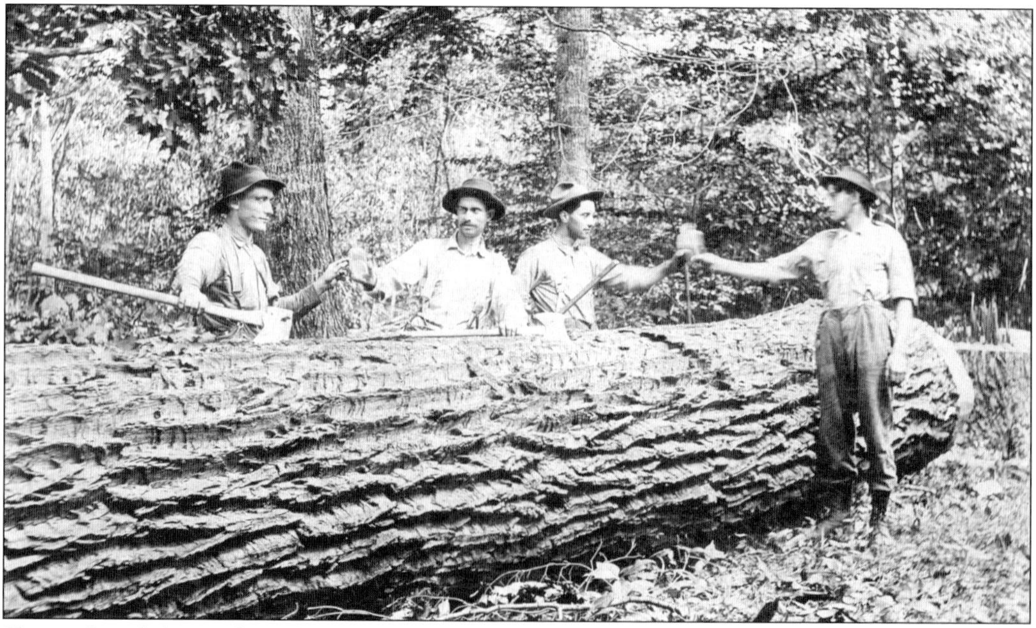

Shown from left to right, John Feathers, Albert Albrite, Sam Zirk, and Charles Albrite celebrate their work with a quick toast in 1910. The 1885 Rockingham County Atlas shows six sawmills in Brocks Gap: German River Road near Shaver School, near Criders Post Office, near present-day Green Valley Clinic, near the Bergton cut-off, near Riverside Church, and up Yankeetown. (Private collection.)

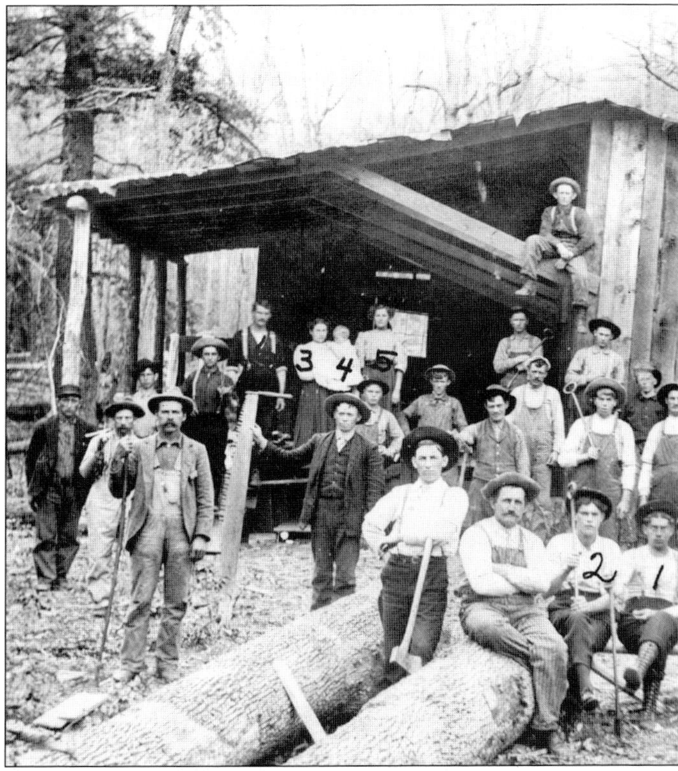

Logging provided cash wages for families. Clara Dove Albrite (3), holding her daughter Lettie, was camp cook around 1907; she is assisted by her husband, William "Bill" Albrite next to her (6) and his sister Hannah (5). The two other men identified are Jacob "Jake" Albrite (1) and Charles Albrite (2). Living in the camps could be dangerous: once, as Clara was walking down a path to the spring, Bill saw a copperhead strike at her, but it missed. (Laura Custer Early collection.)

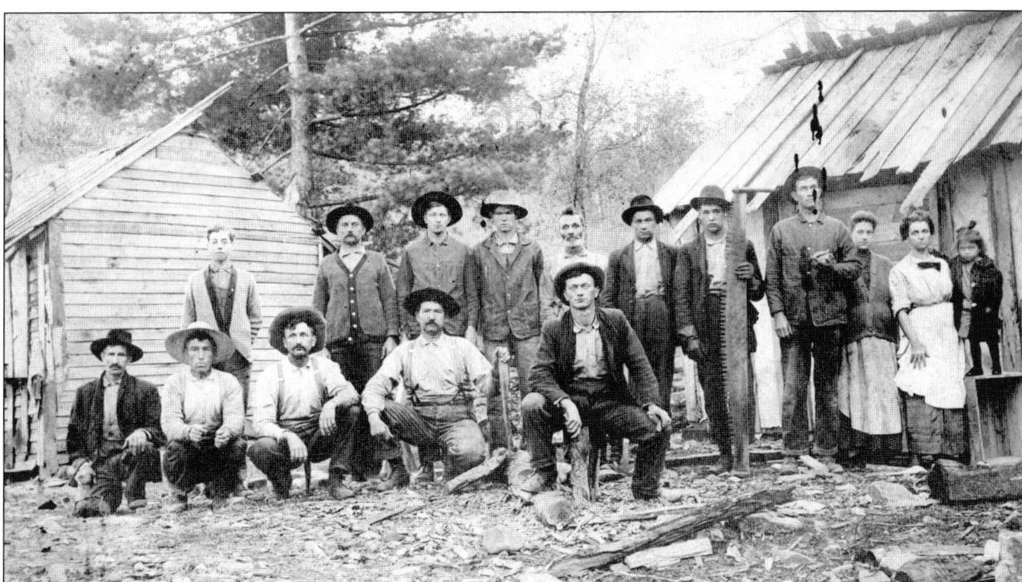

Housing for the lumber workers was crude; they could often hear rattlesnakes rattling warnings under their shanties at night. The following workers are pictured from left to right: (seated) unidentified, George Reedy, James Custer, Charles Turner, and unidentified; (standing) two unidentified people, Joseph W. "Joe" Fawley, Nimrod Turner, two unidentified people, Charles V. Fulk, John A. "John Hen" Fawley, Effie Roadcap Fulk, Lena Roadcap Fawley, and Audrey Albrite Parks. (Private collection.)

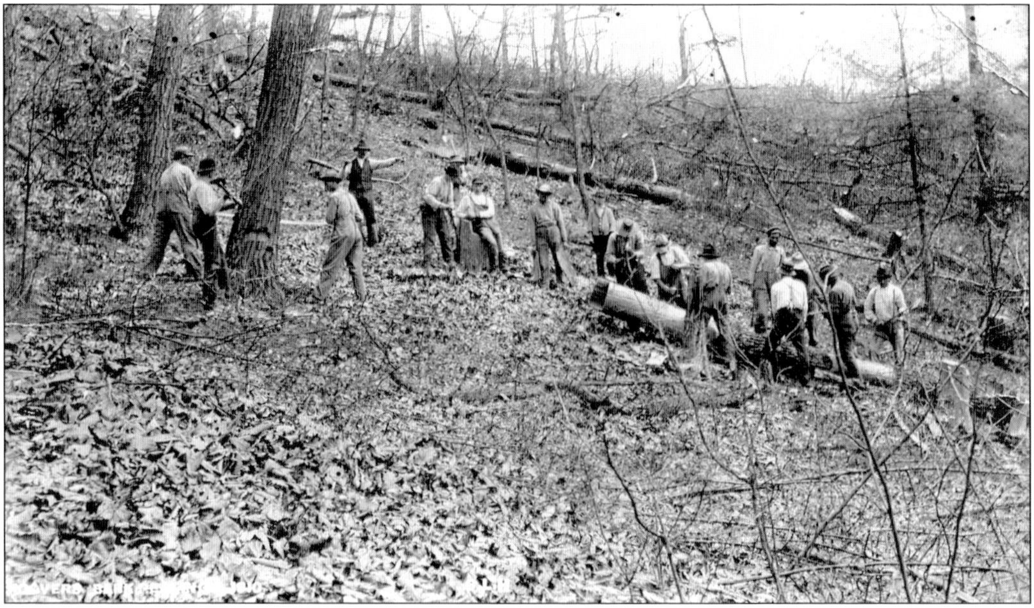

Chestnut oak bark was sold to make tannic acid for tanning leather. These unidentified men show the whole peeling operation at Hoover Bark Peeling in 1910. In 1917, wages were $1.50 to $2 per day plus good board. There were bark thieves, too. In 1889, Gen. John E. Roller charged four different men with destroying stands of chestnut oaks for the bark. (Vivian Hiser collection.)

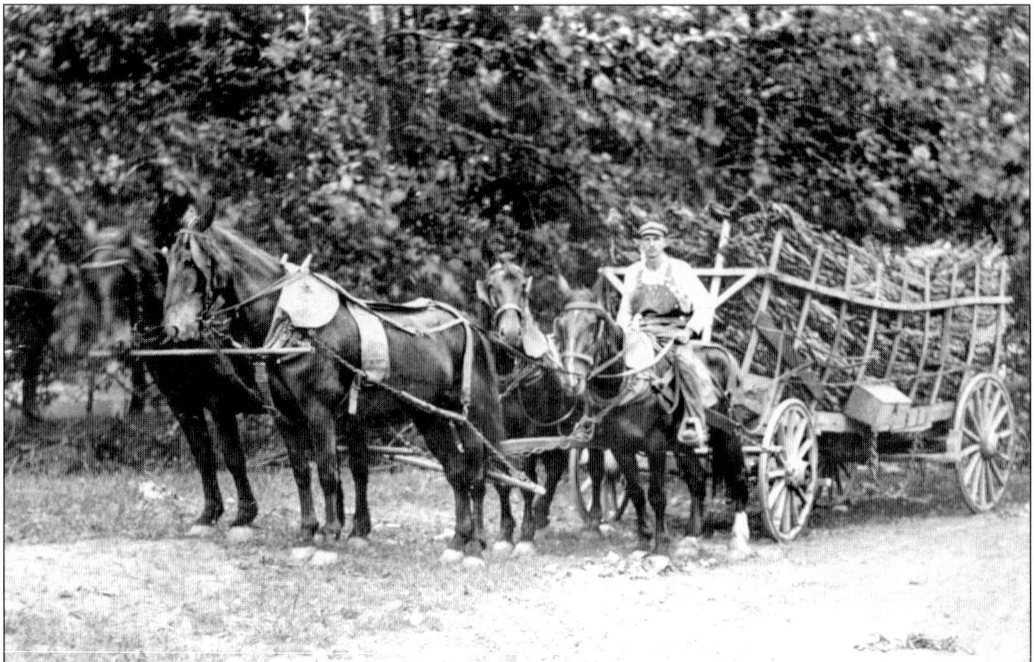

Robert G. "Bob" Nazelrod hauls a load of peeled bark. Notice the homemade bark racks on the wagon. (Sharon Smith Bollman collection.)

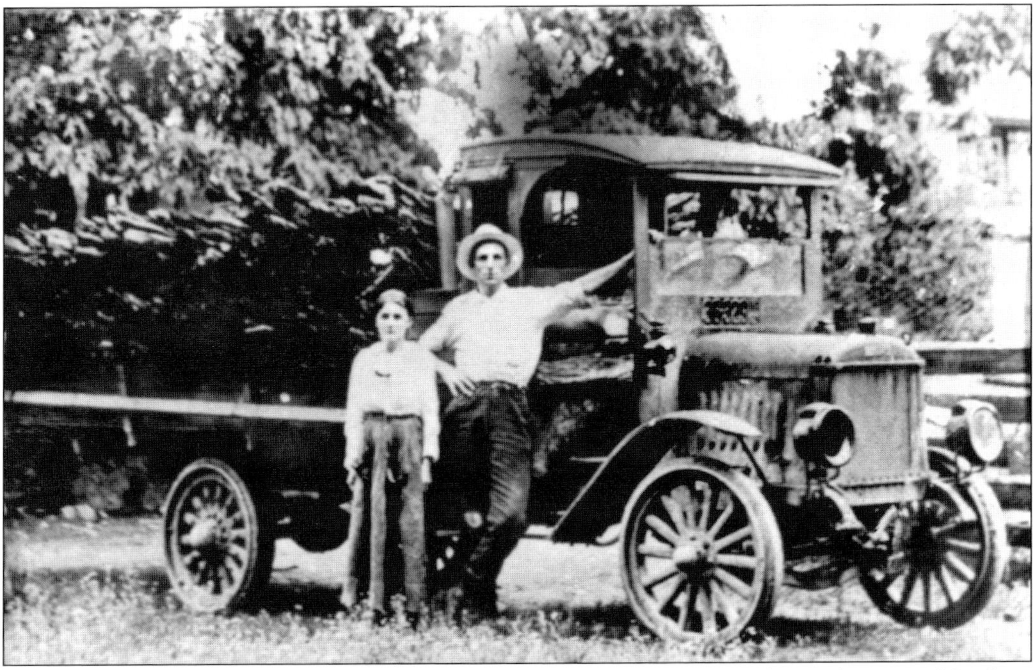

Robert B. "Rob" Turner was born on top of the Shenandoah Mountain five miles west of Criders. In 1922, he moved from the mountain to Criders, where he engaged in stock and poultry raising. He and his wife, Lena Lantz Turner, stand beside a load of bark that probably came from the mountain before 1922. (Gloria Turner Ritchie collection.)

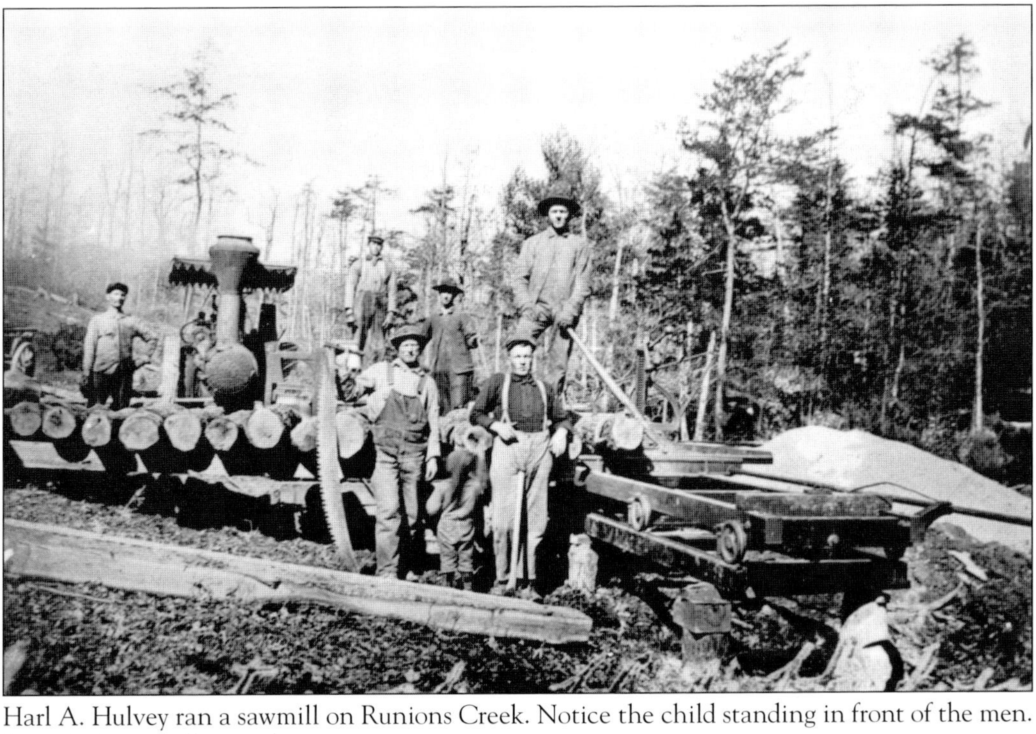

Harl A. Hulvey ran a sawmill on Runions Creek. Notice the child standing in front of the men. (Reuel Tusing collection.)

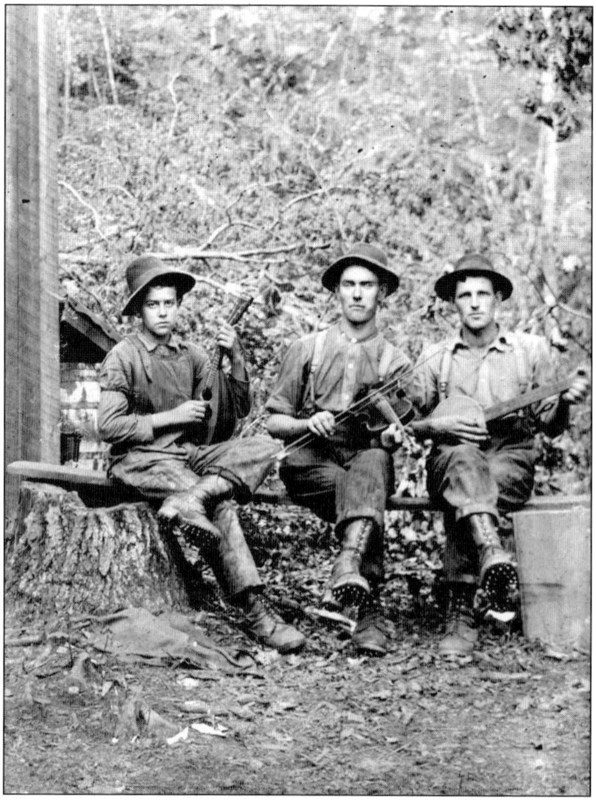

Logging camps were not all work and no fun. These three unidentified men are ready to provide some music for the evening. Notice that they are still wearing their logging boots and their seats are a board placed across two stumps. (Private collection.)

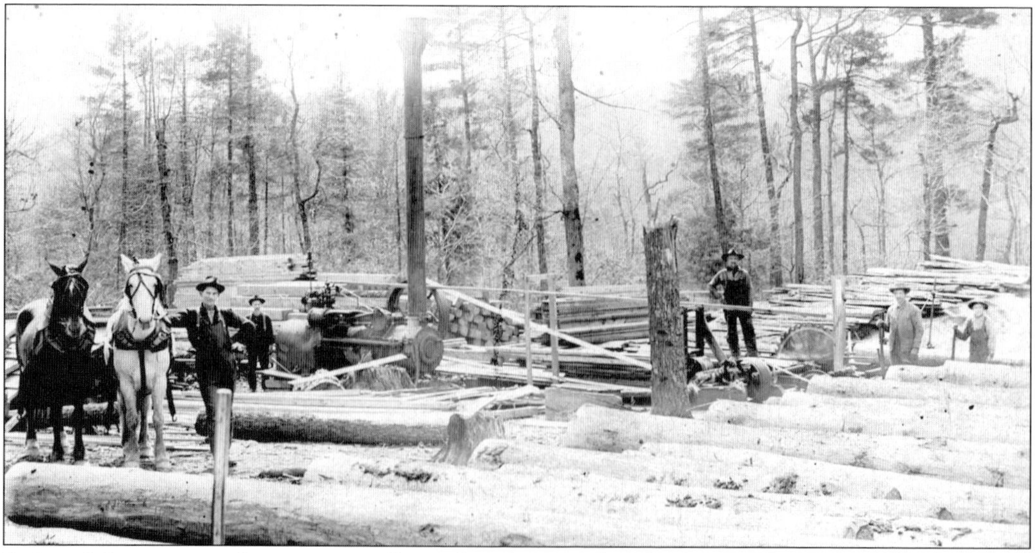

Safety did not come first in sawmills, and some men lost limbs in accidents. Notice the tall smokestack, finished railroad ties, and the long log in the foreground of this 1915 sawmill photograph. Bark from the peeled logs was probably sold to a tannery. However, the stacked lumber in the background shows that they did not let the lumber go to waste. William "Bill" Albrite is on the far left. (Private collection.)

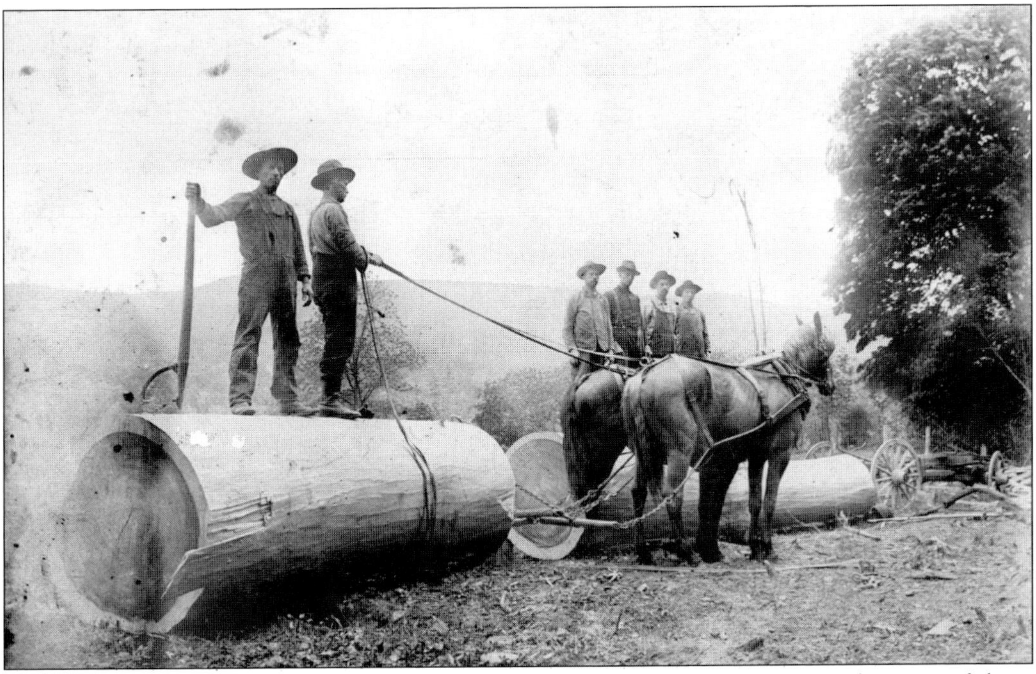

These large logs were peeled and on the way to the sawmill about 1910. The identities of these men are unknown. (Private collection.)

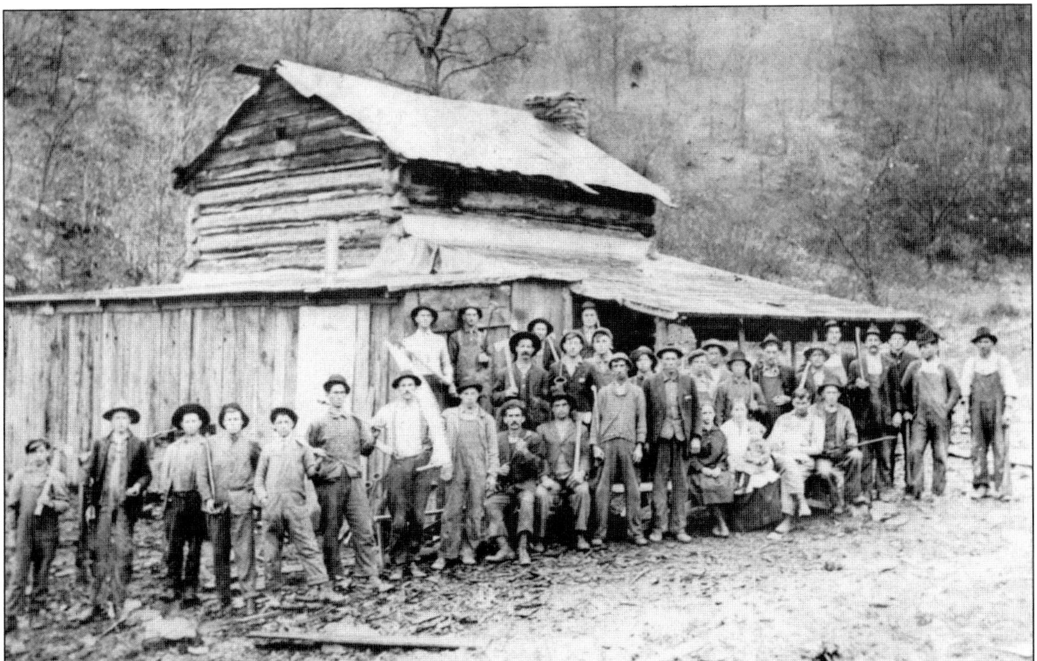

Israel Mongold lived in Mongold Hollow near Bergton, where he owned several hundred acres of land. His lumber camp employed local men. The fourth man standing from the right is Cal Moyer, and Harvey Moyer is second from the right. On the back row far left are John Stultz and Sam Stultz. (Wilma Stultz Smith collection.)

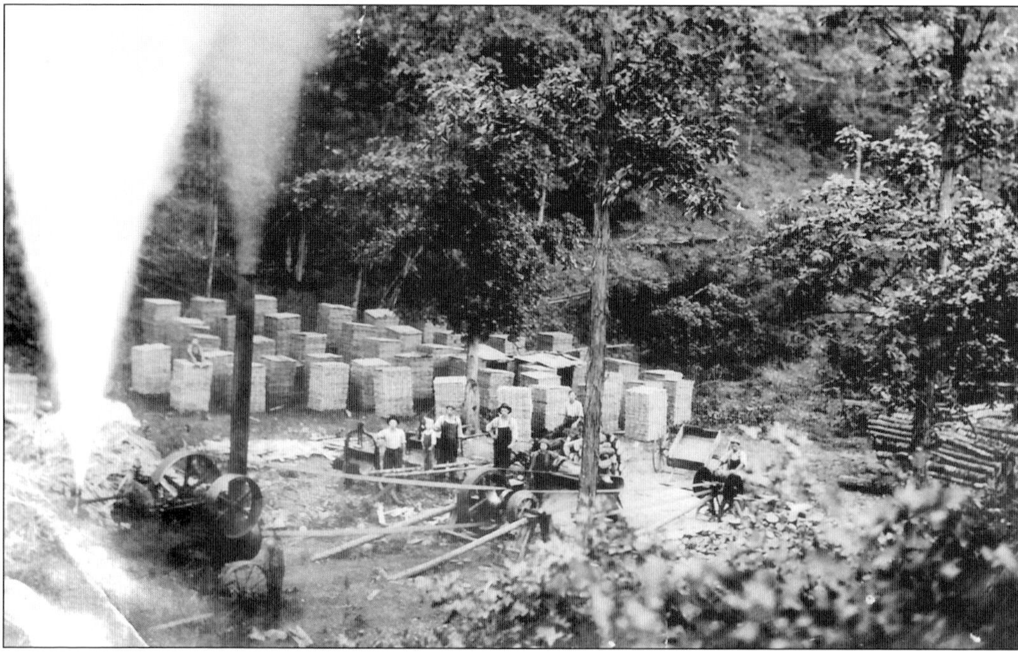

Isaac F. Moyer was a farmer, sawyer, and large landowner in Bergton. He also operated a chicken coop factory and a stave mill. He was nicknamed Ike Arbuckle because he served so much Arbuckles coffee in his lumber camps. This is a photograph of his stave mill operation at Bergton. (Vita Souder Fulk collection.)

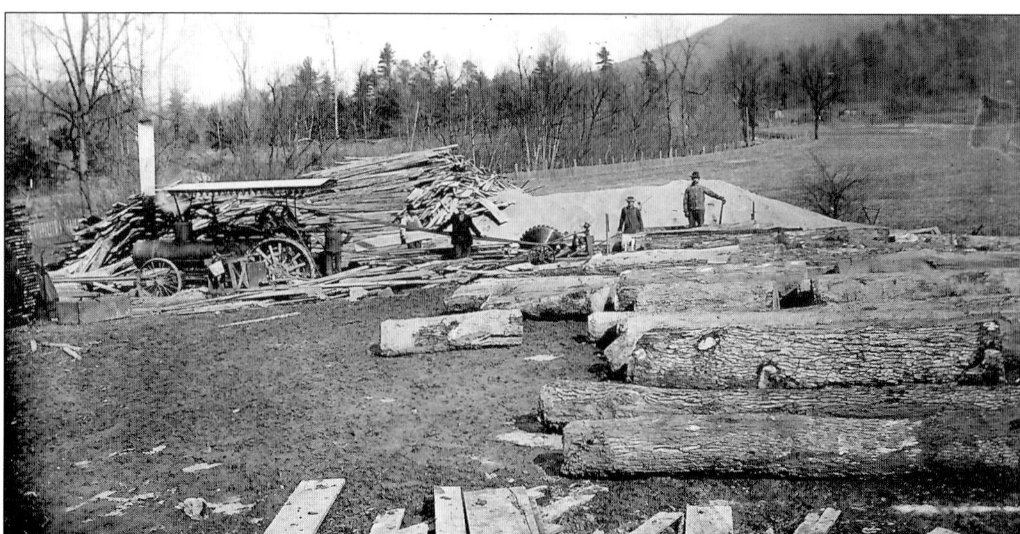

As early as 1888, investors were considering building an extract factory in Brocks Gap. In January 1903, the Allen Extract Company announced construction at the Harper place, with Gen. John E. Roller as one of the chief supporters. They expected to make 200 barrels of tannic acid per week. Nathan C. Runion's sawmill near Miller's Knob cut lumber for the extract factory. (Matthew E. "Bud" Miller collection.)

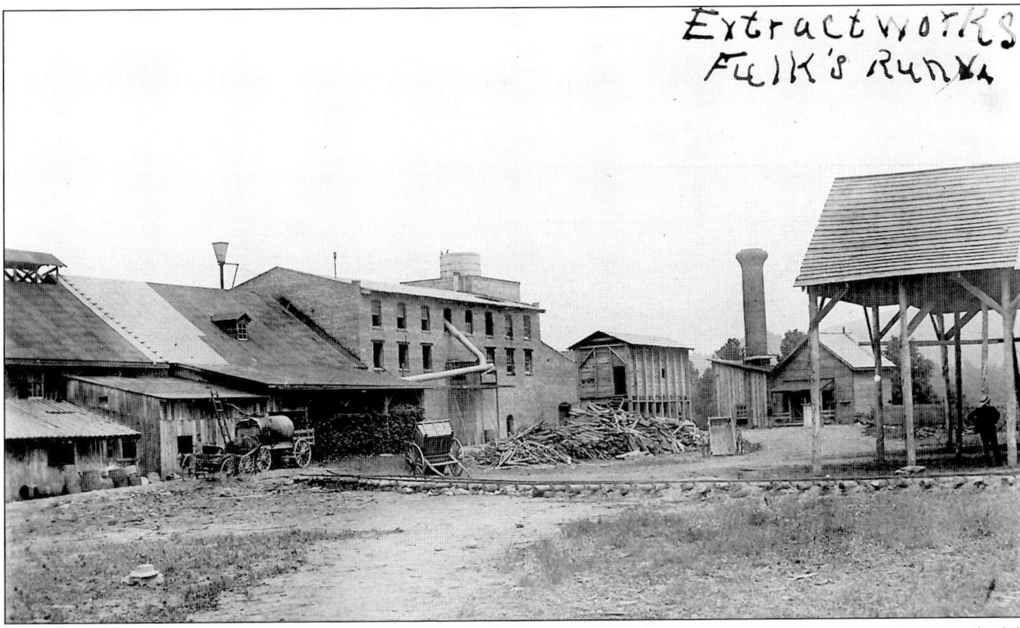

Allen Extract Company became Excelsior Oak Extract Works once it was in operation, probably about 1904. It employed engineers, maintenance men, a bookkeeper, blacksmiths, and laborers. In 1907, fire destroyed the office, commissary, and engine house for total damages of $500; a bucket brigade saved the rest of the factory. This undated photograph shows a tram railway in the middle of the yard. (K. B. Getz collection.)

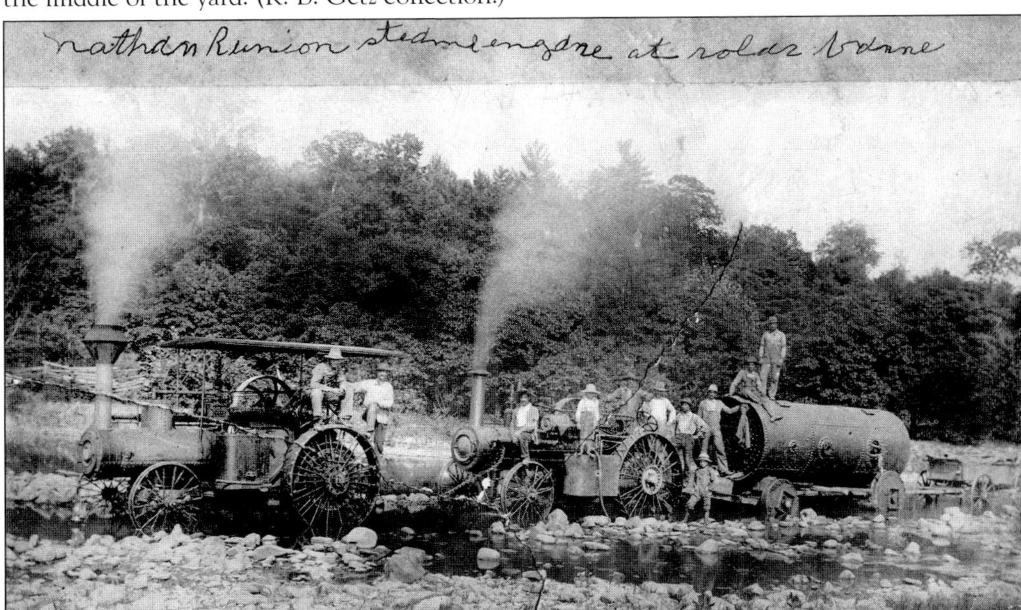

The Extract, or "Ooze Factory," as locals called it, employed blacksmith Nathan C. Runion and his steam engines. It provided income for factory workers, farmers who sold produce, loggers who supplied bark, and teamsters who drove the finished product to Broadway. It closed about 1920, and the bricks, which had been made from clay in a nearby field, were used in a building in Broadway. (Matthew E. "Bud" Miller collection.)

E. D. Root. N. Laurent. A. A. Hyde.

E. D. ROOT & CO.,

Lumber Manufacturers,

BROADWAY P. O., BROCKS GAP, VA.

Announce to consumers of Lumber, that they have their Machinery now in full operation, and that they are prepared to furnish Lumber of all kinds at their Mill, at short notice, and at prices which are the very lowest. Having recently introduced the latest improved machinery for the manufacture of

SHINGLES,

they would call the attention of the public to the beautiful White Pine Shingles they are turning out, which are not inferior to those known as the "Michigan Shingle." These Shingles are put up at the Mill in packages, of 250 and sold very low, according to grade, with 25 cents per M. added for delivering at Broadway. A sample of them can be seen at Basore & Shearer's, Broadway, our local Agents, with whom orders can be left. Also, samples can be seen at the office of the Spirit of the Valley.

All orders thankfully received and promptly attended to. E. D. ROOT & CO.,
oct 18-tf Broadway, Va.

E. D. Root from Connecticut bought 13,000 acres and set up a timber business with two partners on Marshall Run. By 1879, his operation made staves and 8,000 to 10,000 shingles daily; a tram-railway went several miles into the forest to bring logs to the mill. Root had a hotel and 12 buildings. Because he was a Northerner, the area became known as Yankeetown. (*Spirit of the Valley*.)

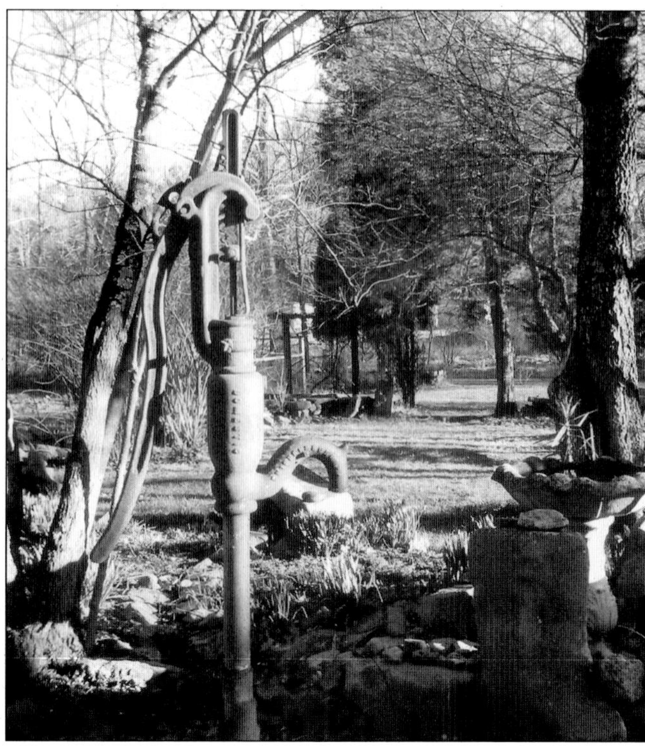

Mr. Root and his operation made Yankeetown a popular place for young people to gather on weekends in the 1880s. Root was editor of *The Broadway Enterprise* newspaper in the 1890s while his lumber mill was still making pine shingles. Though none of Root's buildings remain, this pump and foundation stones may mark the hotel site. Marbles and small artifacts have also been found here. (Mary Ann Yarsinske, photographer.)

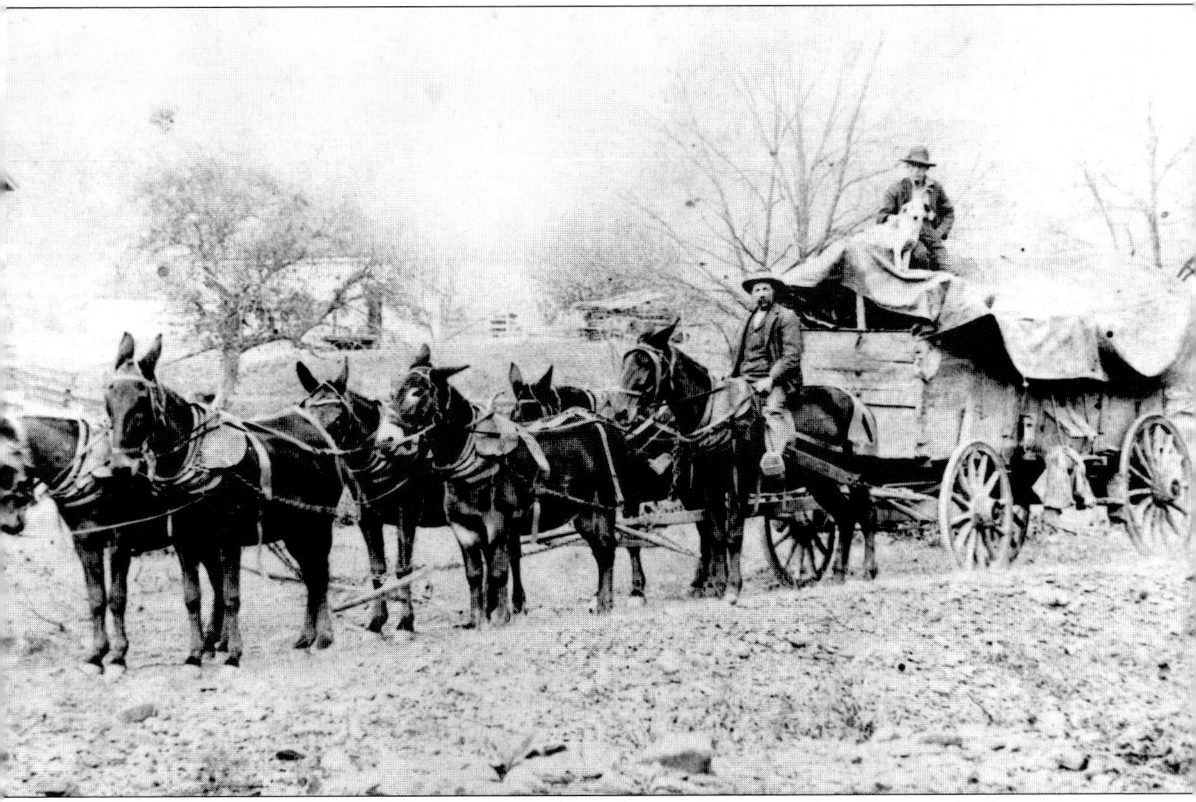

Local teamsters hauled Argentinean rawhides from the train depot in Broadway to the Lost City Tannery. The trip took two and a half days with six-mule team wagons, loading in Broadway in the morning and spending nights in "Strooptown" near Broadway and at William Albrite's near Fulks Run. The wagons arrived at Lost City the third day. Here, Noah Kline stops his mule team beside the J. Mosee Albrite place with a load of finished hides en route to the railroad at Broadway. Charles "Charlie" Albrite is on the wagon. Although they were less attractive, mules were preferred over horses because they were harder working, ate less, and would never overeat to the point of getting sick. (Private collection.)

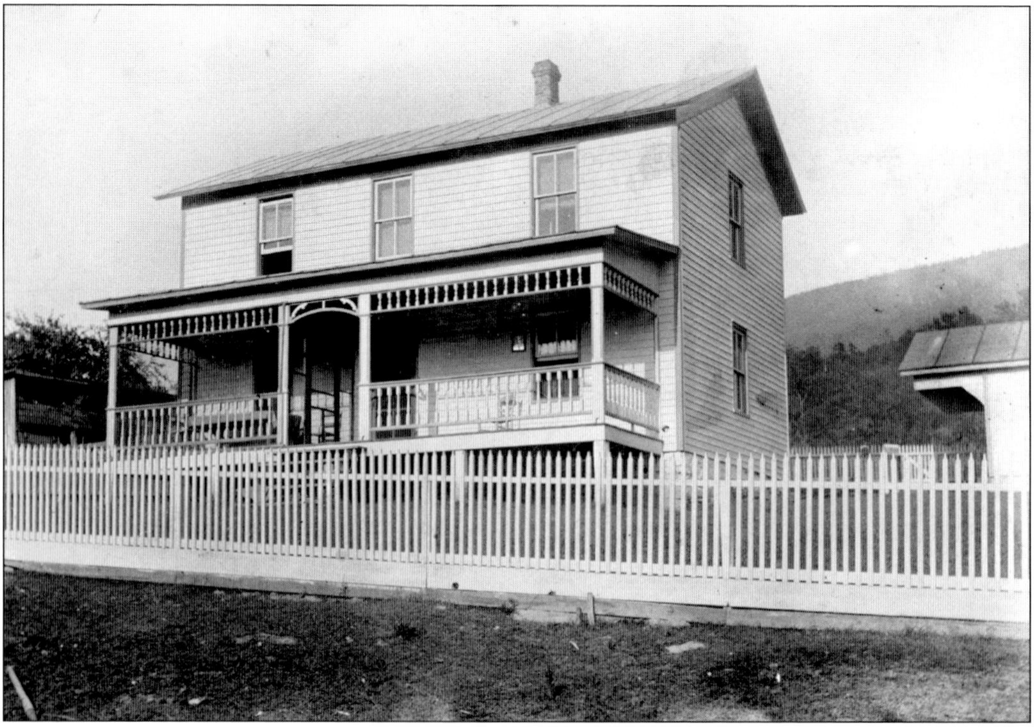

A screened porch made pleasant outdoor dining at Clara Albrite's boarding house for teamsters. How a man cared for his animals was a mark of his character. When a lazy teamster failed to remove all his mules' harnesses for the night, saying, "I'll just have to put them on again tomorrow," other teamsters threatened him until he finished his work and allowed his mules to rest. (Private collection.)

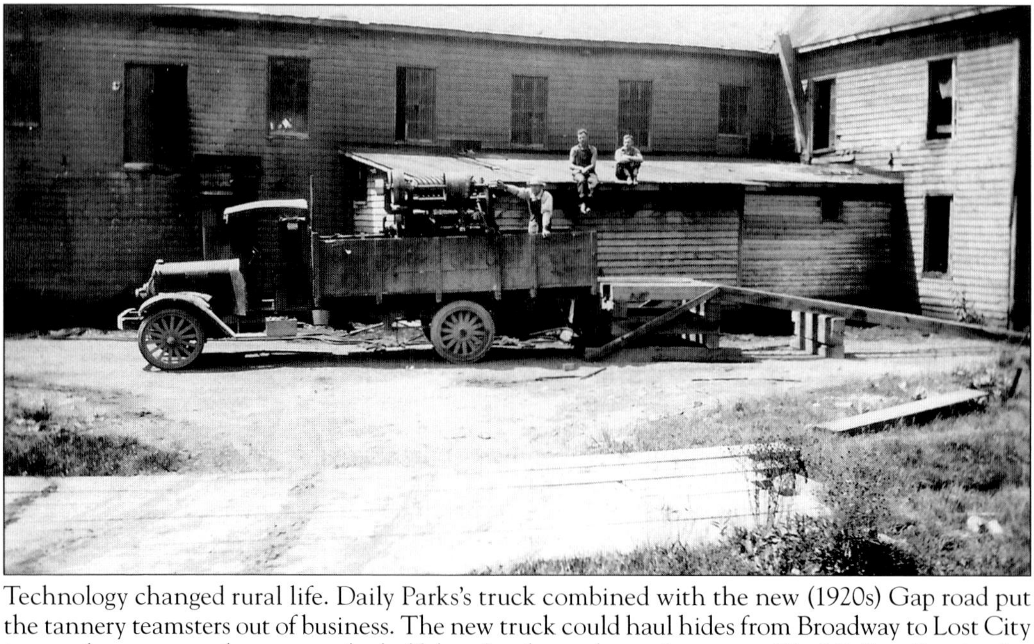

Technology changed rural life. Daily Parks's truck combined with the new (1920s) Gap road put the tannery teamsters out of business. The new truck could haul hides from Broadway to Lost City in one day, compared to two and a half days for the mules and wagons. (Carl Fulk collection.)

Seven

Post Offices and Stores

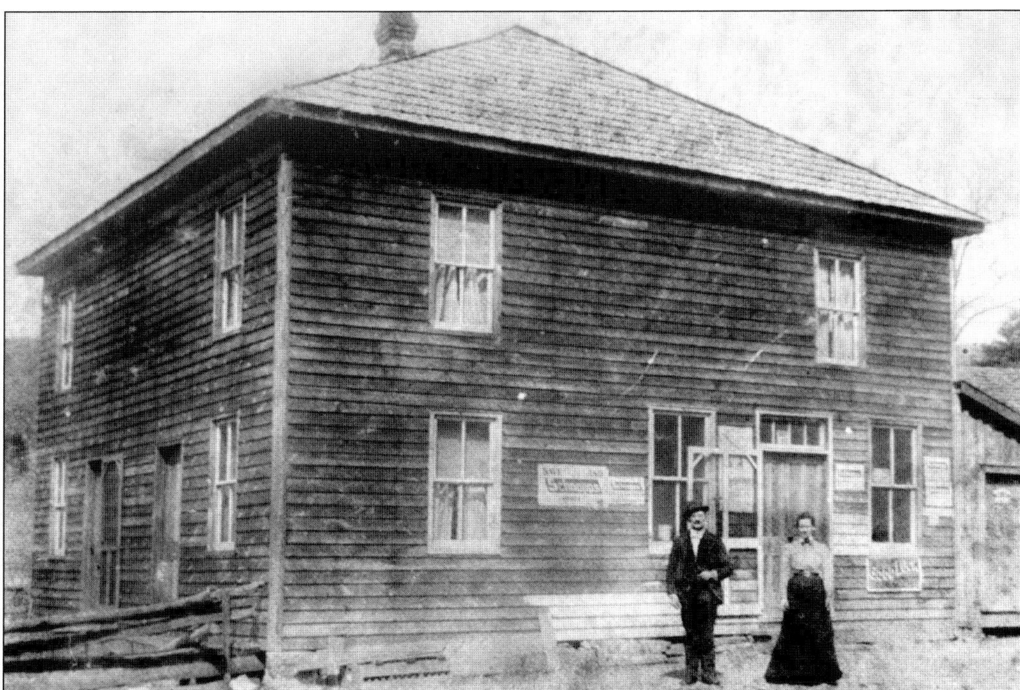

As of 1826, one post office served all of Brocks Gap, with Isaac Riddle as postmaster. In 1858, with Samuel Cootes as postmaster, the office's name changed from Brocks Gap to Cootes Store. Many post offices were opened from 1880s until the 1930s. Tunis Post Office, shown here with Postmaster and Mrs. John H. Custer, operated on Runions Creek from 1900 to 1907 with four different postmasters. (Viola Ritchie Sager collection.)

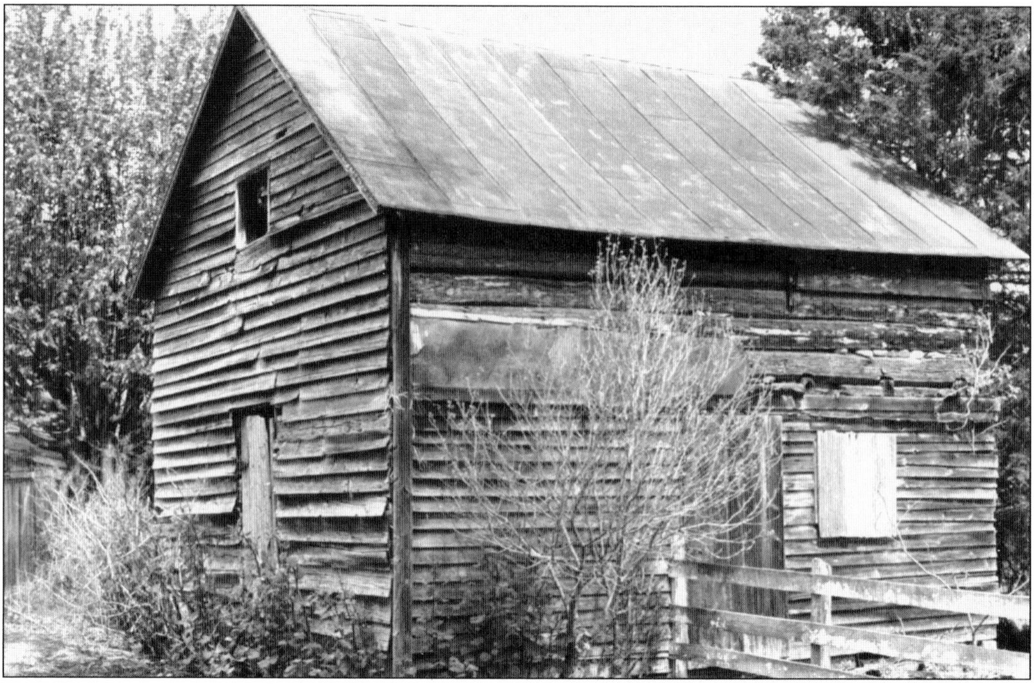

In 1873, George W. Fawley operated the first Fulks Run post office out of Adam H. Fulk's log home near present-day Fulks Run Elementary School; the office moved whenever the postmaster changed. Fawley was replaced in 1881 by William Fulk, who was replaced in 1892 by Jacob D. Custer. William H. Souder took over in 1895, and William Fulk in 1897. Samuel A. Crider was postmaster from 1914 to 1947. (Pat Turner Ritchie, photographer.)

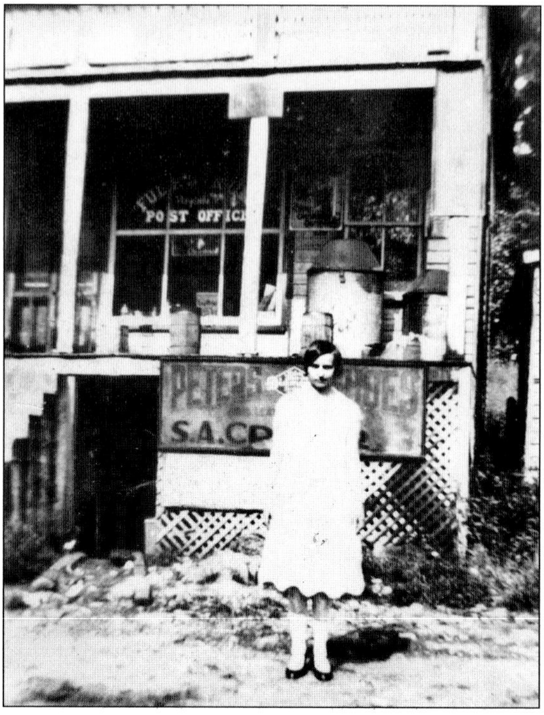

Georgia Custer Fulk, daughter of former postmaster Jacob D. Custer, stands in front of Fulks Run Post Office when it was housed in Samuel A. Crider's store at the mouth of Dry River around 1920. (Velma Crider Dove collection.)

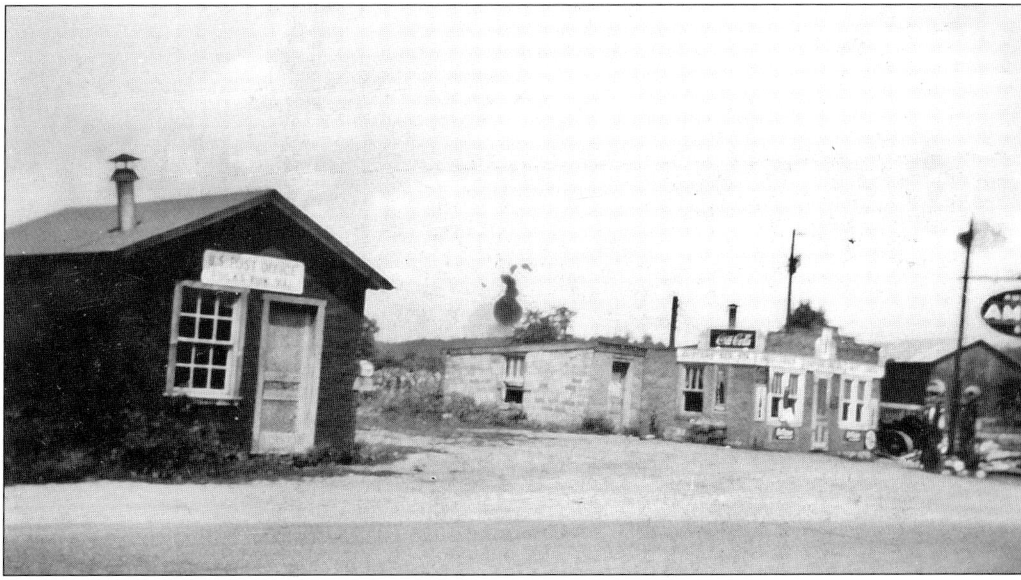

When Dulaney A. Custer was Fulks Run postmaster in 1947, the office was in the building on the left, beside Custer's Service Station, owned by Millard "Pete" Custer. Pete first had a store on the 1920s road under the hill from this location. He had to relocate his home and business when Route 259 was moved in the 1940s to its present location. (Ruth A. Turner collection.)

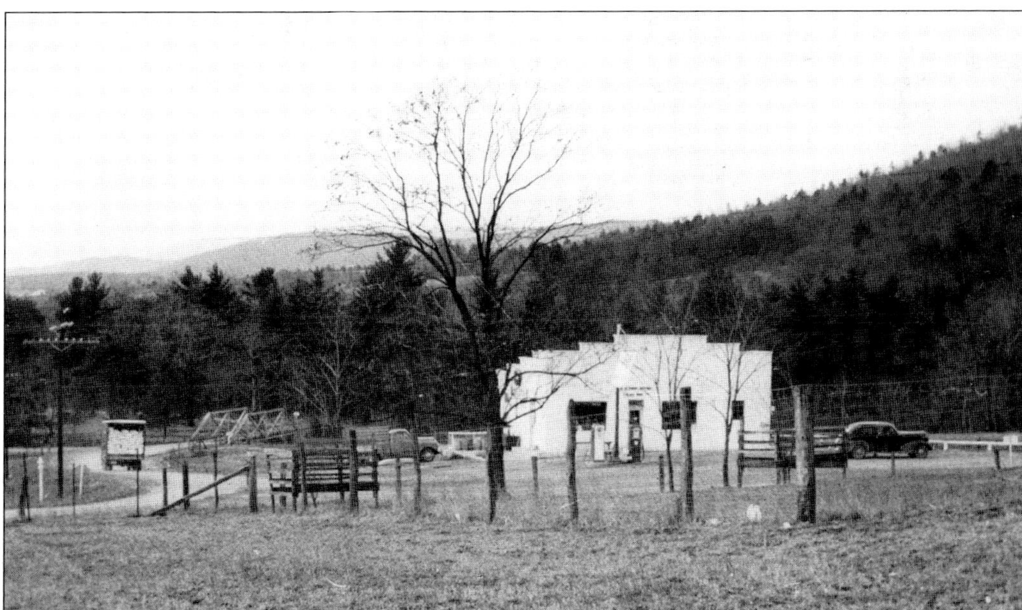

When Garnett R. Turner became postmaster in 1947, the office continued at Dulaney Custer's for two years until Garnett built Fulks Run Grocery. In 1949, the office moved to a corner room of the new store building. In addition to the store/post office, this photograph includes the iron bridge on Highway 612 and a feed truck loaded with 100-pound sacks of poultry feed. (Garnett R. Turner, photographer.)

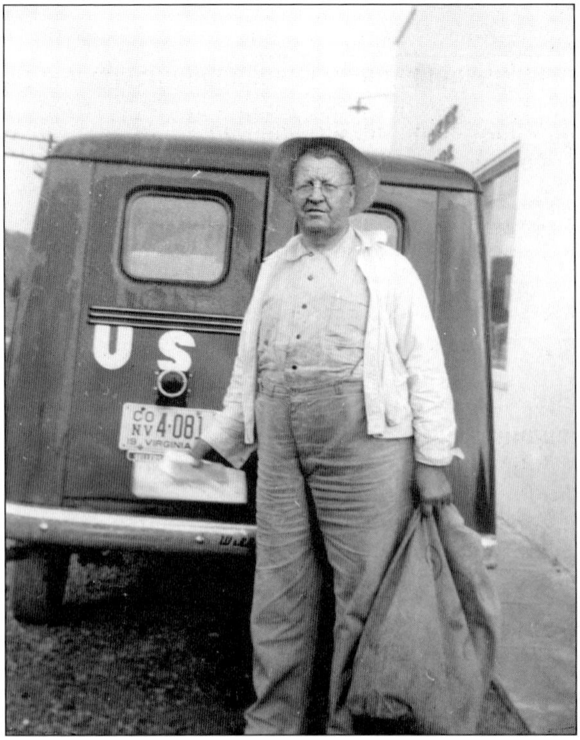

Arthur "Bunk" Runion was the star route mail carrier between Broadway and Fulks Run in the 1950s. Lena Albrite Turner had begun to paint "US Mail" on his truck, but a new baby interrupted the paint job after "US." For this photo, Arthur stood in front of the blank side so that the unfinished paint job would not be noticed. (Garnett R. Turner, photographer.)

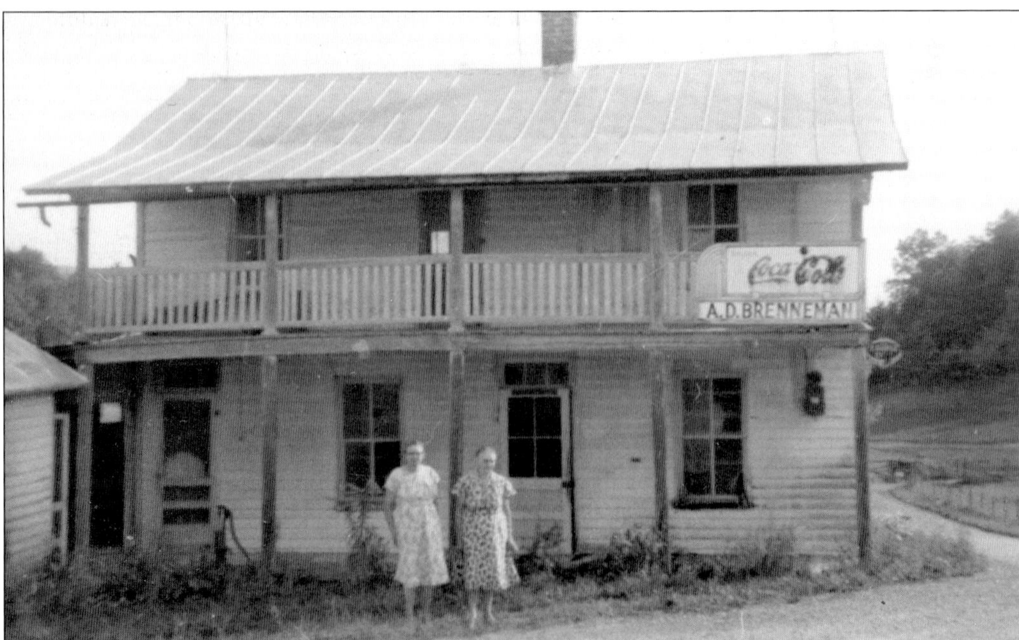

Genoa's first postmaster in 1897 was Charles E. Custer, who wanted the new office to be named "Custer." The office stayed in the Custer family (Samuel Custer and John H. Custer) until 1912. A. D. "Doug" Brenneman was postmaster from 1912 to 1937. In this 1968 photograph, Doug's stepdaughters, Velma Turner Cooper (left) and Ruth A. Turner, stand outside the building that had served as the post office, store, and their home. (Ruth A. Turner collection.)

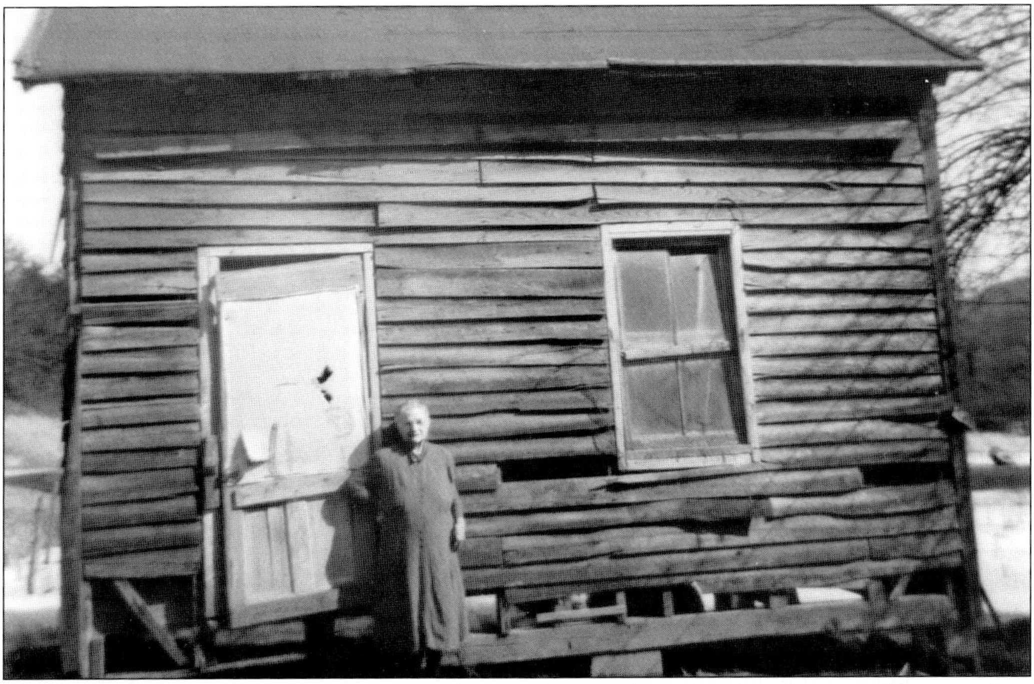

Established in 1908 by Sidney E. Hoover, Palos was three and one-fourth miles west of Genoa. Mary C. Kirkpatrick, pictured beside the former Palos office in 1961, served as Palos's last postmaster from 1916 until closing. Hoover Post Office was near Palos from 1890 to 1910 and had five different postmasters; Hoover's first postmaster was David E. Hoover and its last was Luther Kirkpatrick. (Norman C. Shifflett, photographer; Peggy Ann Shifflett collection.)

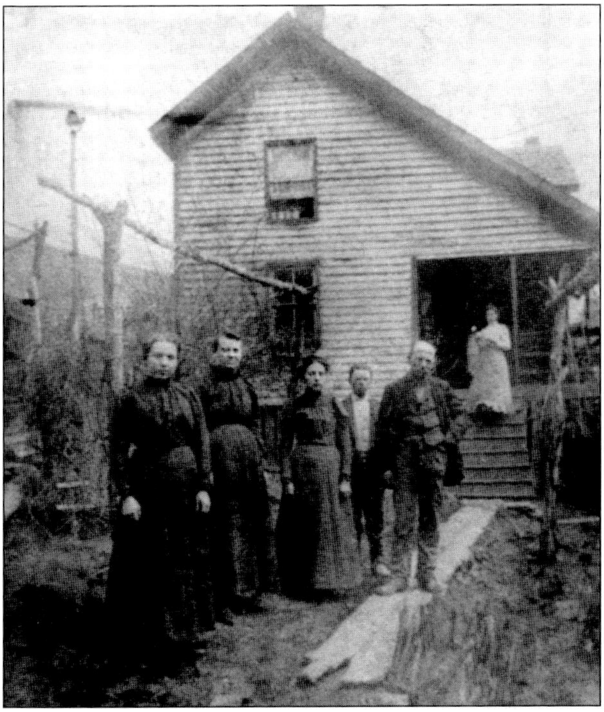

Paul Post Office on the Shenandoah Mountain served 50 people and was 15 miles from Fulks Run, 10 miles from Criders, and 10 miles from Fort Seybert, West Virginia. Established in 1905 with Adam M. Turner as postmaster, Paul had two other postmasters (Daniel M. Turner and Luther Ritchie) before being discontinued in 1911. The Luther Ritchie family stands outside their home/post office. (Ruth Ritchie collection.)

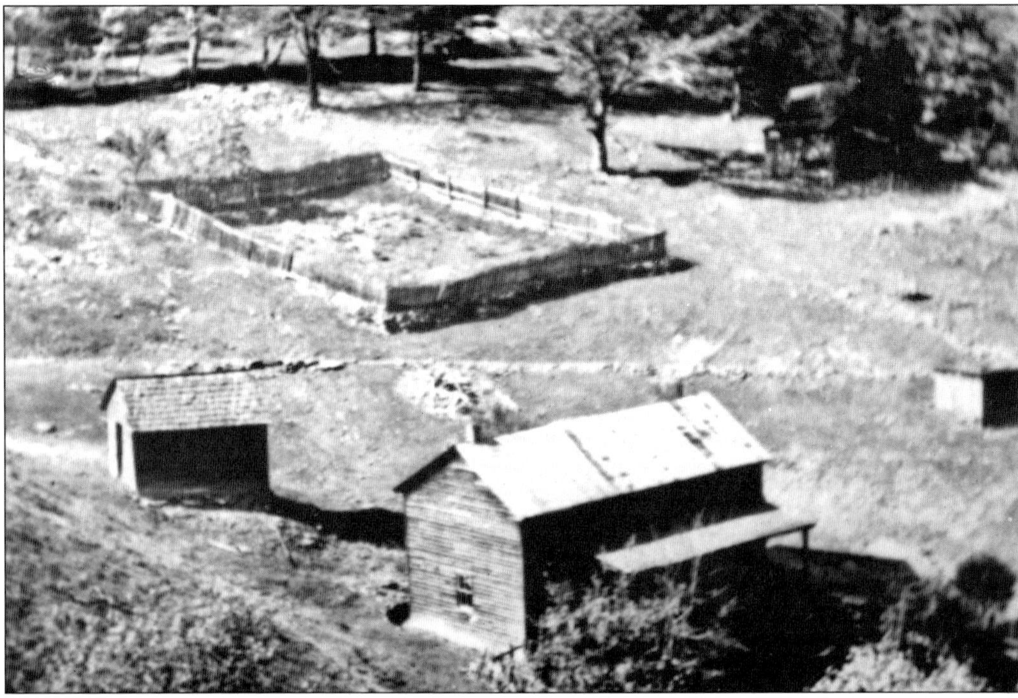

The other end of Shenandoah Mountain was also heavily populated. In 1891, Jonas Dove applied for a new office named Star Lick, located at his mountain home, to serve 50 people. This office was six miles from Peru, West Virginia, six miles from Dovesville, and just on the Virginia side of the West Virginia state line. Jonas was postmaster from 1891 to 1896, when mail was transferred to Dovesville. (Luke Dove collection.)

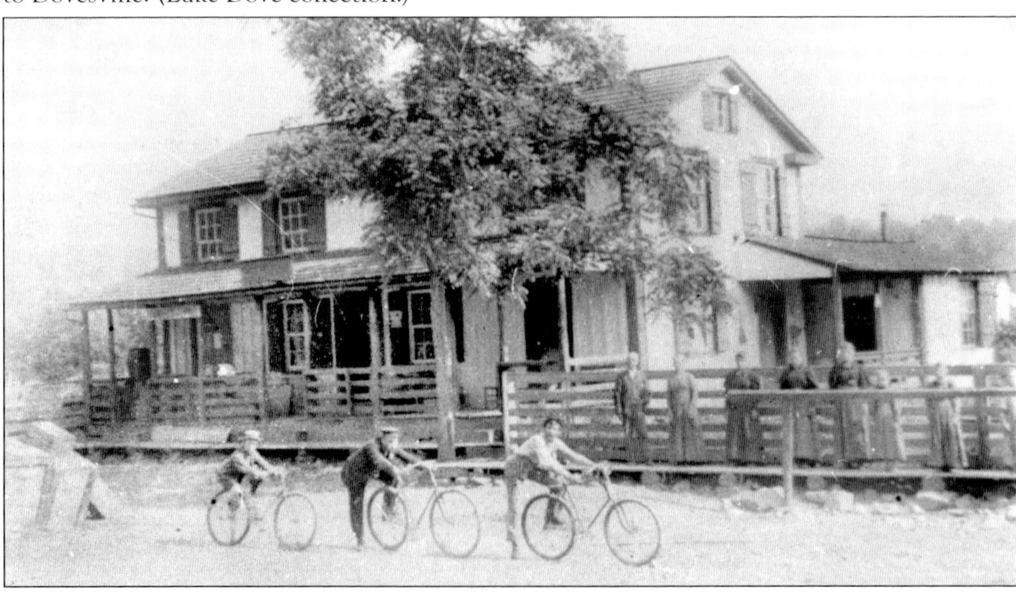

In 1880, when William "Riley" Crider applied for a new post office, he suggested it be called "Crider's Store" because of its location in his store. It was approved as Criders and served 200 people. Crider held the office for 21 years, followed by seven postmasters in 10 years. In this early photograph of Crider's Store, Riley and his wife, Susan, are on the walk. (Nellie Siever Ritchie collection.)

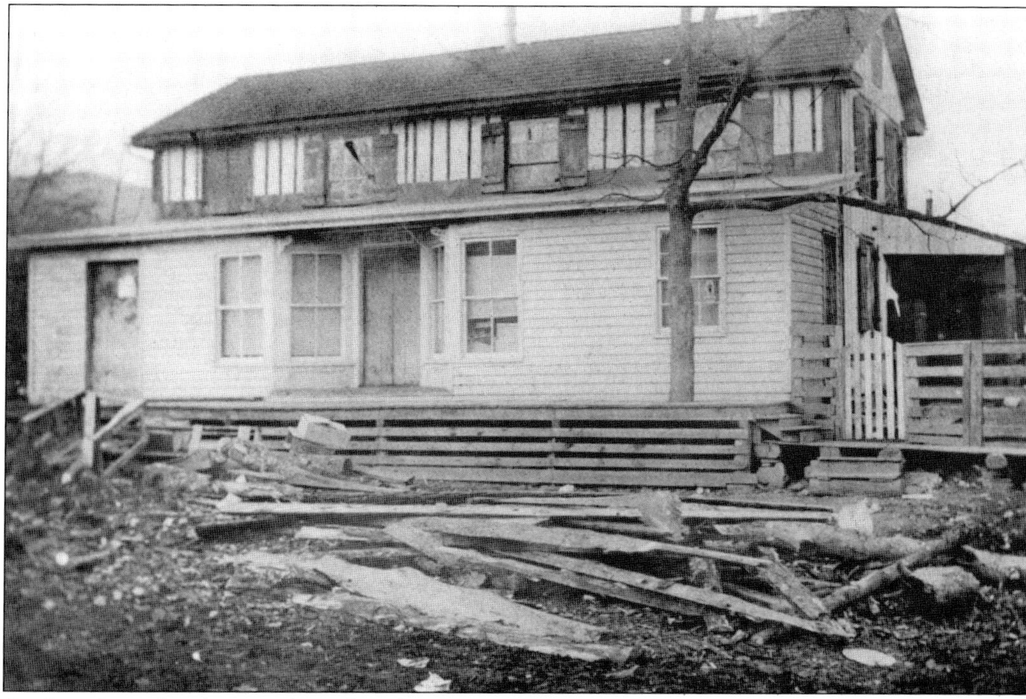

Crider's Store has been enlarged and remodeled since 1881, when it became a post office/store/home. With this remodeling, the porch was enclosed, but the wooden walk to the right was still in use. Beginning in 1912, Joseph W. Stultz held the office for 40 years before retiring. Janet R. Turner took over the office in 1952. (Leota Moyers Stultz collection.)

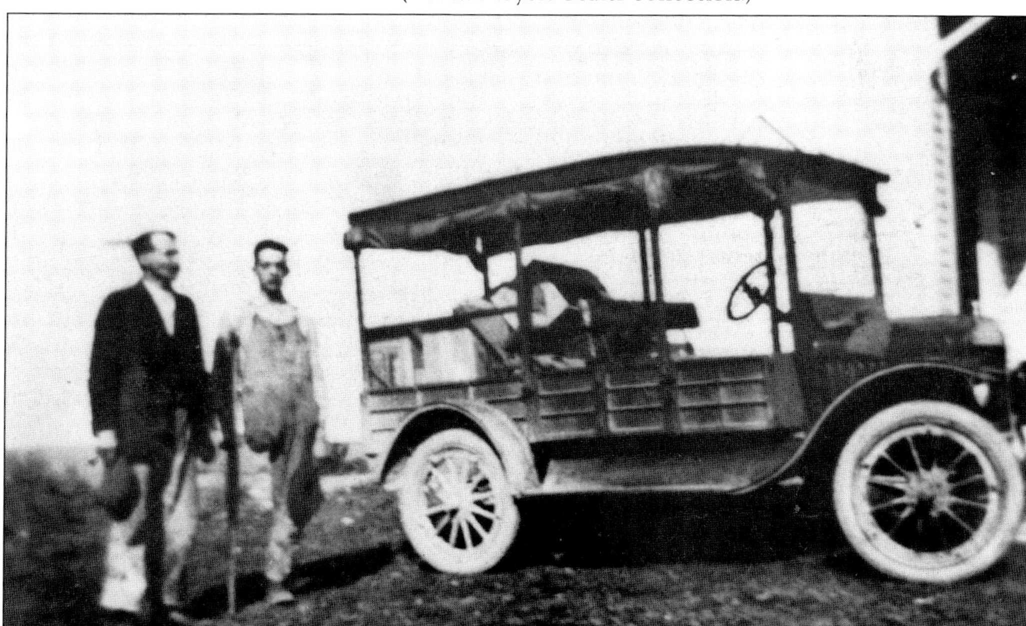

Luther Wittig and Ed Miller built this mail truck for D. Luther Turner of Bergton in 1923. Turner and Albert Miller admire the new truck at Riverside United Brethren Church. (Garner Turner collection.)

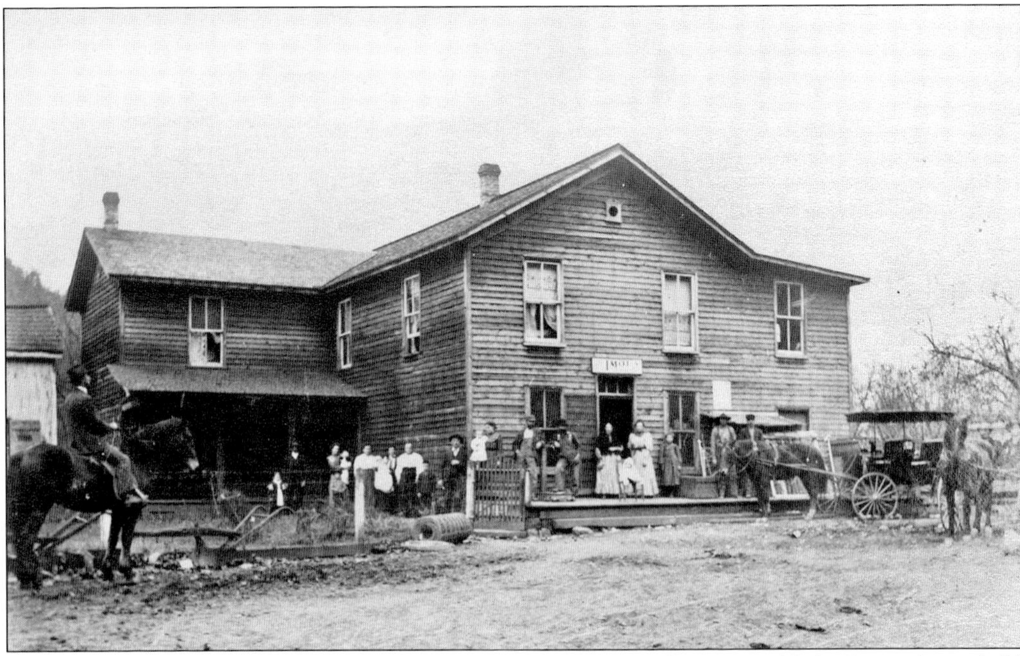

German immigrant Ulrich Wittig was postmaster when Dovesville was established in 1850, probably in his log store building near the store pictured here. The office was discontinued in 1866, but reopened in 1872 with Ulrich's son George as postmaster for the next 35 years. In 1898, the post office was on the north side of the North Branch of the Shenandoah River, at the junction with Crab Run. (Anna Lee Wittig Lantz.)

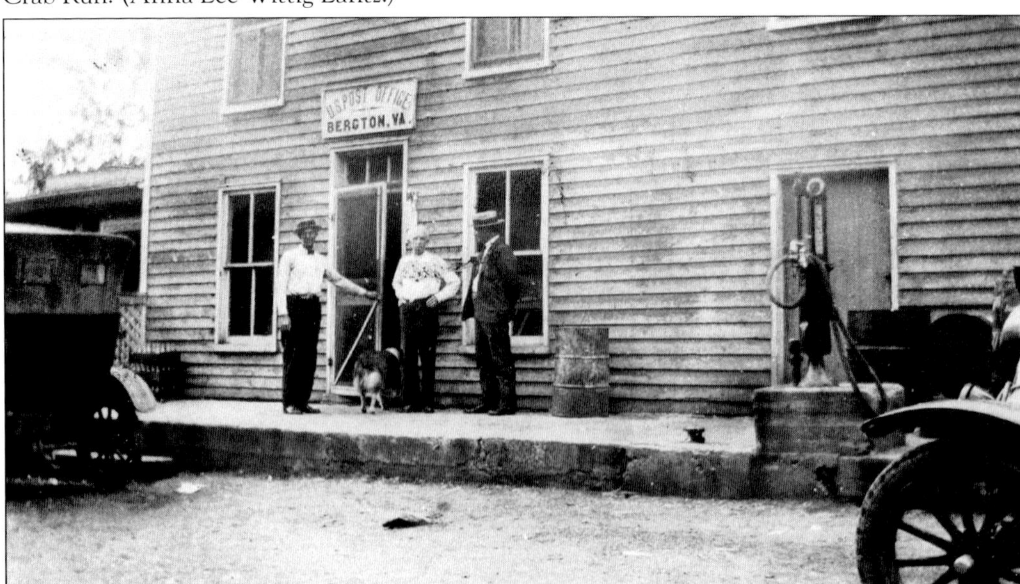

Without moving from the building, Charles L. Souder was postmaster of three different post offices. From 1907 until 1923, he was in charge of Dovesville. Then, for a brief time between 1923 and 1924, the name Dovesville was changed to West Gap before being changed to Bergton in 1924. The "U.S. Post Office Bergton" sign above the door dates this photograph to after 1924. (Barbara Loomis collection.)

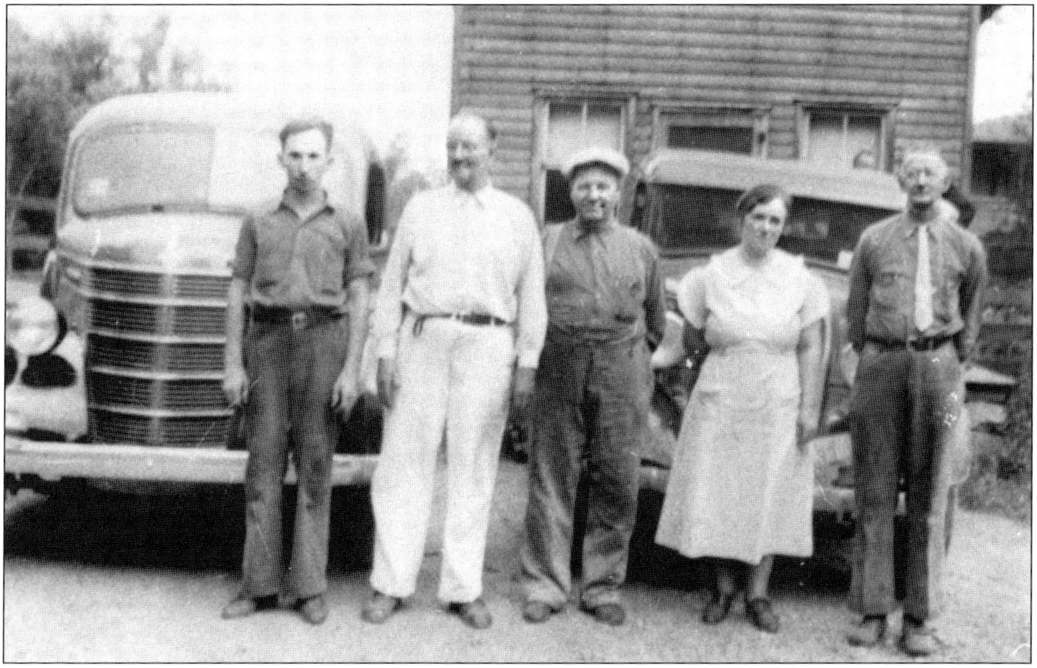

In the 1930s, Herman W. "Big" Turner took mail to Criders and the Shenandoah Mountain. Samuel Fawley carried mail to Crab Run, Highway 259, and back to Bergton. Arthur "Bunk" Runion ran from Broadway to Bergton, Lost City, Lost River, Baker, and back to Bergton, Fulks Run, and Broadway. Grace V. Dove was the Bergton postmistress. Clarence See took mail to Mathias and to Moorefield, West Virginia. (Garner Turner collection.)

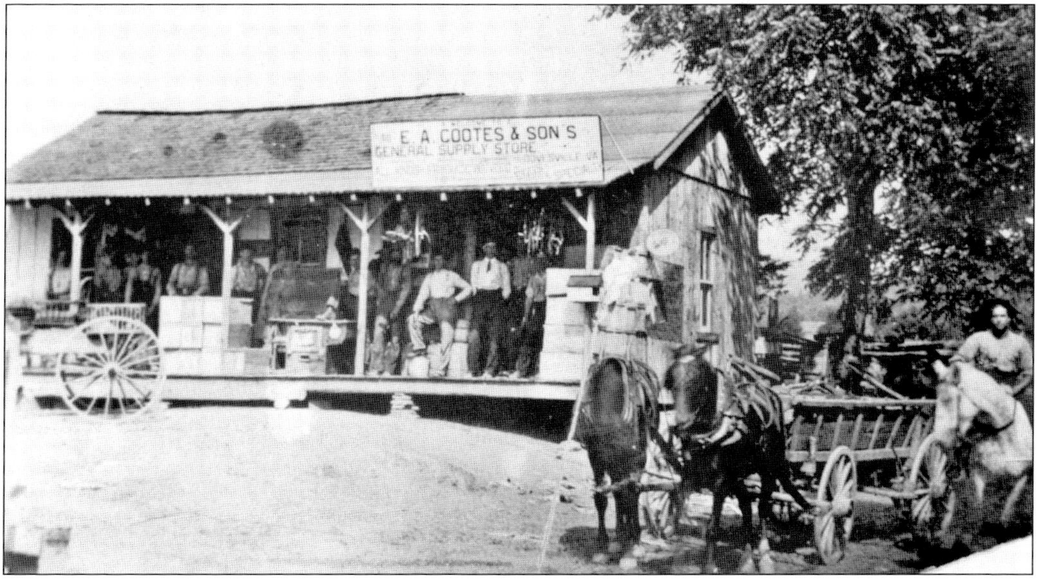

E. A. Cootes from the Cootes Store area operated a store in Dovesville near Robert Hottinger's present-day home. The "General Supply Store" sign says all kinds of produce are wanted. Most stores bought wild berries, nuts, and animal hides from customers and sold them in town. His store was prosperous; a later photograph shows that a second story was added to the building. (Leafy Runion Miller collection.)

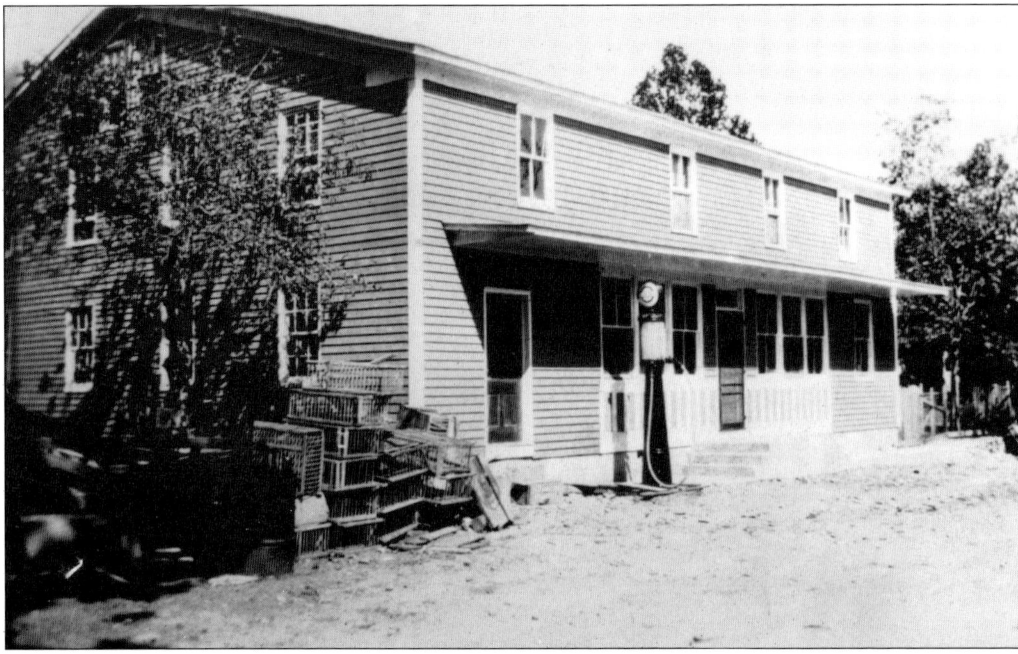

Postmaster Joseph W. Stultz ran the Stultz and Turner store until 1954, when Miller Turner bought it. Joe and his wife, Virginia "Dare" Turner Stultz, enlarged the store and living quarters to board schoolteachers and "drummers" or traveling salesmen. Perhaps the chicken coops were made in Mannie Shoemaker's chicken coop factory; a 1919 news article reported his coops were made with good sycamore rods. (Goldie Ketterman Whetzel collection.)

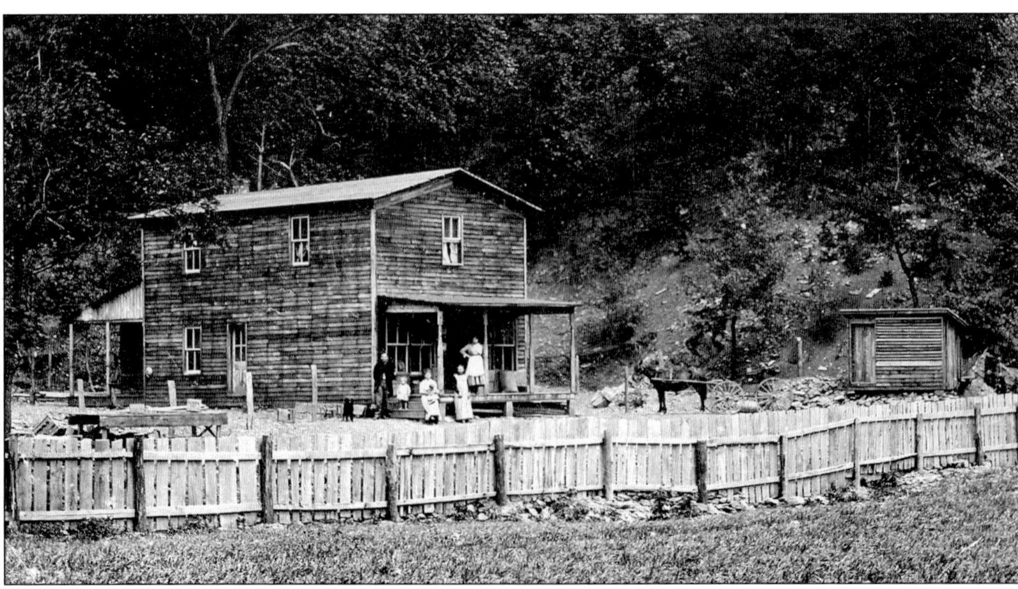

Rev. Joseph Webster "Web" Lantz built this store and residence on German River Road in 1915. The store was on the first floor, bedrooms on the second floor, and kitchen in the back. About 1922, Web moved the old Caplinger schoolhouse to a location near the present-day Criders Post Office, remodeled it, and operated his store from there. (Joseph "Day" Lantz collection.)

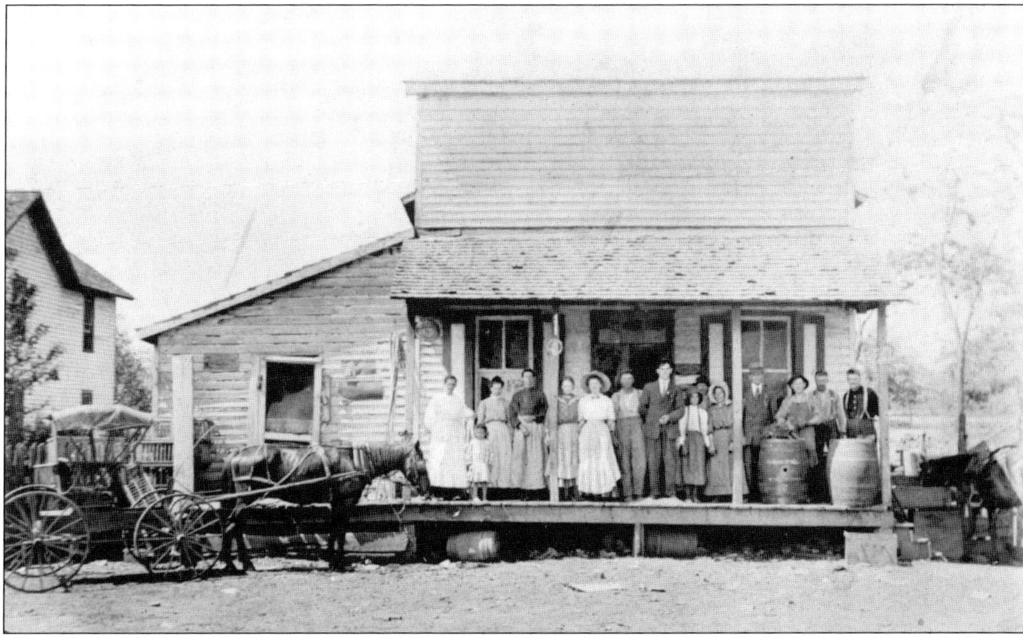

A merchant for 54 years, Jacob D. "Jake" Custer also served as postmaster of Fulks Run from 1892 to 1893 and from 1897 to 1914. This is his store on Dry River after it was enlarged. His home, which is still standing, can be seen at the left. The horse on the right enjoys a fresh drink of water from the trough. (Georgia Custer Fulk collection.)

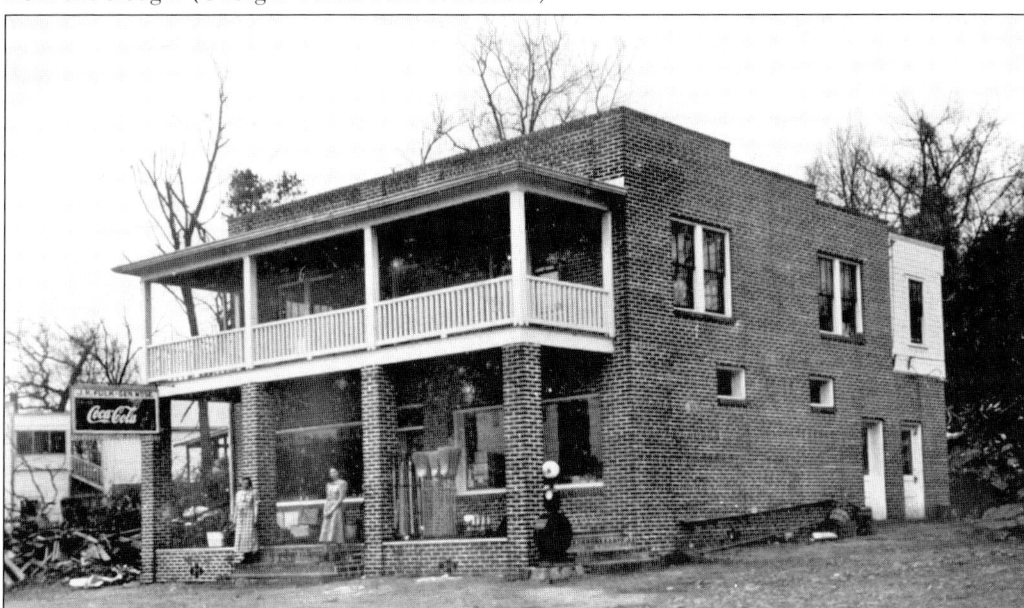

John Kelly and Georgia Custer Fulk built this new brick building for their store at Little Dry River Road in Fulks Run. The business had started in a frame building across the Shenandoah River owned by Georgia's father, Jacob "Jake" Custer, who moved the store to a white frame building on the same lot as the brick store. The Fulks operated their store until retiring around 1946. (Georgia Custer Fulk collection.)

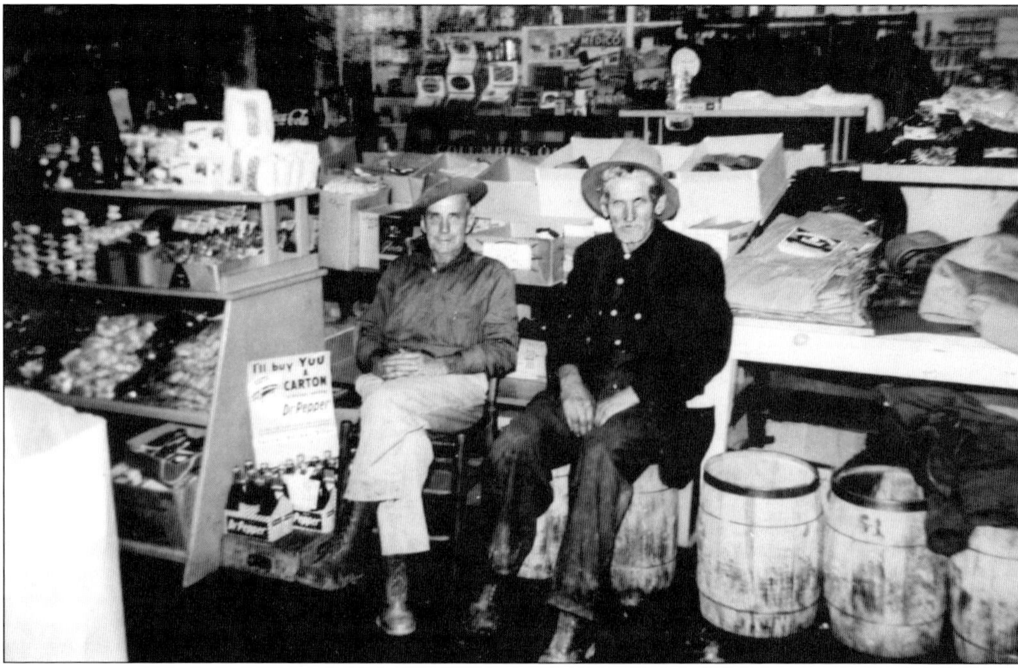

Shopping was not the only reason to go to the store. Country stores were a place to exchange news, relax after a hard day's work, and socialize. Jacob R. "Jake" Albrite and Joseph "Joe" Dove take a prominent seat inside the front door of Crider Brothers at Fulks Run so they can see all the customers as they enter. (Lillian Runion Crider collection.)

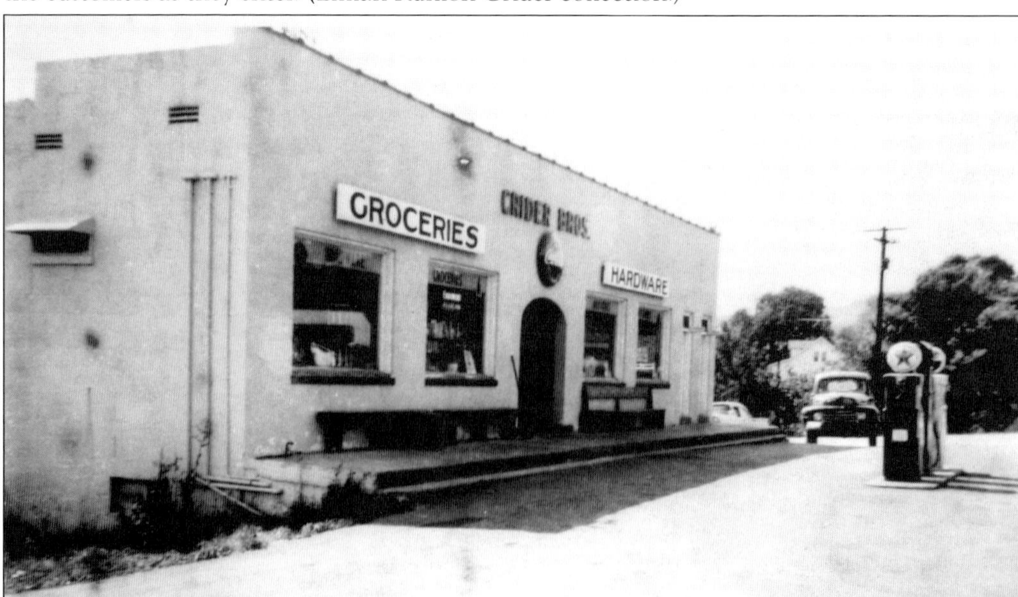

Loy H. Crider and Charles F. Crider were third-generation merchants. Their grandfather, William Riley Crider, was a merchant and the first postmaster at Criders. Their father, Samuel A. Crider, was a merchant and postmaster at Criders for one year and at Fulks Run for 33 years. Loy and Charles built their store on "new" Highway 259 around 1950 and ran it until retiring in 1988. (Lillian Runion Crider collection.)

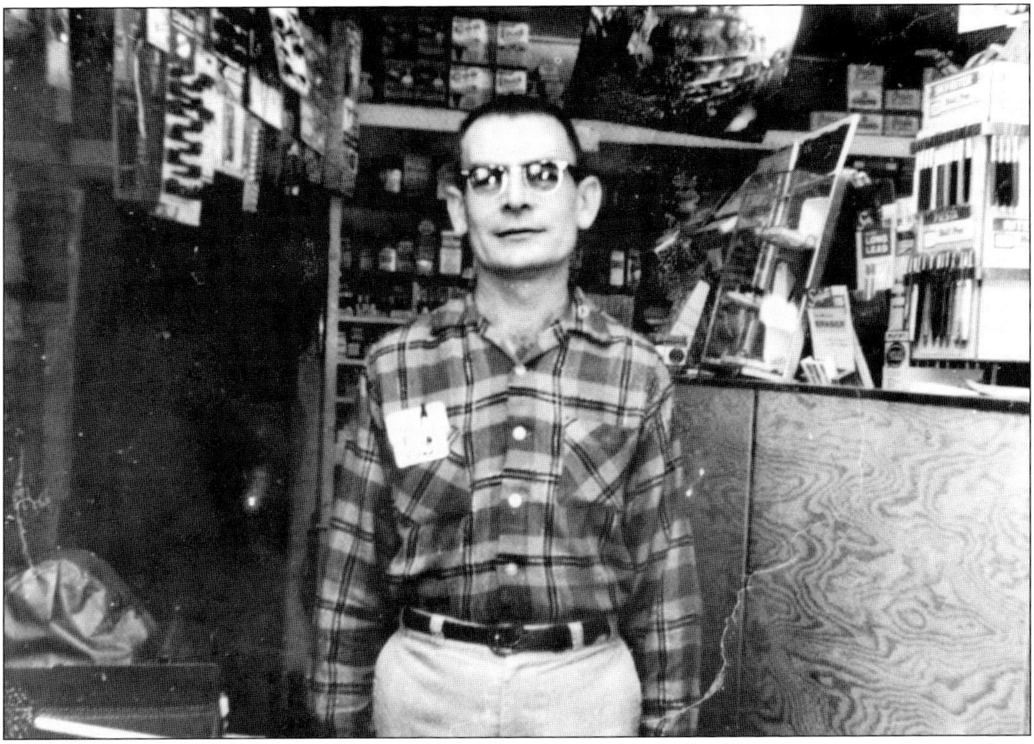

Charles and Loy Crider sold a variety of groceries, hardware, and other goods in their store. This is a photograph of Charles before the store was doubled in size in the mid-1960s. (Lillian Runion Crider collection.)

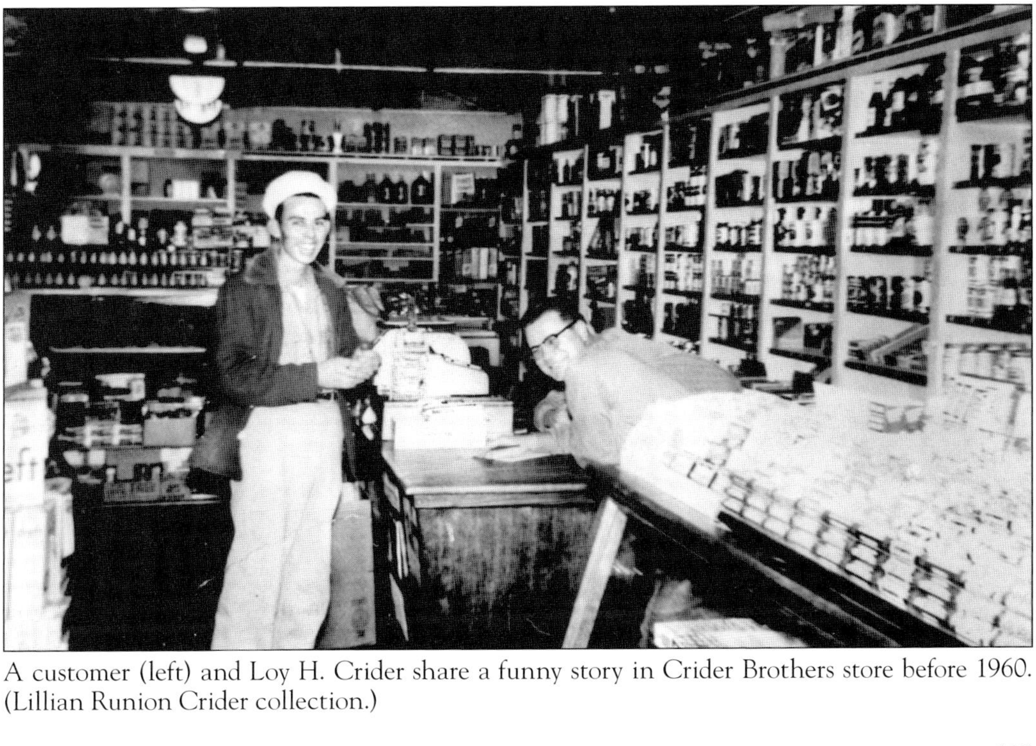

A customer (left) and Loy H. Crider share a funny story in Crider Brothers store before 1960. (Lillian Runion Crider collection.)

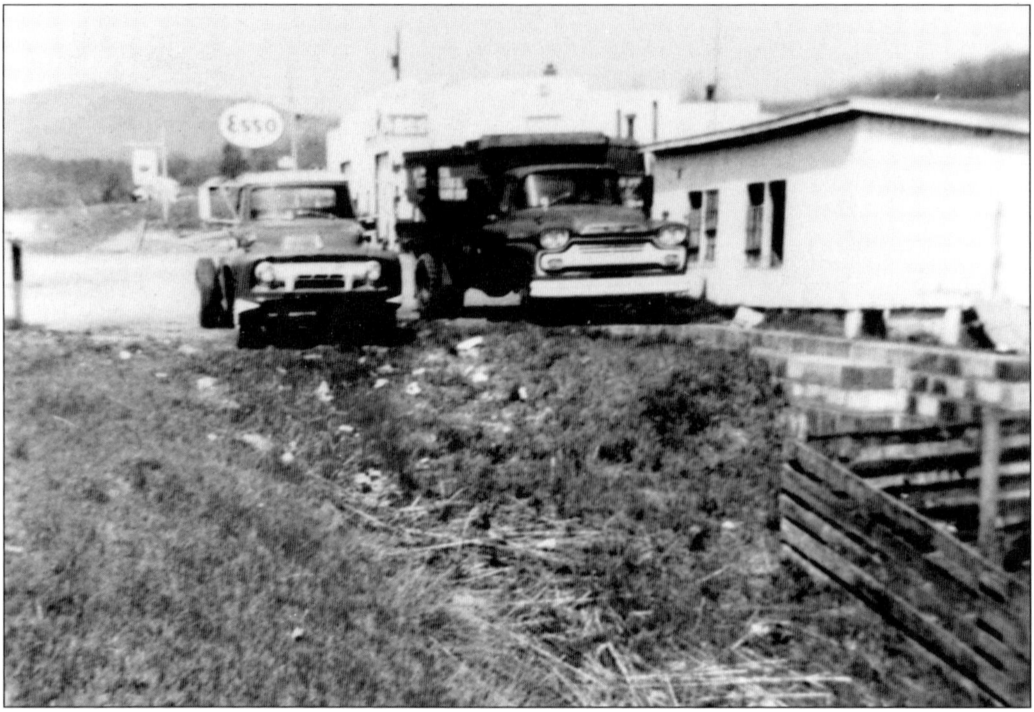

Around 1942, when the "new" Highway 259 was constructed, Melvin C. Estep built a new store at Fulks Run to accommodate his general store and trucking business. This photograph from the early 1950s includes two of the Estep trucks. During the 1950s and 1960s, Robert Bare and then William "Billy" Bare ran the store. (Donna Kline Estep collection.)

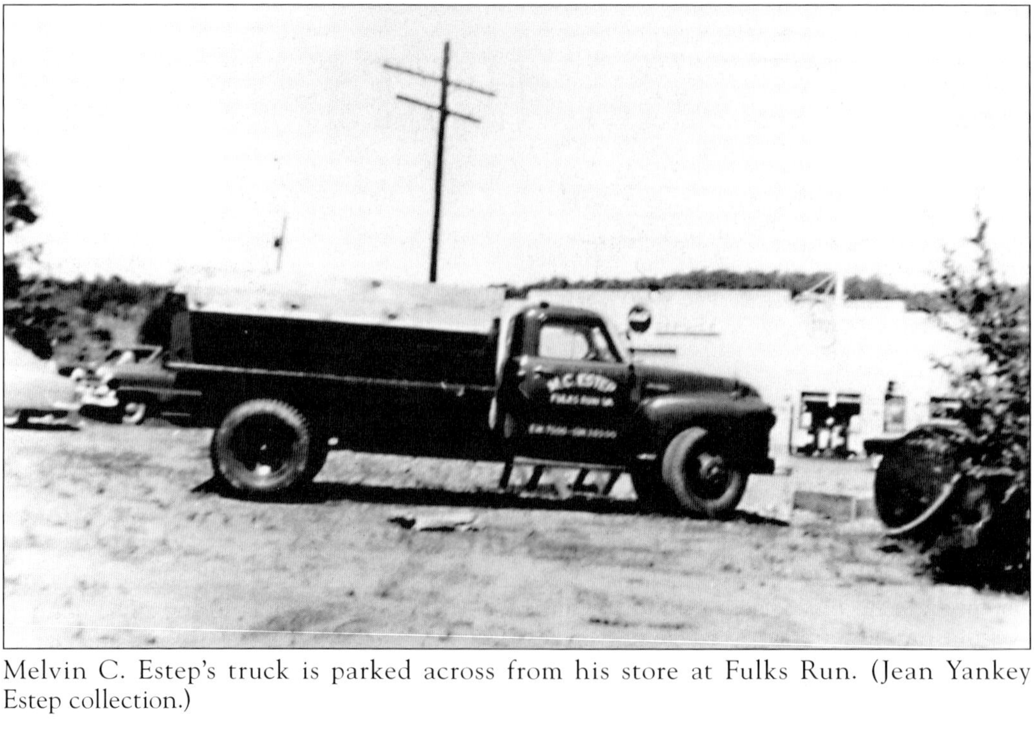

Melvin C. Estep's truck is parked across from his store at Fulks Run. (Jean Yankey Estep collection.)

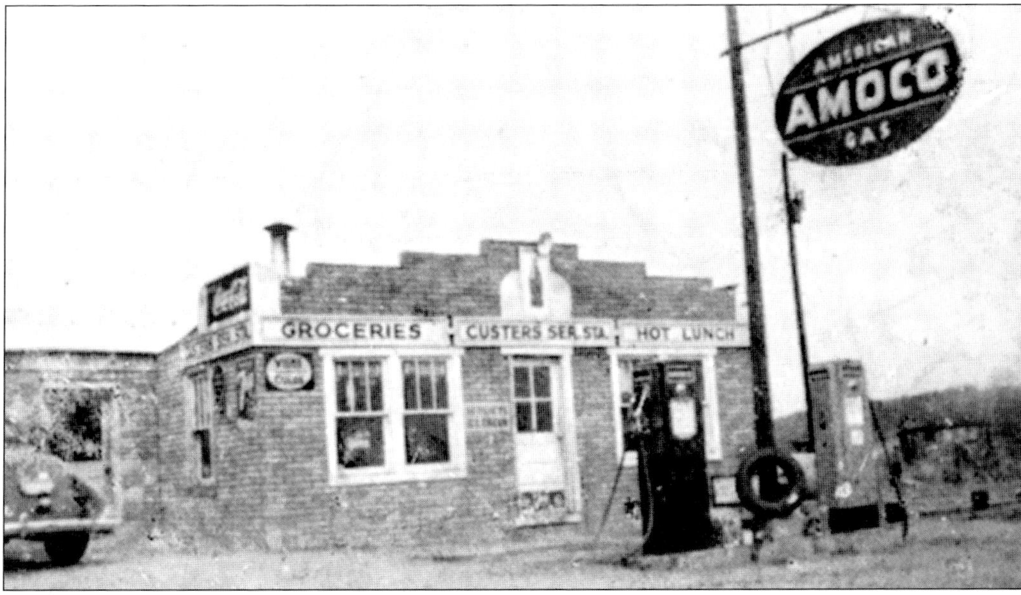

Millard D. "Pete" Custer and his wife, Naomi Fulk Custer, began Custer's Service Station in Fulks Run before 1947. Naomi served meals in a corner of the store. They built a modern building around 1956 that housed a restaurant with a lunch counter and tables. The Custers sold the store to Naomi's brother Matthew Fulk in 1960. (Naomi Fulk Custer collection.)

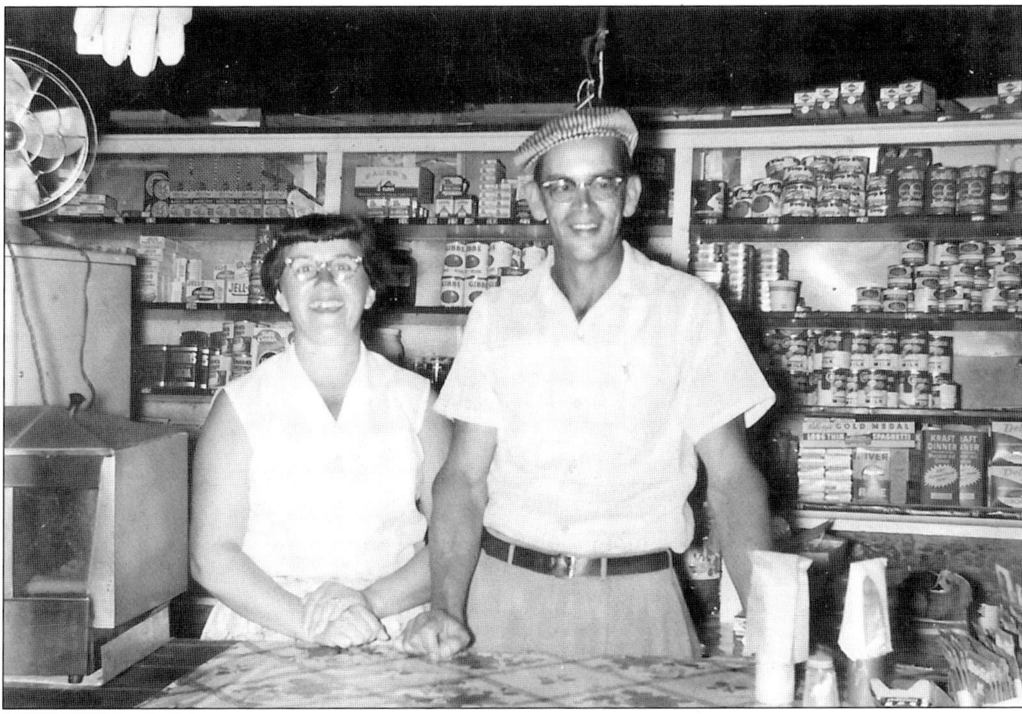

Naomi and Pete Custer pose behind the lunch counter of their restaurant/store. The hot dog machine on the counter was a new convenience. Small paper bags over the mustard and catsup bottles kept the flies away. Other interior photos of the store show it was decorated with hunting trophies. (Naomi Fulk Custer collection.)

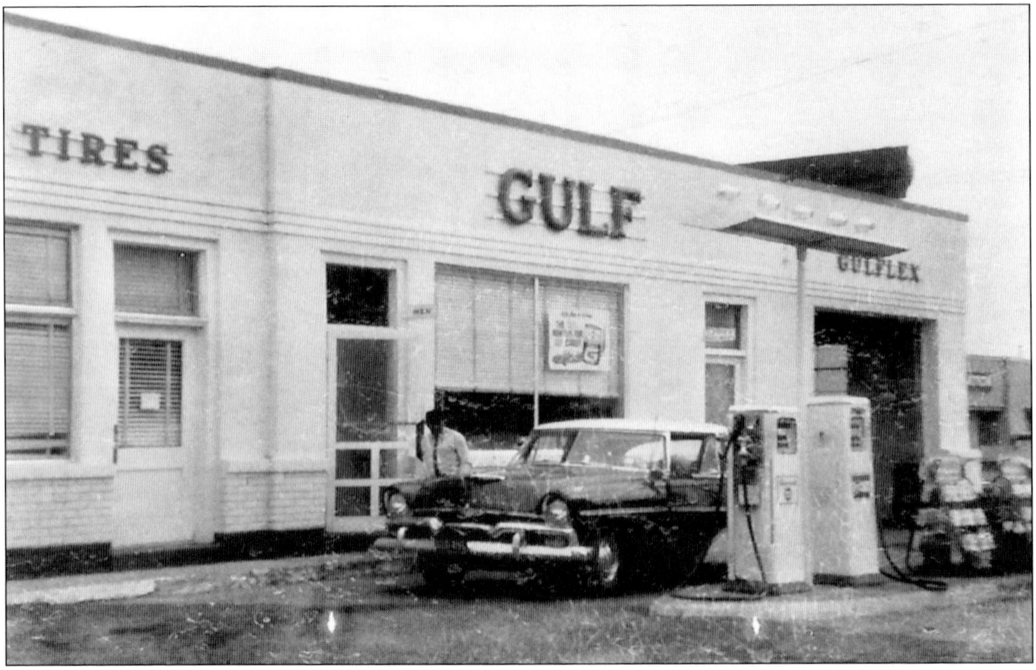

Matthew Fulk bought Custer's Service Station in 1960 and changed the name to Mac's Superette. After the restaurant part of the store was closed, C. McClory "Slim" Southerly used it as a barbershop. Matthew remodeled and enlarged the store about 1965. The store was the largest game-checking station in the state for deer and bear. (Pauline Carr Fulk collection.)

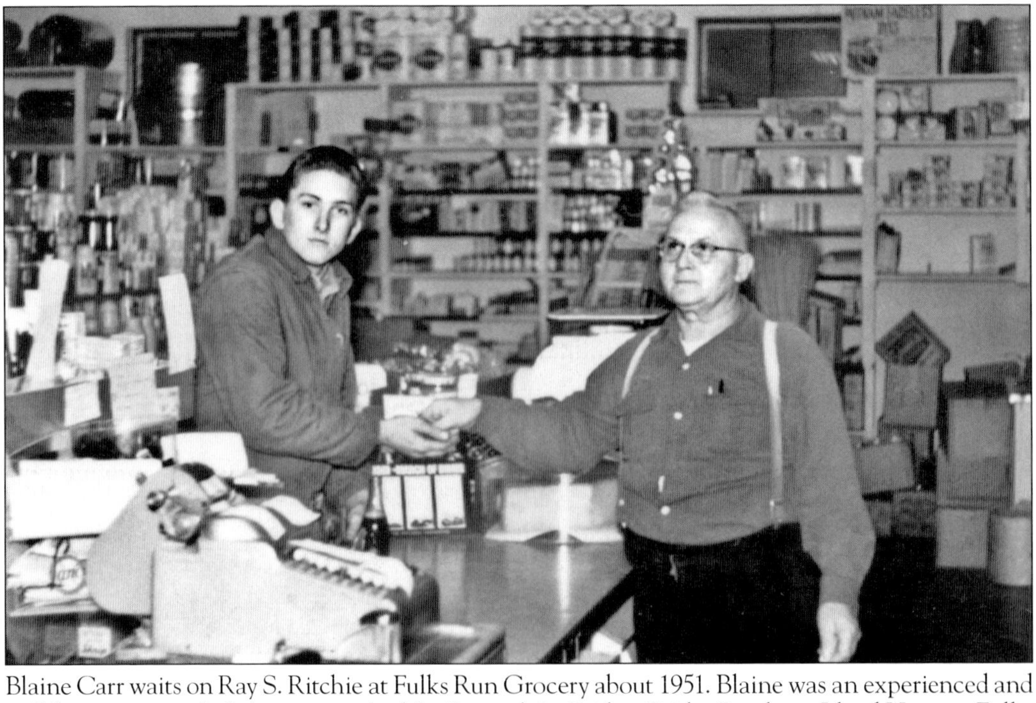

Blaine Carr waits on Ray S. Ritchie at Fulks Run Grocery about 1951. Blaine was an experienced and well-known store clerk, having worked for Samuel A. Crider, Crider Brothers, Lloyd Hoover, Fulks Run Grocery, and Mac's Superette during his long career. (Garnett R. Turner, photographer.)

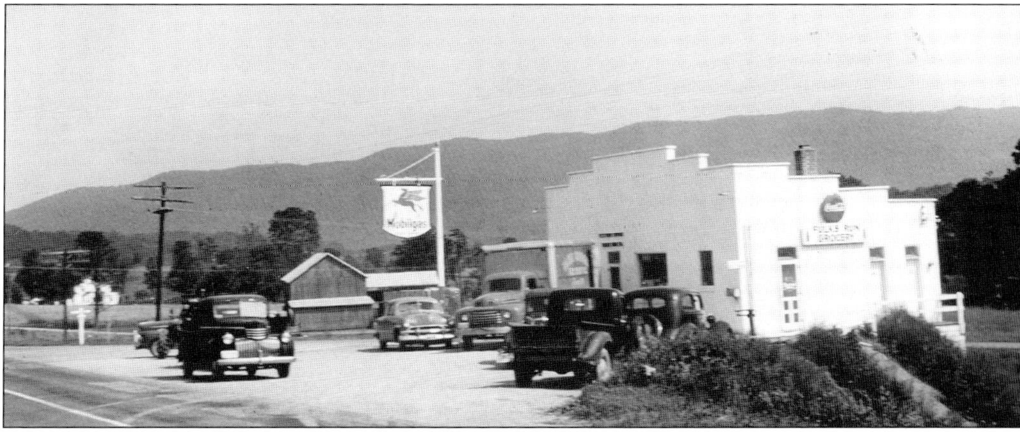

In 1949, Garnett R. Turner built Fulks Run Grocery and Post Office. Early that year, Dr. Charles Hertzler rented the basement for his medical practice until his Green Valley Clinic was completed. When waiting on a customer, the store clerk gathered items on the shopping list, using a long-handled grabber for items on top shelves. Self-service grocery shopping and grocery carts were not common until the mid-1960s. (Garnett R. Turner, photographer.)

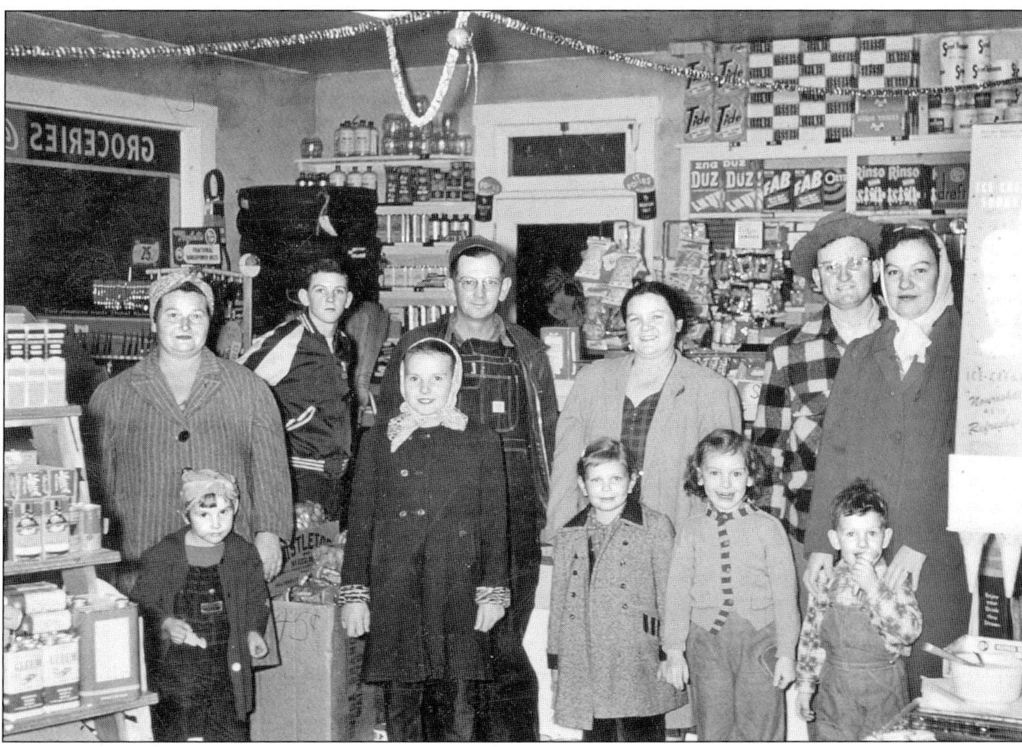

Christmas decorations, including painted bells on the door, created a festive mood at Fulks Run Grocery in 1951. Pictured from left to right are (children, first row) Carol May, Patsy May, Carol Lee Custer, Kay Ellen Turner, and Dennis Turner; (adults, second row) Nellie May, Derwood Custer, Clarence A. Custer, Margaret Fawley Custer, Granvil J. Turner, and Violet Miller Turner. (Garnett R. Turner, photographer.)

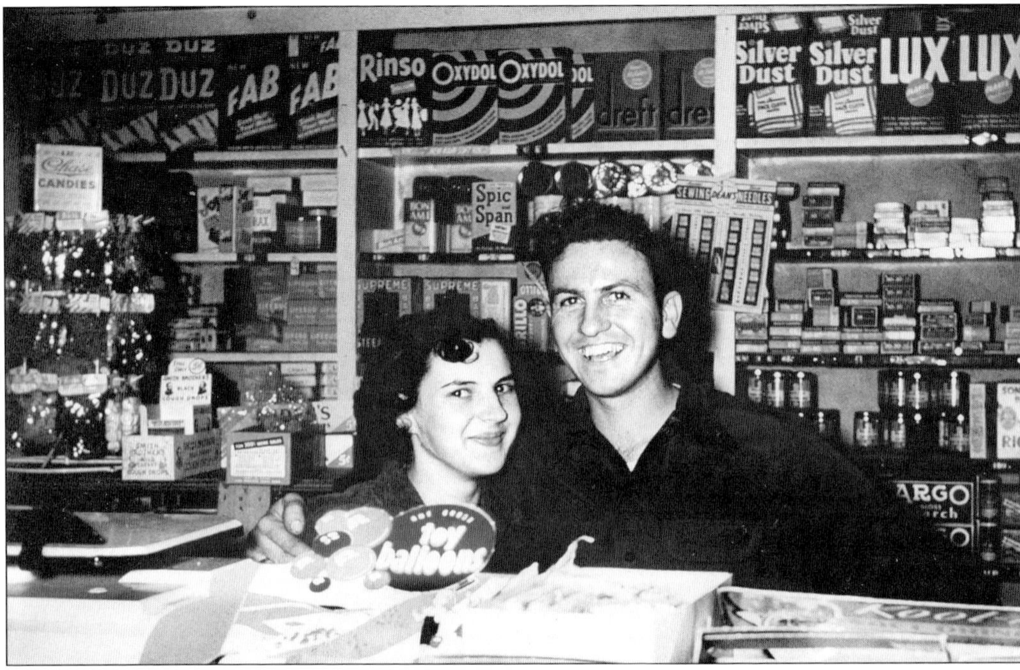

Lena and Garnett Turner pose behind the counter in Fulks Run Grocery about 1950. In addition to groceries, they sold tires, Chippewa work boots, sandwiches, and work clothes. The store was enlarged in 1957 and doubled in size in 1963. Some cleaning brands on the shelves have stood the test of time and are familiar today: Fab, Spic and Span, Bon Ami, and Brillo. (Granvil J. Turner, photographer.)

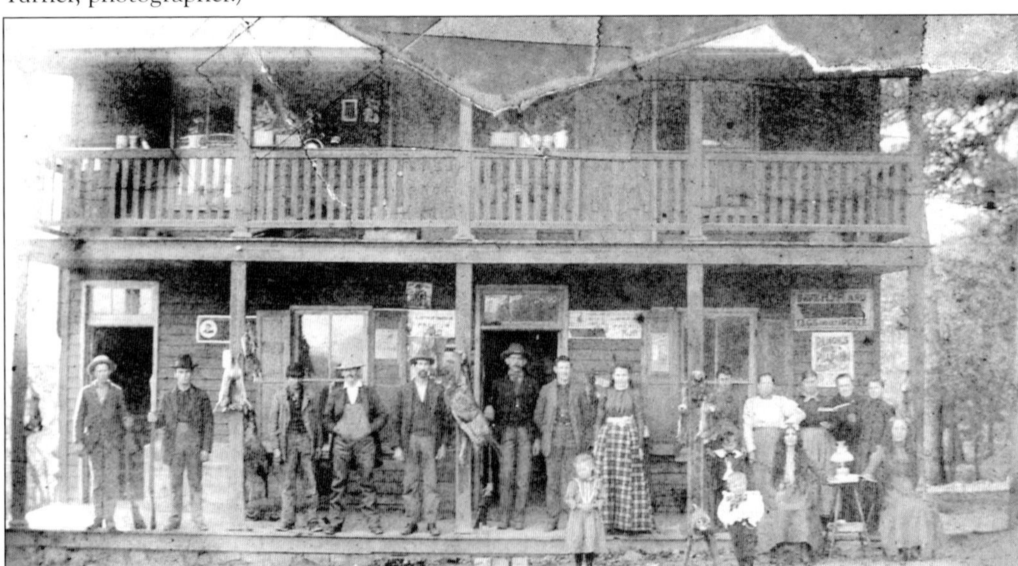

Dewitt F. "Dee" Ritchie built this store at Genoa in 1894 and operated it until 1901, when he and his wife, Verna Trumbo (seventh and eighth from the left), purchased a store near Cherry Grove. George W. and Emma Trumbo Ritchie bought the store and ran it until about 1908. Although this photograph is faded, you can still see the squirrels and turkey hanging from the posts. (Frances Ritchie Deavers collection.)

Abraham Douglas "Doug" Brenneman bought the Ritchies' store in 1908 and ran it until his death in 1955. The store also served as the Genoa Post Office from 1912 until 1937, when it was discontinued. Doug and his wife, Clara Kline Turner Brenneman, constructed a separate building for their kitchen and living room to the left of the store. The buildings burned in the 1970s. (Garnett R. Turner, photographer.)

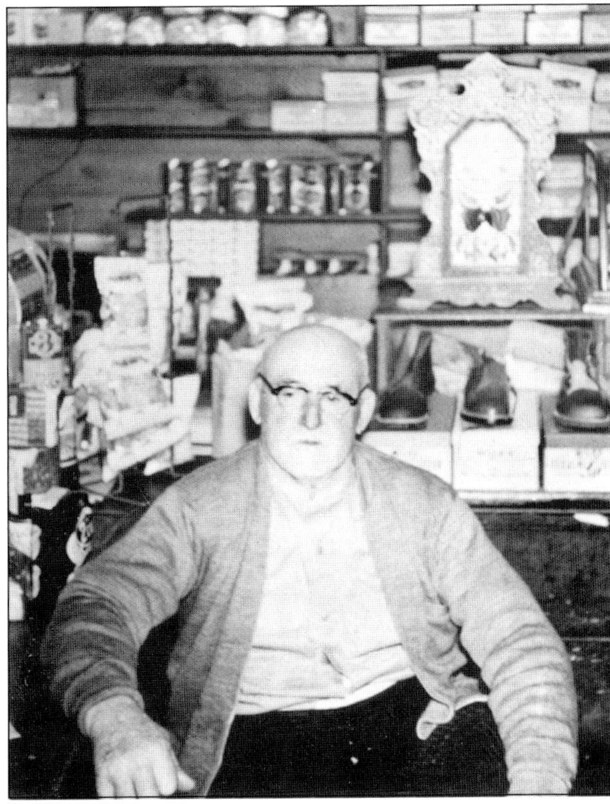

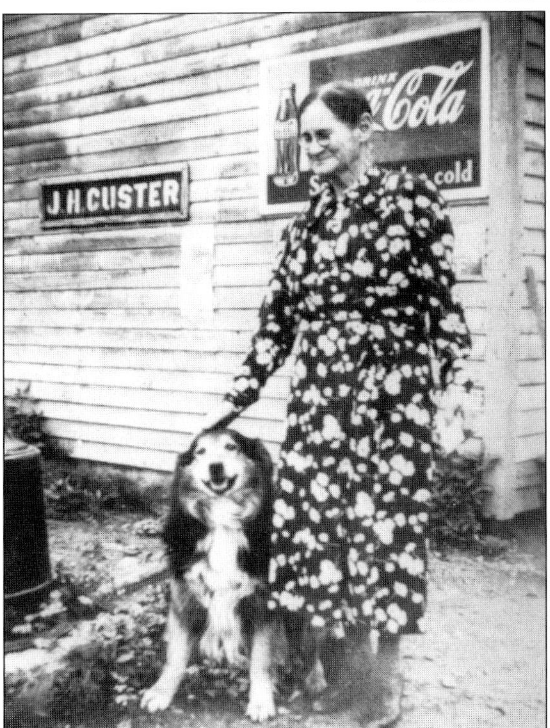

John H. and Elizabeth "Lizzie" Fawley Custer ran a store on Runions Creek before moving to Genoa, where they operated a store on a hill above Genoa School. After John's death in 1935, Lizzie operated the store until her death in 1954. Her store had a feature not found in many present-day stores—a box in the front of the store and one in the back for spitting tobacco juice.

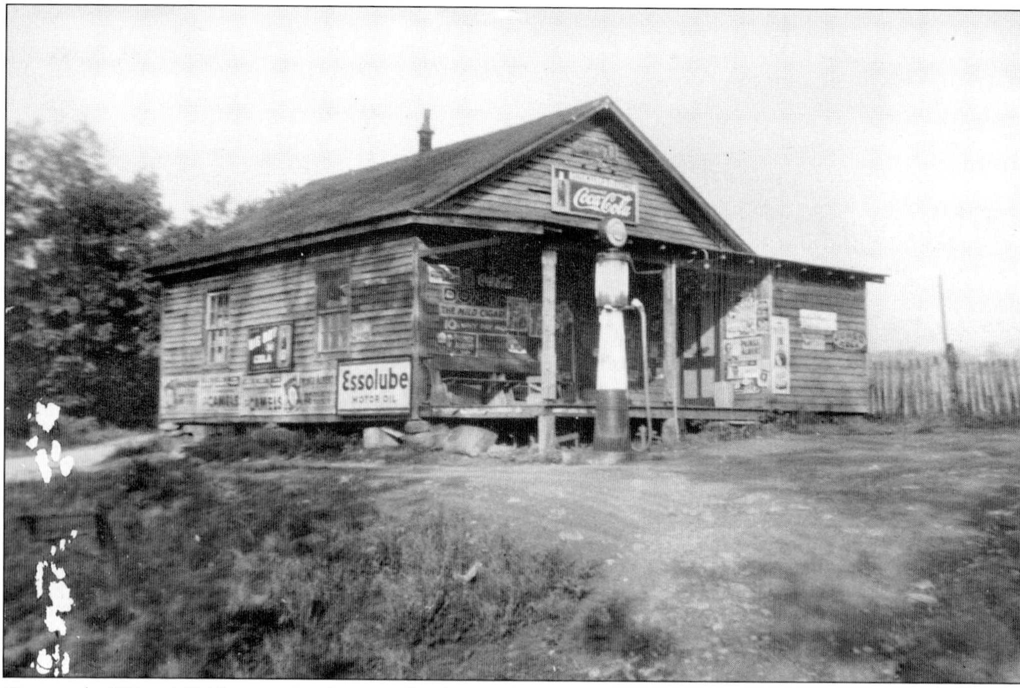

Gertrude "Gertie" Shoemaker's store building first served as the one-room Shoemaker School. When the school merged with Oak Grove to form Genoa School in 1919, Gertie bought the building and moved it to this location on Highway 612. (Janice Shoemaker Fulk collection.)

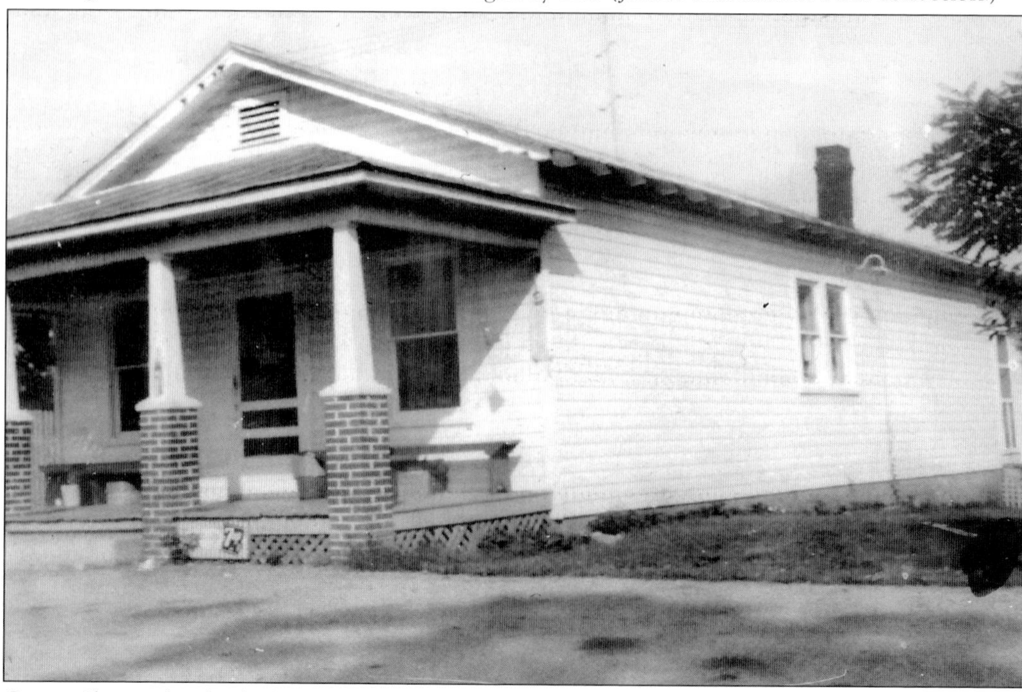

Gertie Shoemaker built this new store building about 1939 and tore down her old store. Her son Ford Shoemaker ran the store after her death. It closed in the late 1960s. (Janice Shoemaker Fulk collection.)

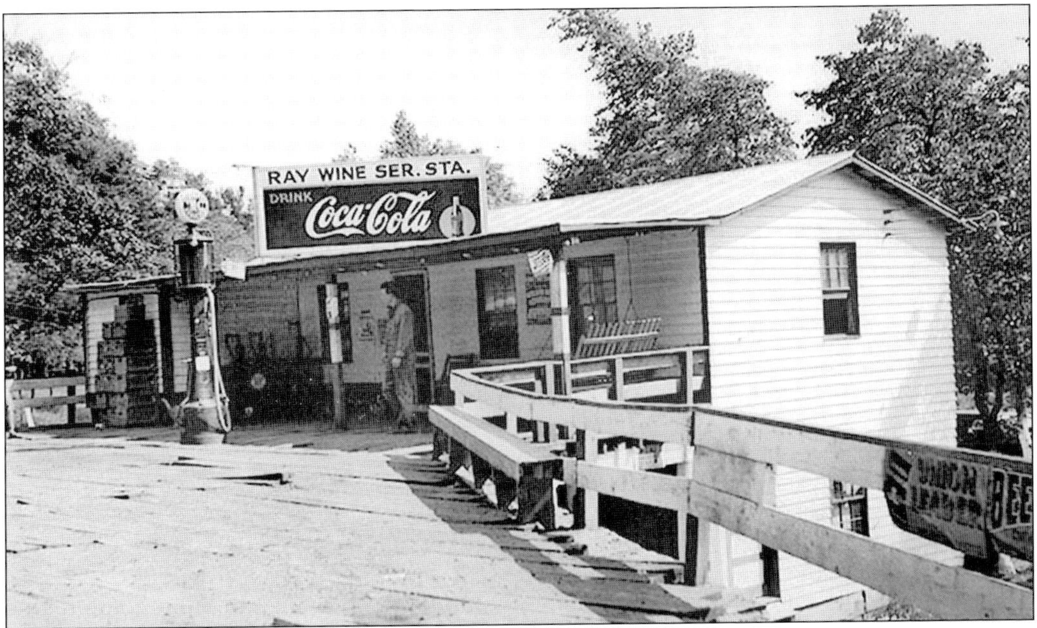

Harry Weatherholtz leased this service station, featuring a wooden driveway and porch swing, to Ray B. Wine. The men pictured are H. C. Weatherholtz (left) and Verco Weatherholtz, sons of Harry T. Weatherholtz. After Ray quit running the station, it sat empty for a long time, and weather and the river took its toll on it. (Robert "Bud" Weatherholtz collection; courtesy of Carol Hepner Turner.)

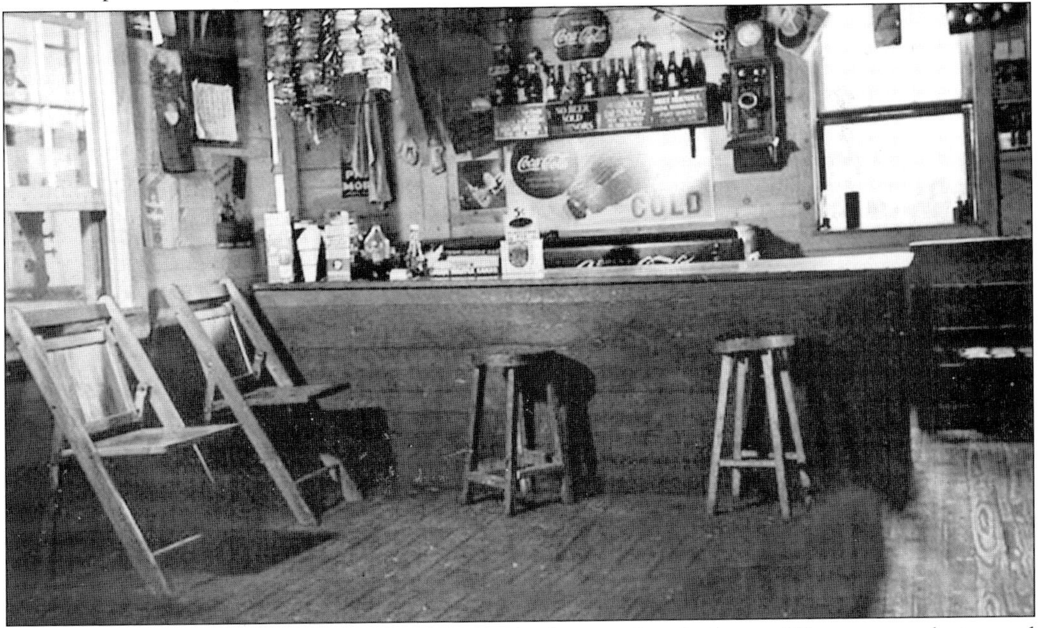

Ray B. Wine's service station at Brocks Gap had a crank telephone. There were chairs and stools for patrons, and air conditioning was provided by an open window. The Coca-Cola cooler probably refrigerated the bottles with cold water. After returning from World War II, Benjamin H. "Bennie" Carr bought the place, tore it down, and built Brocks Gap Service Inc. (Robert "Bud" Weatherholtz collection; courtesy of Carol Hepner Turner.)

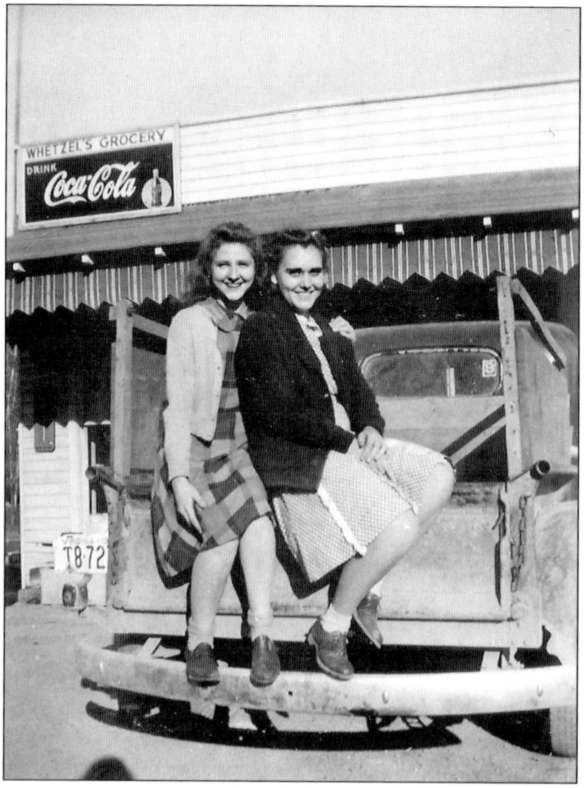

Russel J. "R. J." Whetzel operated a store from the 1930s until the 1950s beside Hooper's old mill building on Crab Run Road in Bergton, near the present-day community center. Helen Whetzel Moyer and Estelle Moyer Dispanet are pictured here. R. J. later remodeled the building into a home, where his daughter Emma Whetzel Wittig currently lives. (Emma Whetzel Wittig collection.)

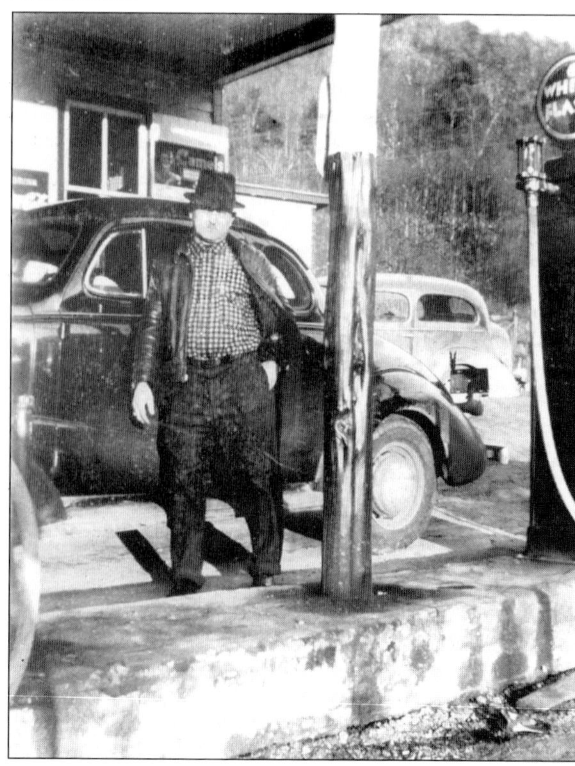

Pete Turner ran a service station at the base of Chimney Rock in the 1930s. Another photograph of the station is on page 125. Hazel Mitchell later used the building for Chimney Rock Rug Shop, where she wove rag rugs for sale. The building was remodeled and currently is a residence. (Private collection.)

Eight

OTHER BUSINESSES

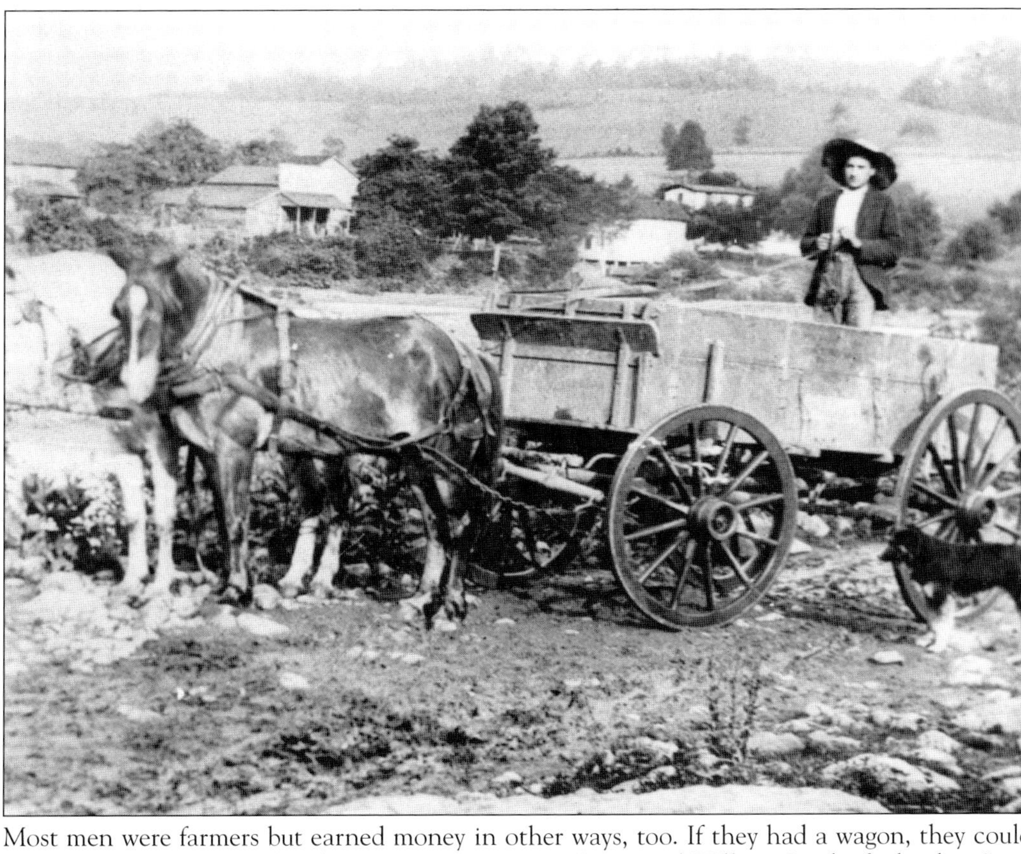

Most men were farmers but earned money in other ways, too. If they had a wagon, they could earn cash hauling for the local store. In 1880, Wittig's Store paid William Snyder for hauling "up," "down," or to Broadway. George W. "Web" Fulk of Fulks Run and his team are pictured on the old Dry River Road with Jacob Custer's store in the background. (Lula Fulk Turner collection.)

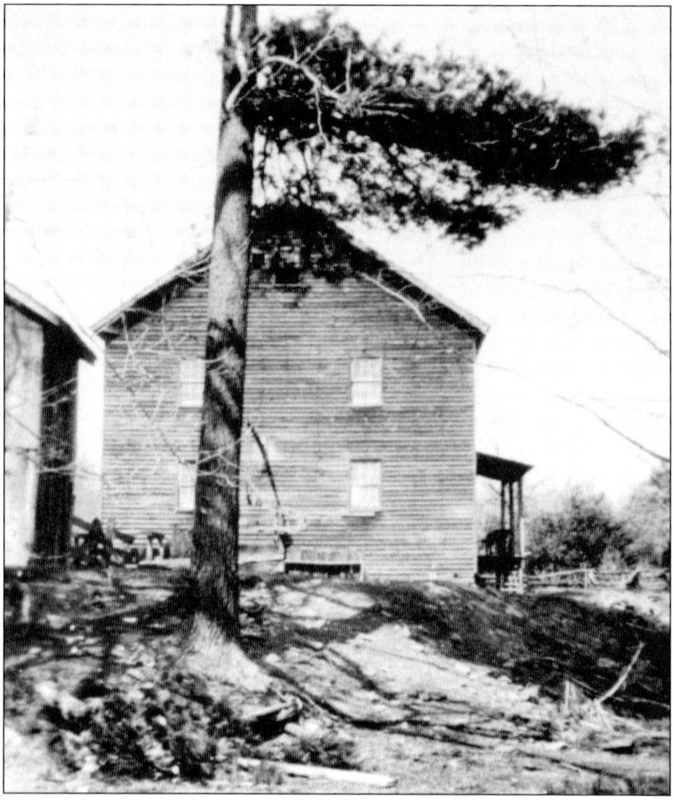

Located next to the present-day Criders Post Office, Hupp Mill was powered by water from the German River and operated until about 1925. A gate in the river dam between the houses of Israel "Doc" Dove and Casper L. Moyers channeled water through a tunnel, under the road, and into the millrace. The millers were Charles B. Hupp, Charles A. Hupp, William F. Hupp, Paul Smith, and Irvin Crider. (Leota Moyers Stultz collection.)

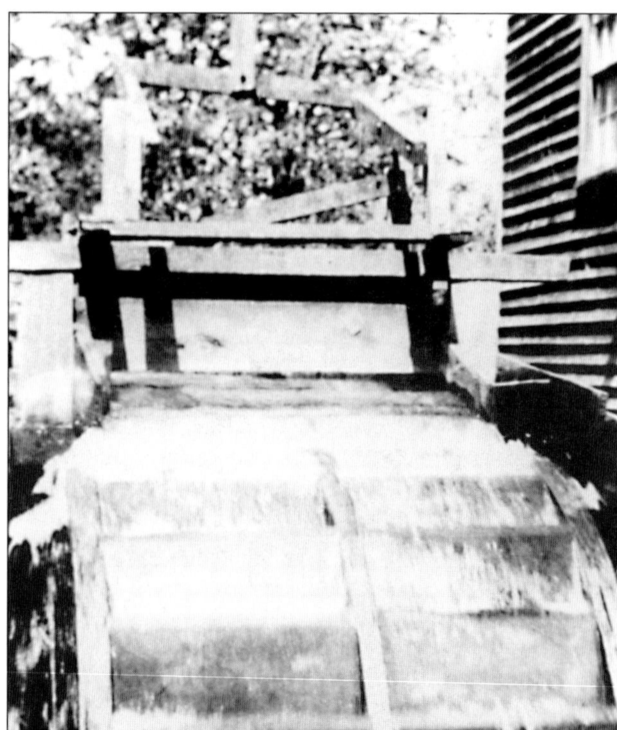

The wooden water wheel at Hupp Mill was wider than most mill wheels. When water was low, a gasoline engine ran it. An earlier grist and sawmill, located a short distance upstream from Hupp Mill, was owned by the Lantz and Caplinger families. When Jacob Caplinger operated the Caplinger Mill in 1870, his mill was worth $500, was water-powered, and ran an eight-horsepower engine. (Lewis H. Yankey collection.)

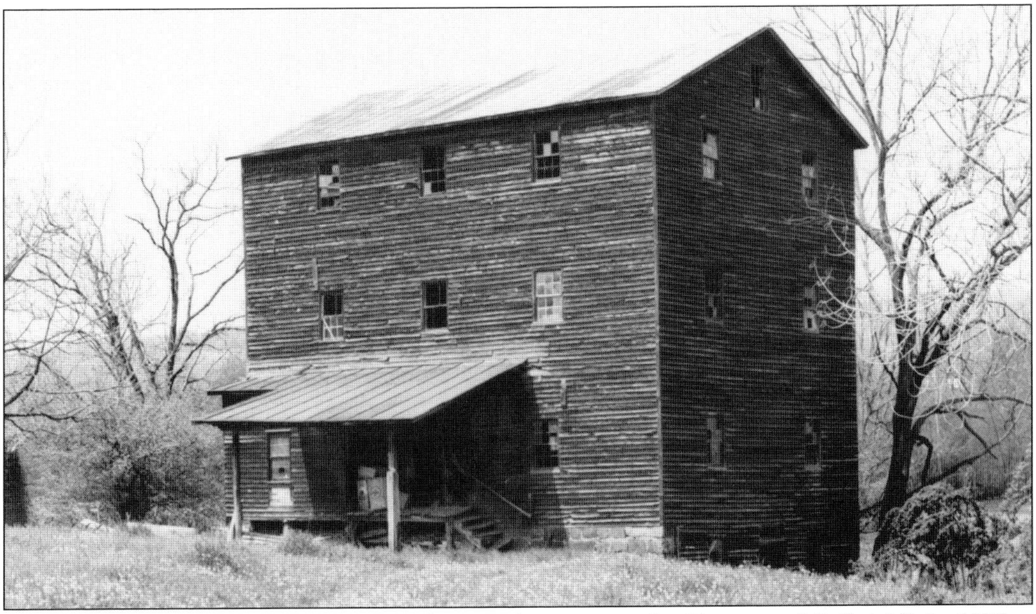

Luther Turner's mill at Fulks Run was chartered in 1911 as the Turner and Fulk Mill. In 1920, a gasoline engine replaced the original steam engine. Luther's son Herman B. Turner remembered when 20 teams of horses and wagons lined up at the mill, waiting their turn. Once, lightening struck the mill, but Herman and others used water from a barrel to extinguish the blaze. (Pat Turner Ritchie, photographer.)

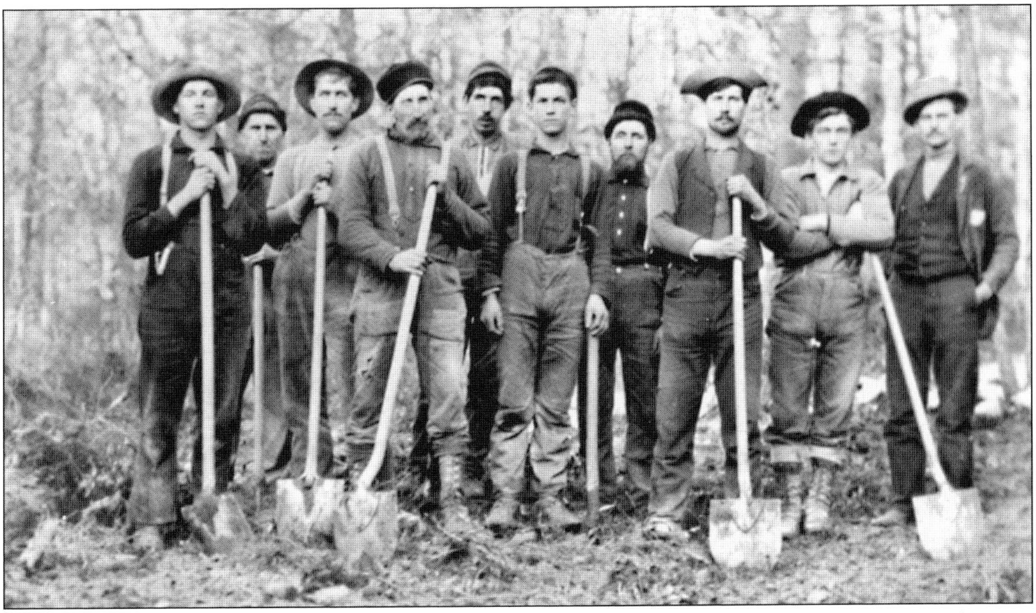

Until after 1900, all able-bodied men over 16 had to maintain public roads near their homes. These men are working on the Ridge Road from Bennetts Run to Criders Post Office. Pictured from left to right are Casper L. Sonifrank, Solon P. "Doc" Halterman, Curtis Lee Smith, Solomon Perry Smith, James "Jim" Yankey, Grover Cleveland Sonifrank, Samuel Daniel "Sam" Halterman, George Adam "Didymus" Smith, Charles William Sonifrank, and Clarence Lantz. (Goldie Turner May collection.)

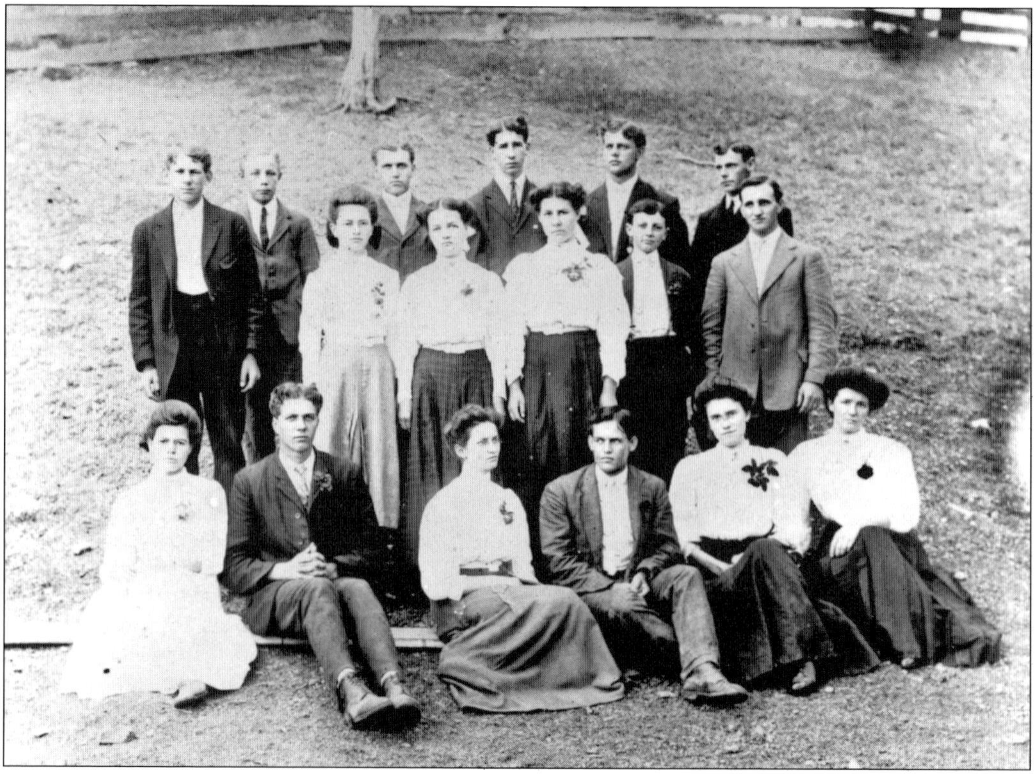

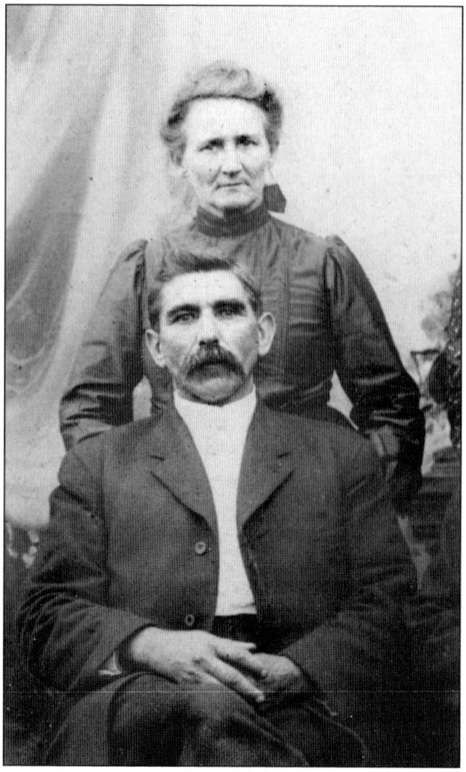

The following group of teachers in 1912 are listed from left to right: (first row) Emma or Effie Souder, George Lantz, Sallie May Sindy, Grant Souder, Hattie Moyers Pope, and Delia Moyers May; (second row) Ada May Hedrick, ? Smith, Minnie Crider Hottinger, Lawson Souder, and John May; (third row) Kenna Moyer, Grant Moyers, Lory Halterman, Russel May, Grover Moyers, and Pearl Wilbur Dove. (J. Ellwood May collection.)

Dovesville undertaker Michael Fink (pictured with his wife, Martha Cullers Fink) sewed coffin linings and body covers for his wooden coffins. His hearse was three times longer than it was wide and was composed of smooth wooden material indented on the sides like a window, with carved filigree at the top corners. The glossy black box, mounted on a two-horse wagon, had a driver's seat high in the front with two kerosene lamps on either side.

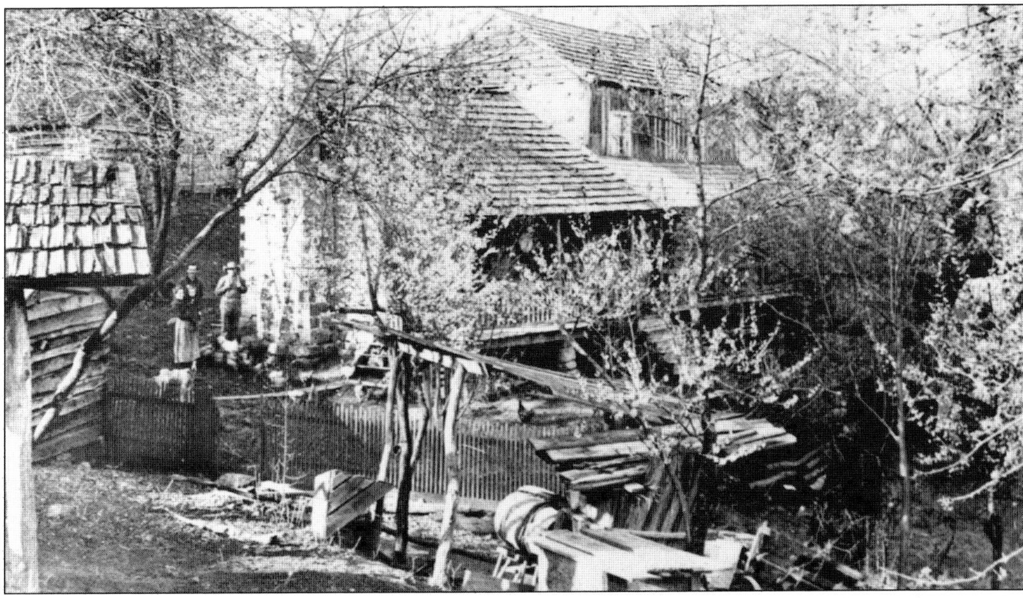

One of the founders of Dovesville Mutual Telephone Company, Savannah "Vannie" Moyers, built his own switchboard in his West Mountain home, pictured here. Dovesville residents strung wires from their homes to the switchboard, using trees for poles. Vannie and his daughter Mae were switchboard operators until about 1952. In 1969, the company merged with Shenandoah County Telephone Company, and homes had dial telephones for the first time. (Lennis Moyers Garber collection.)

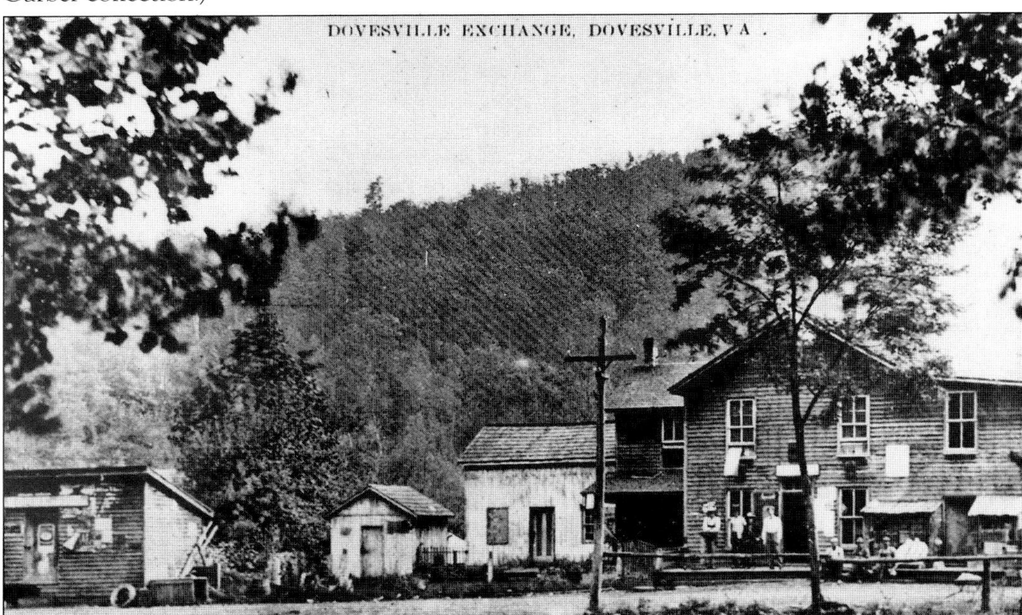

Telephone service in Bergton incorporated in 1905 as Dovesville Mutual Telephone Company. Nine lines served 71 households. Incoming calls rang all telephones on the line but each home had a special coded ring; for instance, one long and two short rings meant a call for Crider's Store. No call was to last more than five minutes, and business messages were not to be delayed by gossip. (J. Ellwood May collection.)

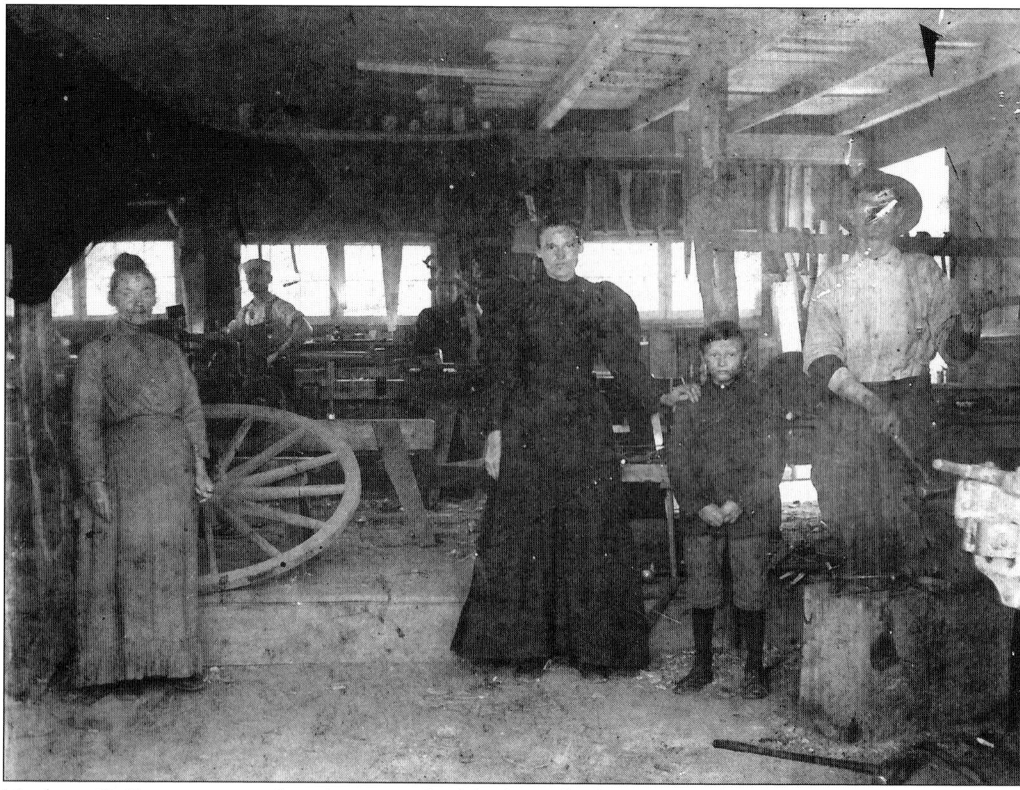

Nathan C. Runion owned and operated a blacksmith shop near Chimney Rock. A photograph of his farm and shop beside Runions Creek is on page 13. His home is still standing, but his shop was demolished for Highway 259 in the 1940s. Pictured from left to right are Mollie Hess Turner, two unidentified men (in back), Asenith F. Davis Runion, Emerson "James" Runion, and Nathan C. Runion around 1900. (Matthew E. "Bud" Miller collection.)

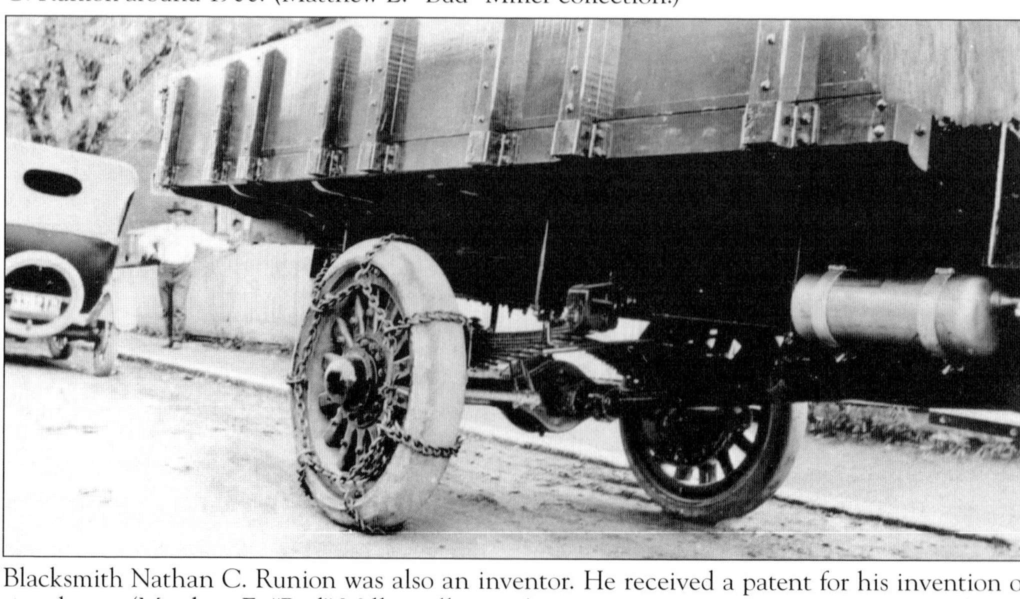

Blacksmith Nathan C. Runion was also an inventor. He received a patent for his invention of tire chains. (Matthew E. "Bud" Miller collection.)

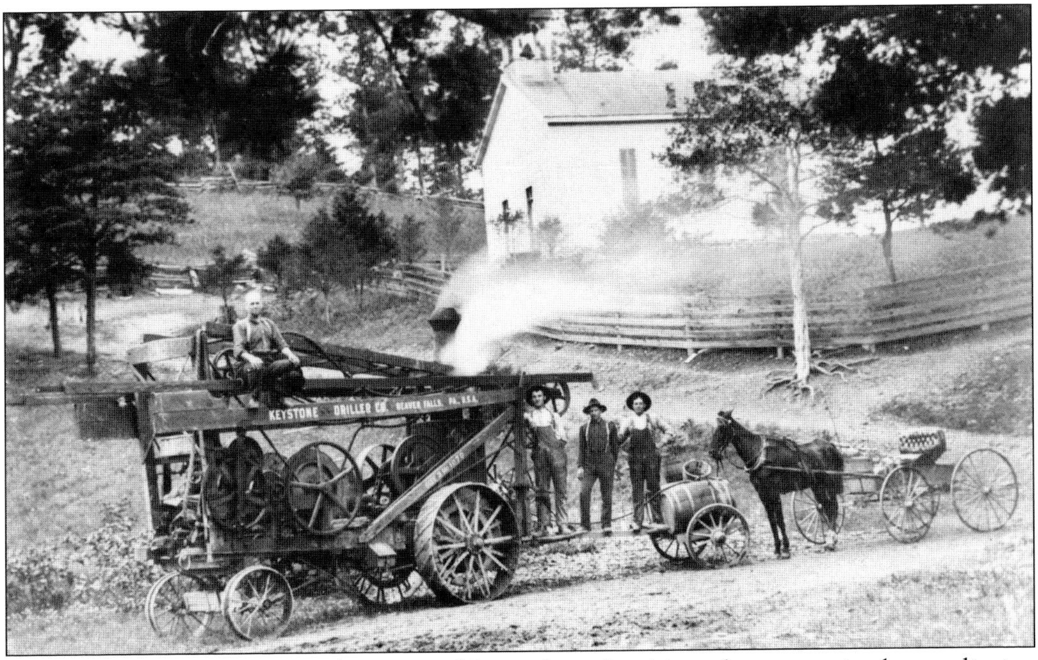

Steam engines made men's work easier and faster, from threshing wheat to sawing logs to digging wells. George W. Whetzel is pictured around 1900 sitting on top of his No. 1070 well-drilling machine from Keystone Driller Company of Beaver Falls, Pennsylvania. Phanuel's Lutheran Church is in the background. (Vita Souder Fulk collection.)

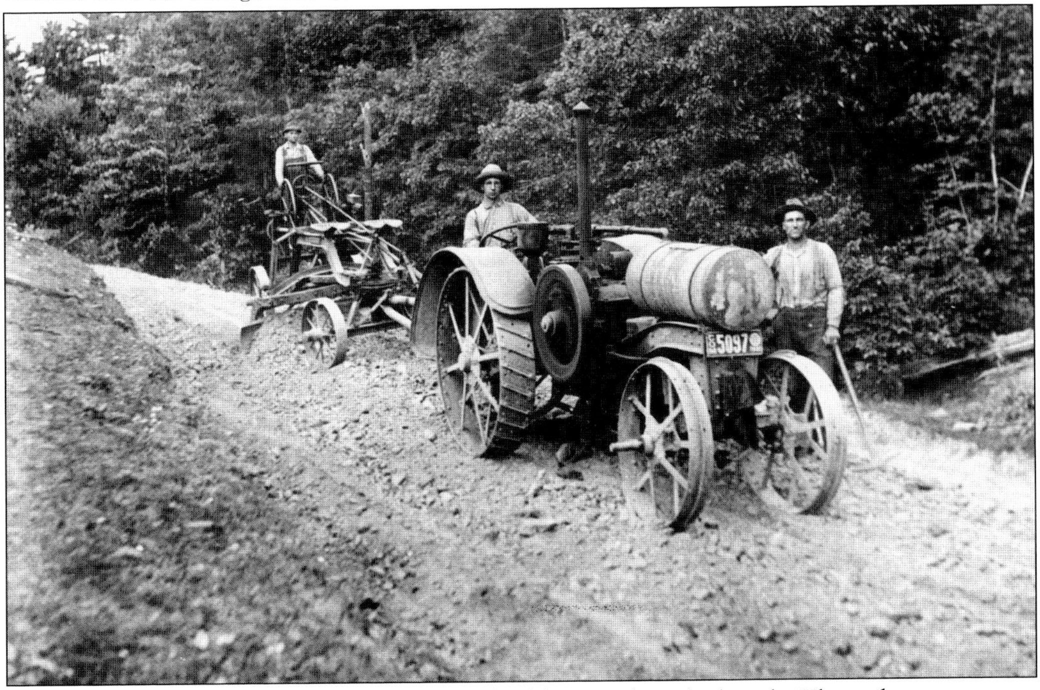

Road graders were a great improvement over building roads with shovels. These three men were constructing a "modern" Crab Run Road near Bergton, perhaps in the 1910s. The workers, from left to right, are H. Kenna Moyer, Russell May, and "Big Cal" Moyers. (J. Ellwood May collection.)

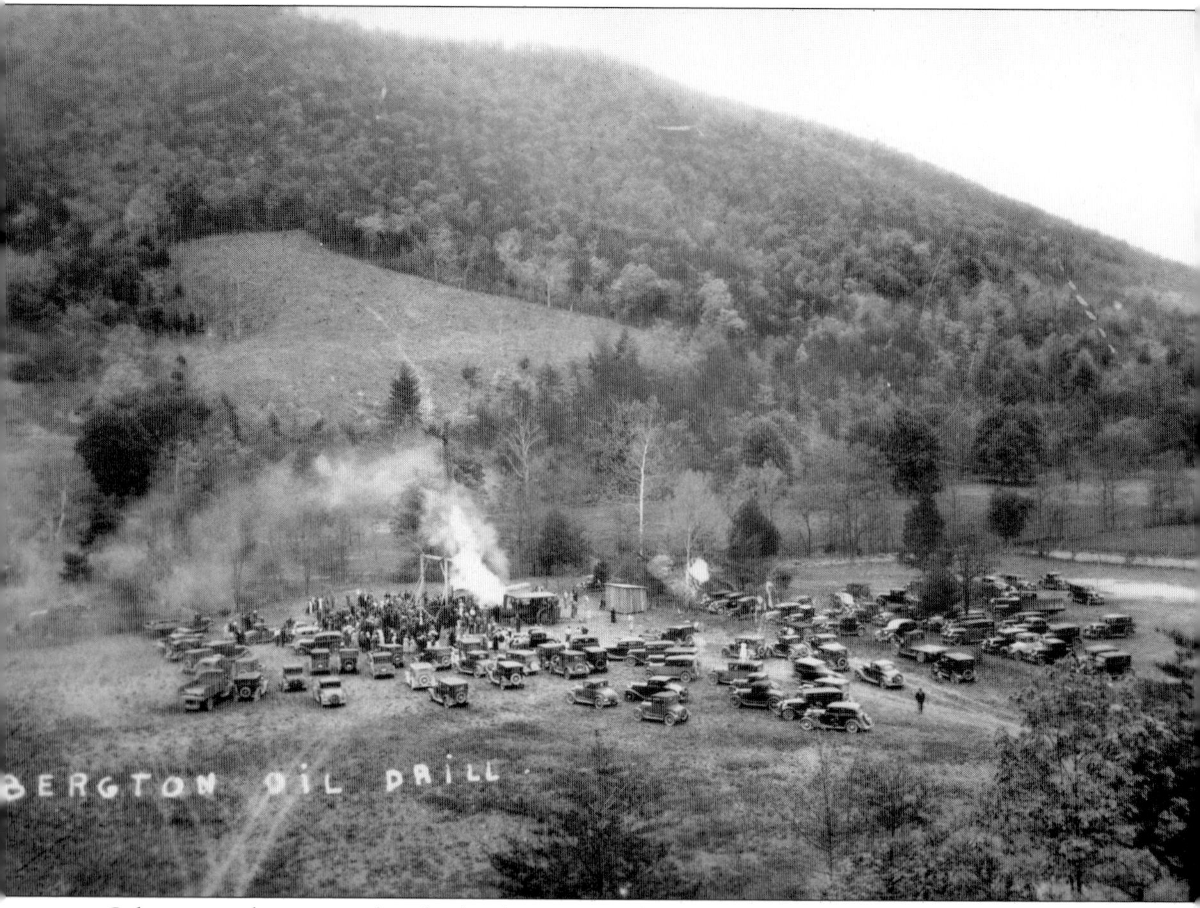

Other natural resources besides lumber attracted attention from developers. In 1936, two oil and gas companies were drilling in Bergton and a third oil company was leasing available farms. Charles L. Souder was the first to cook a meal with natural gas from the well, fixing fried ham, eggs, and potatoes. A popular destination on a Sunday afternoon drive was the gas field to see the flame atop a derrick near the present-day Bergton Fairgrounds. Someone composed the following song about the gas drilling to the tune of "Revive Us Again":

We believe we have gas;
We believe this thing strong;
We all talk it and boost it to help things along.
Rah! For Bergton, shout it out folks.
Rah! For Bergton! Again.
Rah! For Bergton, whoop it up folks, again and again.

(Luke Dove, photographer.)

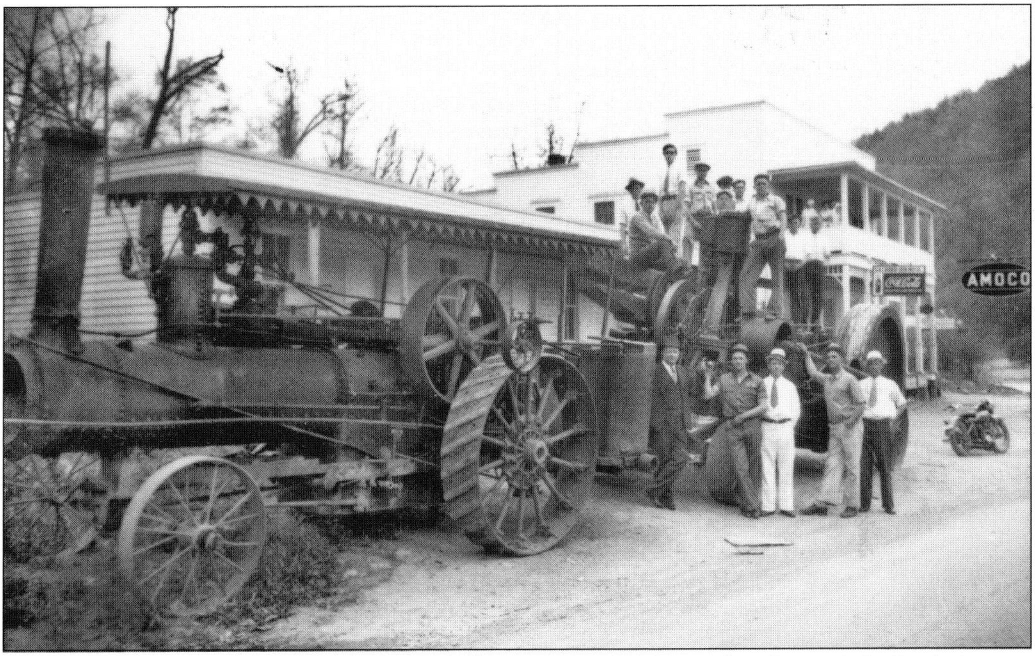

It was a momentous occasion when gas-drilling equipment stopped at Samuel A. Crider's store at Fulks Run on its way to begin drilling for gas in Bergton in the mid-1930s. Photographer Luke Dove wrote on a picture of the drilling site: "Miss Lenora, May 30, 1935, Bergton, VA, began drilling 5:20 p.m." (Luke Dove, photographer.)

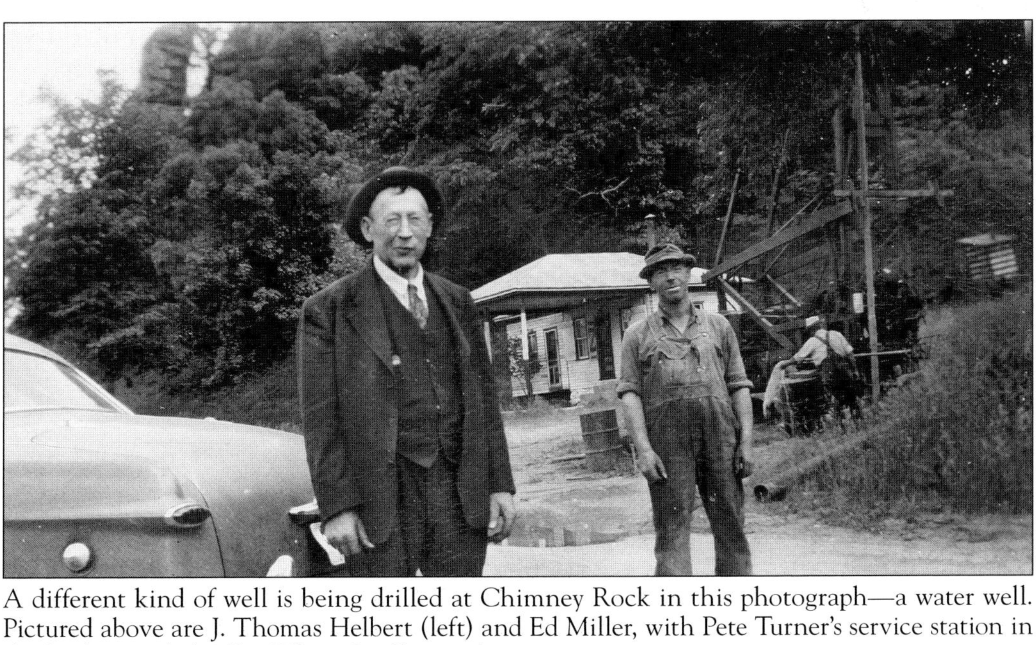

A different kind of well is being drilled at Chimney Rock in this photograph—a water well. Pictured above are J. Thomas Helbert (left) and Ed Miller, with Pete Turner's service station in the background. (Miller Whetzel collection.)

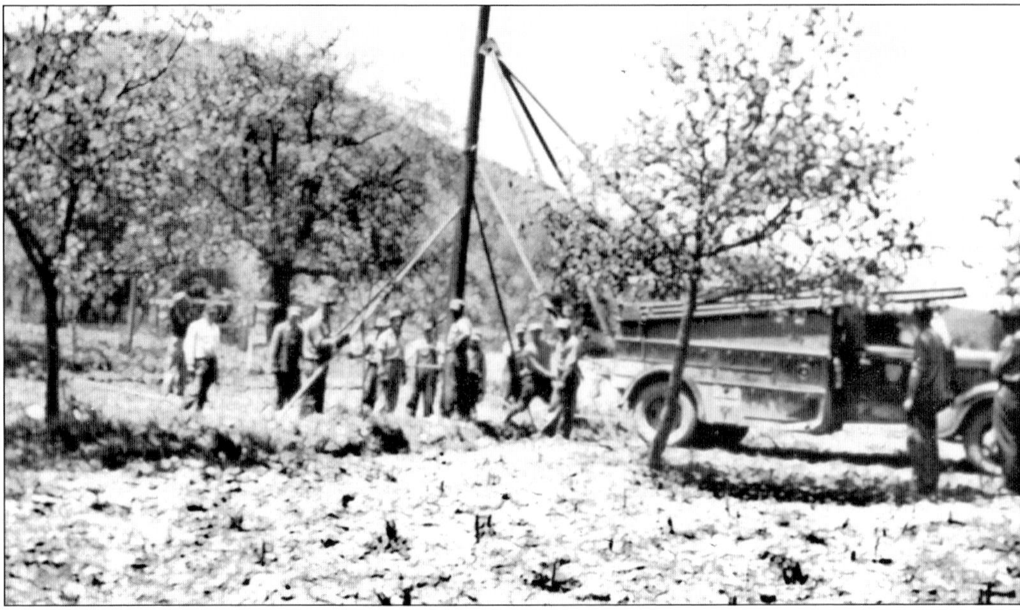

Before electricity came to Brocks Gap, some families bought Delco 32-volt battery systems, which ran water pumps for the barn, house lights, and 32-volt radios. These men are setting electric poles near Bergton. Electricity arrived about 1937 through Shenandoah Valley Electric Cooperative, and the 120-volt system was an improvement over Delco batteries. (Luke Dove collection.)

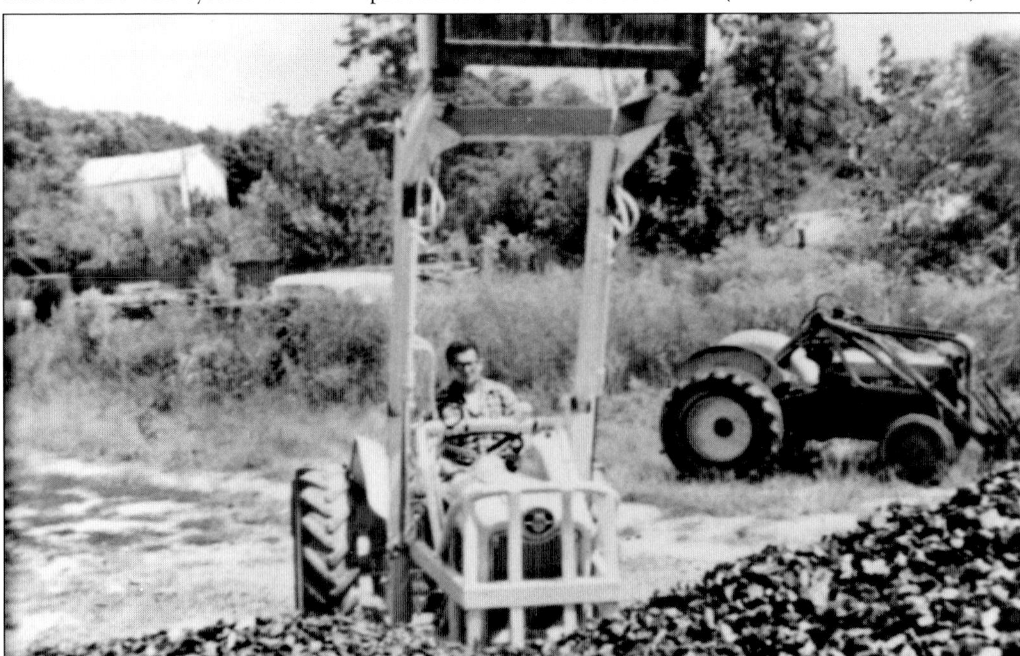

Coal-burning stoves for homes and chicken houses were an improvement over wood-burning ones. Warm Morning coal stoves were common in a number of homes. Eugene "Gene" Estep of Fulks Run began a heating oil and coal business about 1954 and is probably loading his truck with coal for a delivery in this photograph. His business served customers in the Brocks Gap area and in neighboring Hardy County. (Donna Kline Estep collection.)

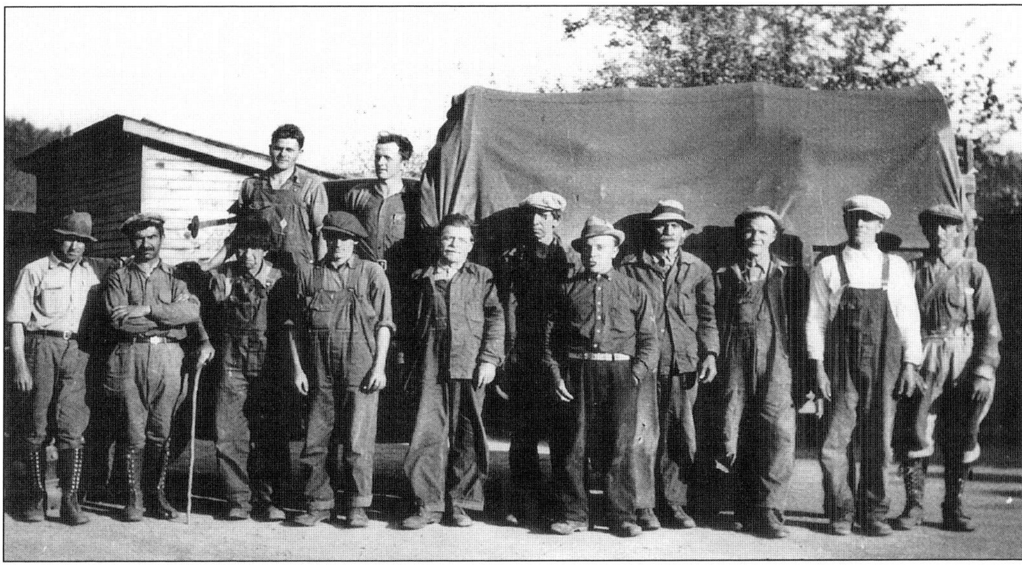

From the 1930s until 1970, a Virginia program paid men to kill gooseberry bushes, which caused a blister rust on pine trees. The following men are pictured from left to right: (first row) Bernie R. Vaughn, Seymour W. Smith, Jasper Dove, Elmer Dove, Lee (Faro) Dove, E. "Lee" May, Robert Freed, William "Will" Dove Riggleman, Joseph D. Dove, David Freed, and Samuel Mook; (second row) Allen Siever and Silas Leroy "Lee" Siever. (Irene Smith Yankey collection.)

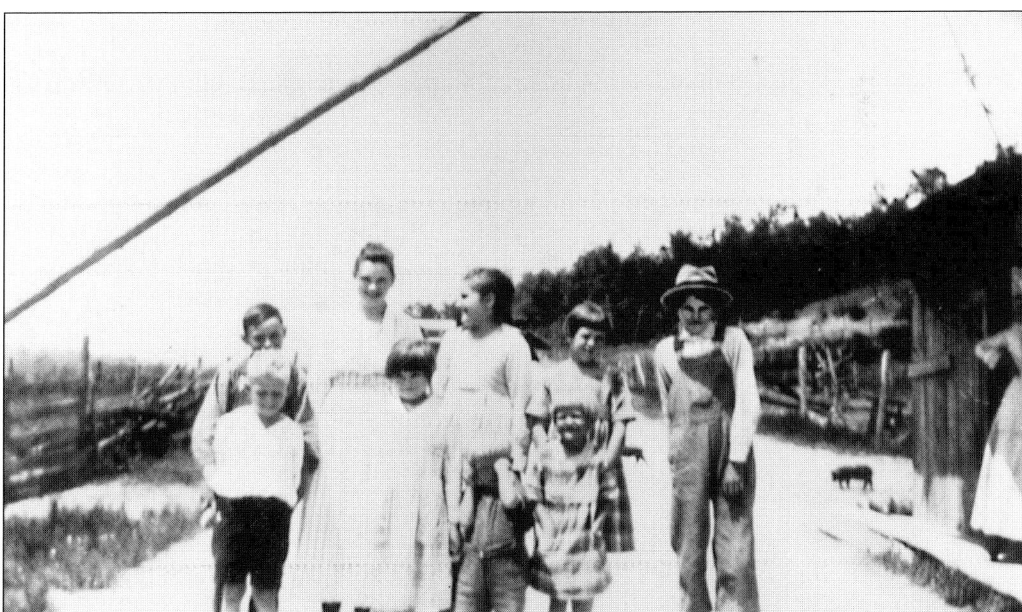

A tollgate was located near Chimney Rock before 1920. The gate's bar is visible on the left. Notice the piglet crossing the road behind the group. The following are pictured from left to right: (first row) Joseph Runion, Willie Turner Phillips, Stanford Runion, and Virginia Fulk; (second row) Owen E. Runion, Leafy Runion Miller, Violet Turner Custer, Mabel Turner Turner, and Ralph D. Runion. (Matthew E. "Bud" Miller collection.)

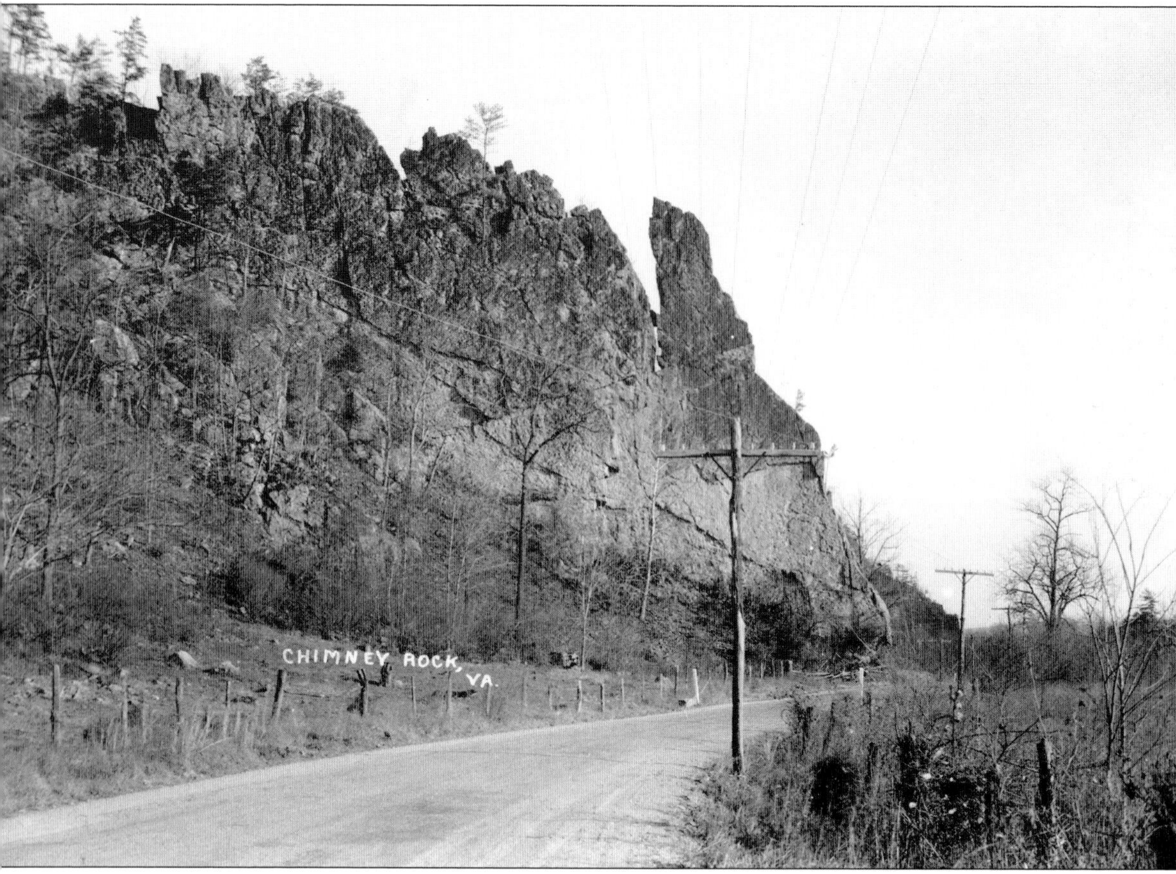

This is the view of Chimney Rock you have as you head out of Brocks Gap, or "out the way." We hope you have enjoyed your visit to our communities and carry with you a little feeling of home from Brocks Gap. (Luke Dove, photographer.)